Skilling Up Vietnam

DIRECTIONS IN DEVELOPMENT
Human Development

Skilling Up Vietnam

Preparing the Workforce for a Modern Market Economy

Christian Bodewig and Reena Badiani-Magnusson,
with Kevin Macdonald, David Newhouse, and Jan Rutkowski

THE WORLD BANK
Washington, D.C.

ISBN (paper): 978-1-4648-0231-7
ISBN (electronic): 978-1-4648-0232-4
DOI: 10.1596/978-1-4648-0231-7

Cover photo: Vietnam *Escuela Nueva* (VNEN) pilot class in Lang Sen Primary School, Kim Lien Commune,
Nam Dan District, Nghe An Province. © Christian Bodewig. Used with permission. Further permission
required for reuse.
Cover design: Debra Naylor, Naylor Design

Library of Congress Cataloging-in-Publication Data

Bodewig, Christian.
Skilling up Vietnam : preparing the workforce for a modern market economy / Christian Bodewig and
Reena Badiani-Magnusson ; with Kevin Macdonald, David Newhouse, and Jan Rutkowski.
      pages cm. — (Directions in development)
    Includes bibliographical references.
ISBN 978-1-4648-0231-7 (alk. paper) — ISBN 978-1-4648-0232-4 (ebk)
1. Employees—Training of—Vietnam. 2. Vocational qualifications—Vietnam. 3. Vietnam—Economic
policy—1975– I. Title.
    HF5549.5.T7B577 2014
    331.11'409597—dc23   2014019254

Contents

Foreword   *xi*
Acknowledgments   *xiii*
About the Authors   *xv*
Executive Summary   *xvii*
Abbreviations   *xxi*

Overview   1
Skills and Development in Vietnam   2
Skills in Demand Today and for the Next 10 Years   6
Preparing the Workforce for a Modern Market Economy   9
Summary and Conclusion   22
References   24

**Chapter 1   Vietnam's Economic Transformation and the Role of
Education**   27
Trends in Vietnam's Labor Market since Đổi Mới   28
The Role of Education in Vietnam's Labor Market   34
Looking Ahead: Skill Needs for an Industrializing Vietnam   39
Summary and Conclusion   45
Notes   47
References   47

Chapter 2   Skills for Current and Future Jobs   49
Shifting the Dialogue: From Education to Skills   50
What Do We Mean by Skills?   57
What Skills Are in Demand and Used in the Urban
   Labor Market?   63
Summary and Conclusion   71
Annex 2A: In Depth   72
Notes   84
References   85

Chapter 3   **Skills Formation and the Importance of the Early Years**   89
               What Do We Know about the Formation of Cognitive,
                   Social and Behavioral, and Technical Skills?   90
               Step 1: School Readiness through Early Childhood
                   Development   97
               Summary and Conclusion   104
               Note   104
               References   105

Chapter 4   **Cognitive and Behavioral Foundation Skills in the
               General Education System**   109
               General Education in Vietnam at a Glance   110
               Step 2: Building Cognitive and Behavioral
                   Foundation Skills in General Education   115
               Summary and Conclusion   128
               Annex 4A: In Depth   129
               Notes   135
               References   136

Chapter 5   **Technical Skills to Promote Employability**   139
               Technical Skills Development in Vietnam at a Glance   140
               Step 3: Building Technical Skills through a
                   Better-Connected System   144
               Summary and Conclusion   162
               Annex 5A: In Depth   163
               Note   165
               References   165

Boxes
1.1   What Are the Barriers to Labor Mobility in Vietnam?   39
1.2   Vietnam's Occupational Changes through the Lens of Skills   43
2.1   Skills Toward Employment and Productivity (STEP) Household
           and Employer Surveys   52
2.2   Defining Skill Gaps and Occupational Skill Shortages   53
3.1   Why Are the Early Years So Fundamental for Building Skills?   94
4.1   Vietnam *Escuela Nueva*   122
5.1   Prospective Students in Rural Areas: Limited Objective Career
           Guidance Information   150
5.2   The University of Danang and Industry Partnership to Improve
           Graduate Employability   156
5.3   Promoting Adult Continuous Education and Training   158

Figures

O.1   Vietnam's Shift of Employment Away from Agriculture,
        1993–2010   2
O.2   Literacy Proficiency of Vietnamese Adults Compared with Peers
        in OECD Countries   4
O.3   Frequency of Problem Solving by Wageworkers, by Occupation   5
O.4   The Three Dimensions of Skills Measured in the STEP Survey   6
O.5   Employers' View of Importance of Job-Related Skills for
        Blue- and White-Collar Workers   8
O.6   The Process of Skill Formation: A Simplified Model   9
O.7   Three Steps in Skills Development   10
O.8   Adult Stimulation and Stunting among Children from Poorer
        and Wealthier Backgrounds   11
O.9   Share of 19- to 21-Year-Olds in Postsecondary Education,
        by Type of Education Received, 1998–2010   17
O.10   Disconnects in Skills Development and Their Causes   18
O.11   Staff Qualifications in Higher Education Institutions   22
1.1   Real GDP Growth in Vietnam and Its Neighbors, 1995–2010   28
1.2   Growth of Labor Productivity in Vietnam Compared with Peers,
        1990–2010   30
1.3   Decomposition of GDP Growth in Contributions from Capital,
        Labor, and TFP, 1990–2010   31
1.4   Share of Vietnam's Workforce in Agricultural and
        Nonagricultural Wage Employment, 1993–2010   31
1.5   Share of Workers in Urban and Rural Areas, 2007–10   32
1.6   Employment Shares in Nonagricultural Occupations of
        Workers Aged 15–64 Years, 2010   33
1.7   Employment Patterns in Vietnam and Its Neighbors, 2008   34
1.8   Educational Attainment of Population by Age Cohort   35
1.9   Highest Level of Educational Attainment by Occupation, 2010   36
1.10   Estimated Education Earnings Premium among Wageworkers,
        1993–2008   37
1.11   Estimated Returns to Education among Wageworkers Relative
        to Lower Secondary Education, 2007 and 2010   37
1.12   Change in Share of Employment by Education Group and
        Urban/Rural, 2007–10   38
B1.1.1 Employment Protection Legislation in Vietnam Compared with
        Other Countries, 2008–10   40
B1.1.2 Labor Market Issues Affecting Businesses' Operations and
        Growth   41
1.13   Percentage Employed in Agriculture and Professional and
        Technical Occupations in Vietnam and Comparator Countries   42
1.14   Trends in the Nature of Tasks in Vietnam's Urban Labor Market,
        1998–2010   43

1.15   Percentage Return to Different Task Combinations, Controlling
        for Education and Demographics   45
1.16   Growth of Employment in Technical and Professional
        Occupations among Different Age Cohorts   46
2.1   Educational Achievement of the Population Aged 20–24 Years,
        2004–10   51
B2.2.1 Problems Businesses Encountered When Trying to Hire   54
2.2   Reported Obstacles to Business Activity   55
2.3   Percentage of Employers Claiming that Job Applicants Lacked
        Skills Required for the Job   56
2.4   Percentage of Individuals Reporting that the Lack of Literacy
        or Computer Skills Has Prevented Obtaining a Job or
        Advancement   56
2.5   Skills Measured in the STEP Survey   57
2.6   Percentage of Individuals, by Literacy Assessment Score   58
2.7   PIAAC and STEP Literacy Proficiency Scores   59
2.8   Literacy Competency Levels   59
2.9   Literacy Proficiency of Vietnamese Adults   60
2.10   Difference between Literacy Proficiency of Older and
        Younger Adults   61
2.11   Use of Numeracy Skills   62
2.12   Importance of Job-Related Skills versus Social and Behavioral
        Skills or Personal Characteristics   64
2.13   Importance of Job-Related Skills among White- and
        Blue-Collar Workers   65
2.14   Percentage of Wageworkers in Different Occupations Who
        Report Having to Problem Solve at Work, by Frequency   66
2.15   Percentage of Wageworkers in Different Occupations Who
        Report Having to Learn New Things, by Frequency   67
2.16   Importance of Social and Behavioral Skills for White- and
        Blue-Collar Workers   68
2.17   Returns to Social and Behavioral Skills, by Occupation Type   69
2.18   Percentage of Wageworkers Who Report Having to Interact with
        Others, Present Ideas to Others, or Supervise Others at Work   70
2.19   Returns to Social and Behavioral Skills for Wage Employment
        and Self-Employment   71
2A.1   Self-Reported Reading Length and Fraction of Correct
        Responses in Literacy Assessment   76
2A.2   Gender Differences in Social and Behavioral Skills and
        Openness to Experience, after Accounting for Education
        and Age   78
2A.3   Gender Gaps in Enrollment in Secondary Education and
        Choice of Fields of Study   79
2A.4   Cognitive Skills: Hanoi versus Ho Chi Minh City   80
2A.5   Social and Behavioral Skills: Hanoi versus Ho Chi Minh City   81

2A.6   Technical Skills: Hanoi versus Ho Chi Minh City   82
2A.7   Index of Openness to Experience and Conscientiousness,
            by Education Level and Age   83
3.1   The Process of Skill Formation   90
3.2   Changes in Cognitive Skills as Children Age   93
3.3   Step 1 in Skills Development: Promoting School Readiness
            to Help Children Learn in School   98
3.4   Percentage of 5-Year-Olds in the Lowest Decile of Each
            School Readiness Domain   99
3.5   Percentage of Children under 5 with Low Height for Age   100
3.6   Preschool Enrollment Rates across Regions in Vietnam,
            2011–12   103
4.1   Step 2 in Skills Development: Developing the Cognitive
            and Behavioral Skills Foundation   110
4.2   Net Enrollment Rates and Enrollment by Wealth Quintile   111
4.3   Mean 2012 PISA Mathematics Scores, Selected Cities
            and Countries   112
4.4   PISA Mean Mathematics Scores, by Subscale, 2012   113
4.5   Math and Language Test Scores of Children of Different
            Backgrounds   113
4.6   Gross and Net Secondary Enrollment Rates in Vietnam
            and Neighboring Countries   116
4.7   Private Spending on Secondary Education, 2010   117
4.8   Changes in the Number of Teachers and Students in Primary
            Schools, 2005–10   119
4.9   Primary Teachers' Professional Training and Correlation of
            Student Test Scores and Their Teachers' Ratings   124
4A.1   Ratio of Lower Secondary Teachers' Salary to GDP per
            Capita, 2008   134
5.1   Step 3 in Skills Development: Building Technical Skills
            for Employment   140
5.2   Percentage of 19- to 21-Year-Olds in Postsecondary Education,
            1998–2010   141
5.3   Higher Education Gross Enrollment Rates   142
5.4   Percentage of University Graduates Employed within
            Six Months of Graduation   143
5.5   Percentage of Internal and External Training, by Size of Business 144
5.6   Percentage of Employees Receiving Training, by Education
            and Employment Type   145
5.7   Disconnects in Skills Development and Their Causes   146
5.8   Percentage of University Graduates, by Field of Study and
            Returns to Field of Study   147
5.9   How Workers Find Jobs   151
5.10   New Vocational Training Programs and Their Funding, 2012   155
5.11   Staff Qualifications in Higher Education Institutions   159

5.12   Private Spending on College Education, by Income Group, 2010   161
5.13   Percentage of Higher Education Students Receiving Fee
            Exemptions, by Income Quintiles, 2006–10   162
5A.1   Functions of the Vietnam Tourism Certification Board   164

Tables

O.1   A Three-Step Agenda for Skills Development in Vietnam   23
B1.2.1   Tasks and Types of Occupations Conducted in Different
               Skill Brackets   44
2.1   Social and Behavioral Skills: The Big Five Personality and
               Motivational Traits   63
3.1   Feeding Practices for Young Children   100
3.2   Activities to Promote Learning and School Readiness in the
               Past Three Days   101
4A.1   PISA Assessments of Vietnamese 15-Year-Olds and Their
               Peers in OECD and Other Economies, 2012   129
4A.2   Korean Education Development Focus, Policy Goals, Major
               Concerns, and Resources, 1948 to Present   132
5.1   Ranking of Information Sources Used to Make Study Decisions
               among Students in Urban and Rural Areas   149
5.2   Focus of Employer-Education Provider Linkages   152
5.3   The Republic of Korea: Example of National Competency
               Standards for One Occupation   157

Foreword

Vietnam finds itself in a critical moment in its economic and social development process. After a period of remarkable economic growth and poverty reduction over the past two decades, Vietnam has recently joined the ranks of middle-income countries. This achievement has triggered a debate among policy makers and the public at large on what it will take to continue the country's success story over the next decade and beyond. Featured prominently in this debate are education and the skills of the workforce. Like across much of East Asia, there is wide consensus among Vietnamese society that good education is necessary for personal and national advancement. Vietnam's "Socio-Economic Development Strategy" for 2011–20 identifies developing a highly skilled workforce as one of its breakthrough areas. *Skilling Up Vietnam* is a contribution to the ongoing national policy debate on how to strengthen skills development in middle-income Vietnam to keep up with changing demands as the economy modernizes, industrializes, and diversifies.

In preparing its workforce for a modern market economy, Vietnam can build on strong foundations. Significant efforts to expand educational attainment over the last two decades have equipped a large share of Vietnam's adult population, especially among younger cohorts, with good basic literacy and numeracy skills. These skills have enabled ever more workers to find employment in the nonagricultural sector, which in turn has been an important driver of the country's rapid development and poverty reduction. But as Vietnam's economy continues to modernize, it will increasingly produce jobs that involve fewer manual and routine tasks and more skill-intensive, nonmanual, and nonroutine tasks. This book presents evidence on the evolving skill needs of the business sector in the dynamic urban Vietnam today.

The analysis presented in this book reveals that Vietnamese businesses care about three dimensions of skills: technical, cognitive, and behavioral. When recruiting, employers look first for technical skills such as in engineering. But employers are also looking for cognitive skills and behavioral skills. They want workers who can think critically, solve problems, work well in teams, and present their work in a convincing manner to clients and colleagues. Such skills are predominantly developed early in life, suggesting that an appropriate skills development strategy needs to aim at interventions along the life cycle, from early childhood through formal schooling age into adulthood.

In line with the country's strategic vision, the Communist Party of Vietnam has recently approved a resolution on fundamental and comprehensive education and training reform. The resolution lays out many reform directions put forward in this book. They include expanding early childhood education and enrollments in full-day schooling, preventing early school leaving after primary and lower secondary education, and modernizing the curriculum and teaching methods to help Vietnamese students to become more effective problem solvers, critical thinkers, communicators, and team workers. As the details of the reform get elaborated and implementation takes shape, the book can serve as a reference to guide action.

Skilling Up Vietnam is written for a wide audience of stakeholders in Vietnam, ranging from students and parents to business leaders and government officials. The message is that developing a skilled workforce ready for a modern market economy is not just the business of the government. It is everyone's business. But the book is also aimed at a readership beyond Vietnam. It is of interest to anyone studying policies to promote human capital formation with the aim of accelerating economic growth and social development. The analysis presented in this book draws on empirical data collected as part of the World Bank's Skills Toward Employment and Productivity (STEP) skills measurement program. Launched in 2011, this program is building a rich new knowledge base on employers' skills needs and skills profiles of workforces across many countries around the world and on what it takes to prepare workforces for productive employment in fast-changing economies. This book's analysis of the case of Vietnam will provide a significant contribution to the understanding of skills development in emerging economies.

Victoria Kwakwa
Country Director for Vietnam
The World Bank

Acknowledgments

This book was written by a World Bank team led by Christian Bodewig and Reena Badiani-Magnusson. David Newhouse, Christian Bodewig, and Reena Badiani-Magnusson wrote chapter 1. Reena Badiani-Magnusson, Jan Rutkowski, and Kevin Macdonald wrote chapter 2. Reena Badiani-Magnusson and Christian Bodewig wrote chapter 3, with inputs from Kevin Macdonald. Christian Bodewig wrote chapters 4 and 5, with inputs from Kevin Macdonald. Shang Gao and Kai Partale (tourism sector specialist at the European Union–funded Environmentally and Socially Responsible Tourism Capacity Development Programme) prepared the "In Depth" sections on the Republic of Korea and on occupational standards in the tourism sector, respectively. Vo Kieu Dung prepared the box on the University of Danang and its partnerships with industry. Nguyen Tam Giang collaborated with Hoang Xuan Thanh and a team from Ageless Consulting on a joint Oxfam and ActionAid Vietnam study, funded by the U.K. Department for International Development (DFID), which yielded evidence on the factors influencing education choice. Emanuela di Gropello and Mai Thi Thanh were core team members at the concept stage and helped shape the analytical agenda for the report. Dung Doan and Bhagyashree Katare provided analytical support for chapter 1. Nguyen Minh Nguyet and Anna Coronado provided administrative support to the team. Carolyn Goldinger edited the report.

The book was first published in Vietnam in November 2013 as the World Bank's *Vietnam Development Report 2014*. This version of the book is updated to reflect new literacy assessment data and data on Vietnam's performance in the 2012 Programme for International Student Assessment (PISA). It was prepared under the guidance of Victoria Kwakwa, country director for Vietnam, and Luis Benveniste, education sector manager for East Asia and Pacific. The preparation benefited from excellent comments from peer reviewers Ariel Fiszbein, Mamta Murthi (at concept stage), and Omar Arias (at completion stage) as well as from James Anderson, Michael Crawford, Gabriel Demombynes, Vo Kieu Dung, Deepak Mishra, Lars Sondergaard, Xiaoqing Yu, and many others. The team acknowledges extensive comments and advice received throughout preparation from Caine Rolleston from the Young Lives research team at Oxford University. The team thanks participants in numerous consultation meetings with Vietnamese citizens, employers, policy makers, education practitioners, and development partners, both online in coordination with the VietnamNet online newspaper and face-to-face, for their advice and views that shaped the hypotheses and the messages in this book.

This book would not have been possible without data from the World Bank's Skills Toward Employment and Productivity (STEP) skills measurement project, which collects information on workforce skills in multiple countries across the world, including in a first round in Vietnam, Yunnan Province of China, the Lao People's Democratic Republic, Sri Lanka, and Bolivia in 2011–12. The Vietnam surveys were managed by Maria Laura Sanchez Puerta and Alexandria Valerio from the World Bank's Human Development Network under the oversight of Ariel Fiszbein, then the network's chief economist.

About the Authors

Christian Bodewig is a sector leader for human development in the World Bank's Europe and Central Asia regional department, where he coordinates the Bank's program in education, health, and social protection and labor in Central Europe and the Baltics. He has led analytical and operational programs in education, skills, labor markets, and social protection in Vietnam and Central and Southeastern Europe. Mr. Bodewig is also a coauthor of the World Bank study *Skills, Not Just Diplomas: Managing Education for Results in Eastern Europe and Central Asia*. He holds degrees in economics and political economy from University College London and the London School of Economics.

Reena Badiani-Magnusson is an economist in the World Bank's East Asia and Pacific Human Development Unit. She has worked on social protection design and delivery, poverty and inequality, labor markets, and impact evaluations in India, the Republic of Congo, the Republic of the Union of Myanmar, Thailand, and Vietnam. Prior to joining the World Bank, she consulted or worked for the International Crops Research Institute for the Semi-Arid Tropics, the Organisation for Economic Co-operation and Development, Arthur Andersen, and *Statesman's Yearbook*. Ms. Badiani-Magnusson holds a PhD in economics from Yale University.

Kevin Macdonald specializes in economic analysis of education sector investment and policy reform. During the past six years, he has worked with the World Bank, UNICEF, the United Nations Development Programme, and governments and research institutes in more than 20 countries, primarily in East Asia and the Pacific, West Africa, Eastern Europe, and the Middle East. His expertise includes program and policy evaluation, cost-benefit analysis, and capacity building. Mr. Macdonald holds a master's degree in economics from the University of British Columbia in Vancouver, Canada.

David Newhouse is a senior economist in the South Asia Economic Policy and Poverty group of the World Bank and works primarily on issues related to poverty in Pakistan and Sri Lanka. He has previously been a labor economist in the Social Protection Anchor where he co-led efforts to monitor labor markets in developing countries and analyze the policy response to the 2008 financial crisis. He coauthored three background papers to the 2013

World Development Report on jobs and led analytical tasks on jobs and youth employment in Indonesia and Papua New Guinea. Mr. Newhouse holds a PhD in economics from Cornell University.

Jan Rutkowski is a lead economist in the World Bank's Europe and Central Asia Human Development Unit. His work focuses on labor market outcomes and poverty, the determinants of job creation, the impact of regulations on labor market performance, the demand for skills, and the role of labor market information in addressing a skills mismatch and reducing structural unemployment. He has written numerous papers, contributed to books, and coauthored the regional World Bank flagship report *Enhancing Job Opportunities: Eastern Europe and the Former Soviet Union*. Prior to joining the World Bank in 1994, Mr. Rutkowski was a section chief at the Research Center for Economics and Statistics in Poland. He has a PhD in economics from Warsaw University.

Executive Summary

Education has played an important role in making Vietnam a development success story over the last 20 years. In the 1990s and early 2000s Vietnam experienced rapid economic growth. The accelerated growth was driven predominantly by productivity increases that came in the wake of a rapid shift of employment from low-productivity agriculture to higher-productivity nonfarm jobs. Vietnam's economy began to industrialize and modernize. Poverty fell dramatically. And education played an enabling role. Vietnam's committed effort to promote access to primary education for all and to ensure its quality through centrally set minimum quality standards has contributed to the country's reputation for having a young, well-educated workforce. Results from the 2012 Programme for International Student Assessment (PISA) and new evidence from an adult skills survey presented in this book show that literacy and numeracy among Vietnam's youth and young urban adult workforce are strong and exceed those of even some wealthier countries.

Despite its clear progress, Vietnam is facing new challenges. The pace of economic growth and the reallocation of jobs away from agriculture have slowed in recent years. Rather than productivity improvements, capital investments have become the main source of economic growth, but this model is not sustainable for ensuring continued rapid economic growth. The size of its workforce is still expanding, but its youth population is shrinking, which means that Vietnam cannot continue to rely on the size of its workforce for continued success. Instead, it needs to focus on making its workforce more productive and on alleviating skills barriers to labor mobility.

Skilled Workforce Needed for Vietnam's Economic Modernization

Equipping its workforce with the right skills will be an important part of Vietnam's effort to accelerate economic growth and further its economic modernization in the coming decade and beyond. Judging by the experience of its more advanced neighbors, Vietnam's economic modernization will involve a shift in labor demand from today's predominantly manual and elementary jobs toward more skill-intensive nonmanual jobs, from jobs that largely involve routine tasks to those with nonroutine tasks, from old jobs to "new" jobs. And new jobs will require new skills.

These new jobs can already be found in today's labor market, but Vietnam's employers struggle to find the right workers for them. Despite the impressive literacy and numeracy achievements among Vietnamese workers, many Vietnamese firms report a shortage of workers with adequate skills as a significant obstacle to their activity. A majority of employers surveyed for this book said that hiring new workers is difficult either because of the inadequate skills of job applicants (a skills gap), or because of a scarcity of workers in some occupations (a skills shortage). Unlike many countries around the world today, Vietnam does not suffer from low labor demand; its employers are seeking workers, but they cannot find the workers that match their skill needs.

Wanted: Cognitive, Social and Behavioral, and Technical Skills

What skills are in demand in Vietnam's nonagricultural labor market today? Employers identify *technical skills* as the most important skills they are looking for when hiring both white- and blue-collar workers. Such technical skills may be the practical ability of an electrician to do the job. But employers are also looking for *cognitive skills* and *social and behavioral skills*. For example, next to technical skills, working well in teams and being able to solve problems are considered important behavioral and cognitive skills for blue-collar workers. When employers hire white-collar workers, they expect that the employees can think critically, solve problems, and present their work in a convincing manner to clients and colleagues.

In short, Vietnam's new jobs require that workers have good foundational skills, such as good reading and mathematics ability. But to be successful in the future, workers also need more advanced skills that will help them respond to changes in workplace demands. As the remarkable performance of its 15-year-old students in PISA 2012 testifies, Vietnam's education system has a strong track record in producing good foundational skills. But employers' views suggest that it faces greater challenges in producing the advanced skills that will be in greater demand in coming years.

Three Steps for a Holistic Skills Strategy

This book summarizes emerging evidence on the formation of cognitive, social and behavioral, and technical skills. Cognitive skills formation is the most intensive in the first years of life and continues through adolescence. Social and behavioral skills are also first formed in childhood and continue to evolve throughout adult life. Stronger cognitive and behavioral skills will help workers to continuously update their technical skills during their working lives. The need to focus on skills will gain importance as Vietnam's population ages, as production in Vietnam becomes more technically sophisticated, and as workers need to catch up with technological changes occurring during their longer working lives.

What does this mean for Vietnam's education and training system? This book proposes a three-step holistic skills strategy that looks at today's workforce as much as the future workforce.

Step 1: Promoting School Readiness through Early Childhood Development

Vietnam can do more to promote school readiness through early childhood development interventions. Efforts at expanding access to preschool education for 3- to 5-year-olds are showing success, but more attention is needed for children from birth to age 3, in particular on tackling malnutrition. Almost a quarter of the children below the age of 5 are stunted. In Vietnam and around the world, stunting has been found to have a strong negative effect on cognitive skills development. Some stunted children remain behind for the rest of their lives. Vietnam cannot afford that.

Step 2: Building Cognitive and Social and Behavioral Foundation Skills in General Education

Vietnam can further strengthen students' cognitive and social and behavioral foundation skills by promoting more schooling and better schooling in primary and secondary education. Doing so entails expanding enrollments in full-day schooling and preventing early school leaving after primary and lower secondary education as well as renovating the curriculum and teaching methods to help Vietnamese students to become more effective problem solvers, critical thinkers, better communicators, and team workers. Work on a new curriculum is already under way, and Vietnam has adapted a promising model from Colombia called *Escuela Nueva*, which features more group learning and problem solving than the memorization and copying often seen in Vietnamese primary school classrooms today. A pilot under way in 1,500 schools across Vietnam is already showing successes and holds lessons for broader reforms.

Step 3: Building Technical Skills through a More Connected System

Vietnam can build better and more technical skills among its graduates and labor market entrants. Technical skills shortages and gaps are not the concern; rather, they are indicators of a dynamic economy that creates new, more skill-intensive jobs. The concern is whether the education and training system is equally dynamic in adjusting quickly to ensure that the supply of technical skills can keep up with the constant and accelerating evolution of the demand for technical skills.

Ensuring that Vietnamese graduates come with the right technical skills requires that businesses, universities, and vocational schools, and current and prospective students become better connected. Better coordination and partnerships can help improve the *information* about what skills employers need and are likely to need in the future. Better information on graduates' job placements can help future students to choose the best schools, universities, and programs. Occupational competency standards and certification systems can improve the information about the skills that workers possess. More autonomy

Skilling Up Vietnam • http://dx.doi.org/10.1596/978-1-4648-0231-7

in decision making, coupled with accountability for the employability of their graduates (*the right incentives*) and better-skilled staff and equipment (*enhanced capacity*), will help universities and vocational schools respond effectively to the information on employer needs. Scholarship programs can provide more students, including the disadvantaged, with opportunities.

The government can be a help in creating a more dynamic and better-connected skills development system. Rather than planning and managing the education and training system centrally and top-down, the government should help to overcome the disconnects through empowering students, universities, and schools and businesses to make good decisions—by facilitating the flow of information, by providing the right incentives to schools and universities to be responsive to information, and by carefully investing in raising their capacity.

The Need to Act

Vietnam's continued transformation toward a successful industrial, middle-income economy is not automatic or guaranteed. Structural reforms and sound macroeconomic policies will matter in ensuring continued fast change, but so will the quality of Vietnam's workforce. Changes in education and training can take a generation to result in a workforce equipped with the right skills. To ensure that worker skills do not become a bottleneck, Vietnam must act now to modernize skills development.

Preparing the workforce for an industrial economy, however, is not just the government's job. It requires a change in behavior by all actors in skills development—employers, schools and universities, and students and their parents. Businesses and universities need to build close partnerships. Parents need to become more involved in their children's schooling. Students need to experience the world of work before their graduation. In rural areas, all parties need to ensure that children from disadvantaged backgrounds have the opportunity to meet their full potential. The role of government is to facilitate this change in behavior by helping to ensure a better information flow among all the actors; to address capacity constraints, including financing capacity; and to set the right incentives by freeing up universities to partner more effectively with businesses.

Abbreviations

ADB   Asian Development Bank
ALL   Adult Literacy and Life Skills Survey
ASEAN   Association of Southeast Asian Nations
CDA   Cognitive Development Assessment
CECODES   Centre for Community Support and Development Studies
CIEM   Central Institute for Economic Management
DFA   District Fundamental School Quality Level Audit
DFID   U.K. Department for International Development
EDI   Early Development Instrument
EPL   employment protection legislation
FDI   foreign direct investment
FSQL   Fundamental School Quality Level
GDETA   General Department of Testing and Accreditation
GDP   gross domestic product
GPE   Global Partnership for Education
HCMC   Ho Chi Minh City
IALS   International Adult Literacy Survey
ISCED   International Standard Classification of Education
IT   information technology
IYCF   infant and young child feeding
LMC   lower-middle-income country
LSE   lower secondary education
MCST   Ministry of Culture, Sports, and Tourism of Vietnam
MDGs   Millennium Development Goals
MIC   middle-income country
MOET   Ministry of Education and Training of Vietnam
MOLISA   Ministry of Labor, Invalids, and Social Affairs of Vietnam
NCS   National Competency Standard
NGO   nongovernmental organization

OECD	Organisation for Economic Co-operation and Development
PIAAC	Programme for the International Assessment of Adult Competencies
PISA	Programme for International Student Assessment
PPVT	Peabody Picture Vocabulary Test
SABER	Systems Approach for Better Education Results
SAR	special administrative region
SEQAP	School Education Quality Assurance Program
SMEs	small and medium enterprises
SOE	state-owned enterprise
STEP	Skills Toward Employment and Productivity
TE	tertiary education
TFP	total factor productivity
TVET	technical and vocational education and training
UNDP	United Nations Development Programme
UNESCO	United Nations Educational, Scientific, and Cultural Organization
UNICEF	United Nations Children's Fund
USE	upper secondary education
VFF-CRT	Centre for Research and Training of the Viet Nam Fatherland Front
VHLSS	Vietnam Household Living Standards Survey
VLSS	Vietnam Living Standards Survey
VNEN	Vietnam *Escuela Nueva*
VTCB	Vietnam Tourism Certification Board
VTOS	Vietnam Tourism Occupational Skills Standards
WHO	World Health Organization

Overview

Vietnam is a country undergoing multiple transitions. The transition from central planning to a market economy, started in 1986 with the đổi mới (renovation) reforms, is much advanced but not yet complete. The same is true for the transition from an agricultural economy to a modern, industrialized economy. In advancing along these parallel transitions, Vietnam has been counting on one of its biggest assets—its abundant young workforce. But Vietnam is also going through a demographic transition toward an aging society. While the size of its workforce is still expanding, Vietnam's youth population is shrinking. This means that Vietnam cannot continue to rely on the size of its workforce to advance these transitions; instead, it needs to focus on making its workforce more productive.

A skilled workforce is central to the success of Vietnam's economic and social transitions, and, fortunately, there is a long-standing consensus across Vietnamese society on the importance of education. The focus on education is evident in the considerable public and private investments in education and growing levels of educational attainment. There is also, however, an equal consensus that Vietnam still needs to do more to develop the "skills" or "quality" of its workforce—one of the three breakthrough goals of the country's 10-year (2011–20) socioeconomic development strategy. Today, a growing public debate among students, parents, employers, educators, and policy makers is under way on what skills are required in the modern market economy, how to ensure that these skills are developed in future graduates, and how each of the stakeholders can participate in improving the skills of the workforce.

This book seeks to contribute to the public debate on the topic of skills and to inform Vietnam's strategic skills development. Using new survey instruments developed by the World Bank as part of the Skills Toward Employment and Productivity (STEP) project, the book analyzes the demand for skills by Vietnamese employers in the greater Hanoi and Ho Chi Minh City (HCMC) regions, Vietnam's economic growth poles, and assesses the skills profile of the working-age population in urban Vietnam. Based on this analysis, it examines how and when different types of skills are formed and what these data mean for reforming the education and training systems. It proposes a set of policy recommendations along three steps of a holistic skills strategy: first, promoting school readiness through early childhood development; second, building the cognitive and social and behavioral (also called noncognitive) foundation skills in general education; and, third, building technical skills through a more connected system.

Skills and Development in Vietnam

Looking Back: Vietnam's Shift Away from Agriculture and the Role of Education

Vietnam's economy has undergone fundamental structural changes over the last 25 years with a shift of employment from the agricultural sector to wage employment in manufacturing, construction, and services. Since the launch of the đổi mới reforms in the late 1980s Vietnam has experienced rapid economic growth, which catapulted it to middle-income status in 2010 and contributed to a fast decline in poverty (World Bank 2012c). This economic miracle was initially associated with substantial labor productivity increases—GDP (gross domestic product) per employed person more than doubled between 1990 and 2010—that came in the wake of improved agricultural efficiency and a rapid shift of employment out of low-productivity agriculture into higher-productivity non-farm jobs (figure O.1).

Education has been important in supporting and promoting structural change, and Vietnam's population has become increasingly well educated. The fraction of the population with less than primary school has plummeted over time, and those born in the period following the đổi mới reforms have attained higher levels of education than any other generation in the country's history.

Figure O.1 Vietnam's Shift of Employment Away from Agriculture, 1993–2010

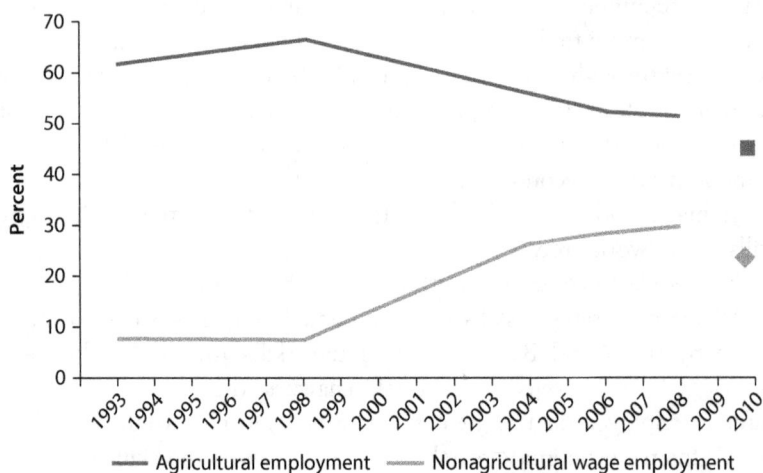

Agricultural employment   Nonagricultural wage employment

Source: World Bank staff estimates using VHLSS 2010.
Note: VHLSS = Vietnam Household Living Standards Survey. The 2010 VHLSS used a new sample frame based on the 2009 census. This captures migration between 1999 and 2009 from rural to peri-urban areas, where fewer workers work in agriculture.

Vietnam's committed efforts to promote access to primary education for all have allowed increasing shares of the population to take advantage of greater economic opportunities. The rise in educational attainment has, however, been uneven across Vietnam. While more and more young people complete primary education, important inequities in access and attainment remain at secondary levels, affecting in particular children from ethnic minority families or those residing in remote areas. A needed expansion in secondary education will come through greater enrollment of the less well-off.

Education has provided most Vietnamese workers with the key basic skills needed to succeed in the workforce: the ability to read and write at an adequate level. In addition to expanding access, government efforts to centrally set minimum quality standards have contributed to achieving good basic education outcomes. New evidence from the STEP surveys shows that literacy and numeracy among Vietnam's students and young adult workforce are widespread and more so than in other countries. It shows that, although older Vietnamese workers trail their peers in OECD (Organisation for Economic Co-operation and Development) countries in literacy, young Vietnamese outperform their peers in many wealthier OECD countries (figure O.2). This evidence is consistent with Vietnam's results from the 2012 Programme for International Student Assessment (PISA), in which 15-year-old Vietnamese students performed strongly in mathematics, reading, and science and did better than the OECD average (OECD 2013b). The message, therefore, is: although inequities remain, Vietnam's basic education system today appears to be doing a fine job at imparting key basic skills for the majority of its students. Increasingly well educated, young Vietnamese workers today have stronger basic skills than previous generations.

Looking Ahead: Modern Jobs and Changing Skill Needs

The pace of economic growth and the reallocation of jobs away from agriculture have slowed in recent years. This slowdown has come in the wake of macroeconomic instability, structural problems in the enterprise sector, and weaknesses in the banking sector. It has affected the labor market, with evidence of a bifurcation that is associated with educational attainment. While well-educated workers are taking advantage of expanding opportunities in the private sector, especially in urban areas, less-educated workers, and particularly those in rural areas, are having difficulties. Less-educated workers and youth from rural areas have a harder time transitioning into the expanding private sector and are often left in the agricultural sector or in informal employment.

Economic growth has not just decelerated; its composition has also changed compared to the early years of đổi mới. Productivity growth was the main driver of GDP growth in the early years of Vietnam's transition, but more recently capital investments have become the main source of economic growth (World Bank 2012b). This model is not sustainable for ensuring continued strong economic growth. Vietnam has every potential to continue its success story and achieve fast growth and convergence in living standards with richer nations in the coming decade and more. But to do so, it will need to promote labor

Skilling Up Vietnam • http://dx.doi.org/10.1596/978-1-4648-0231-7

Figure O.2 Literacy Proficiency of Vietnamese Adults Compared with Peers in OECD Countries

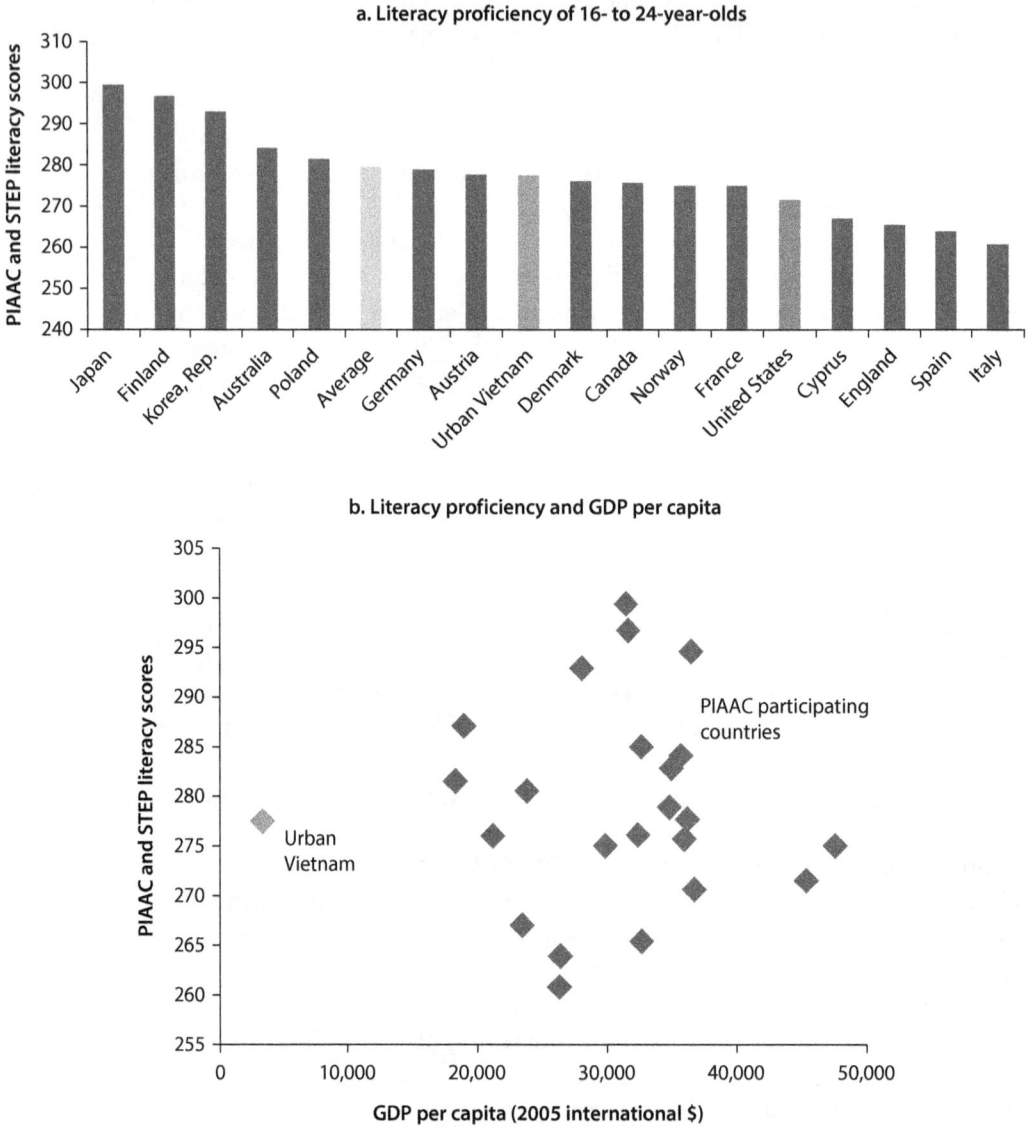

a. Literacy proficiency of 16- to 24-year-olds

b. Literacy proficiency and GDP per capita

Sources: Vietnam estimates from World Bank staff analysis using STEP household survey data. Literacy scores from other countries were measured as part of the PIAAC, and the unadjusted scores are taken from table A2.2a in OECD 2013a. GDP per capita are based on 2005 purchasing power parity and were obtained from the World Development Indicators 2012.
Note: GDP = gross domestic product; OECD = Organisation for Economic Co-operation and Development; PIAAC = Programme for the International Assessment of Adult Competencies; STEP = Skills Toward Employment and Productivity.

productivity growth and foster a continued shift of employment into the nonagricultural sector.

Equipping its workers with the right skills will be an important part of Vietnam's effort to accelerate economic growth and further advance its economic transition. Judging by the experience of its more advanced neighbor, the Republic of Korea, Vietnam can expect a shift in labor demand from today's predominantly manual and elementary jobs toward more skill-intensive nonmanual jobs, from jobs that largely involve routine tasks to those with nonroutine tasks, from traditional jobs to modern jobs. And these modern jobs will require new skills.

Modern skill-intensive jobs are becoming more prominent in Vietnam's labor market and carry high returns. Most nonfarm jobs in Vietnam today are in blue-collar occupations (craftsmen, machine operators, and manual workers) and in the service and sales sector. Better-educated professionals and technicians make up less than a quarter of the nonagricultural workforce. Young graduates are increasingly entering professional and technical occupations, and they report that they need a number of attributes for their jobs: they have to solve problems, learn new things frequently, present ideas or persuade clients at work or interact with noncolleagues (figure O.3). Evidence presented in this book suggests that the nature of tasks performed by Vietnamese workers has been changing from predominantly manual and routine tasks, where workers are asked to perform the same function on a regular basis, toward more analytical, interactive, and non-manual tasks where the type of tasks changes regularly. Workers performing these tasks are also better remunerated than their peers in traditional jobs.

A major problem is that Vietnam's employers are struggling to find the right workers for these modern jobs. The employers report that the lack of workers

Figure O.3 Frequency of Problem Solving by Wageworkers, by Occupation

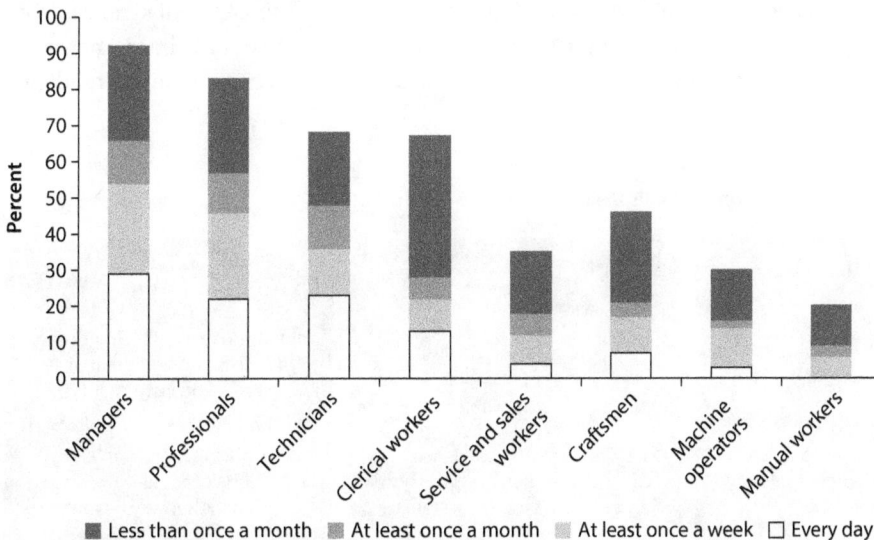

Less than once a month   At least once a month   At least once a week   Every day

Source: World Bank staff estimates using STEP employer survey data.
Note: STEP = Skills Toward Employment and Productivity. The figure shows responses to the following question: "Some tasks are pretty easy and can be done right away or after getting a little help from others. Other tasks require more thinking to figure out how they should be done. As part of this work as [occupation], how often do you have to undertake tasks that require at least 30 minutes of thinking (examples: mechanic figuring out a car problem, budgeting for a business, teacher making a lesson plan, restaurant owner creating a new menu/dish for restaurant, dressmaker designing a new dress)." Respondents were asked to indicate how often they conducted a task of this form. The sample includes only wage employees (*n* = 1,313).

Skilling Up Vietnam • http://dx.doi.org/10.1596/978-1-4648-0231-7

with adequate skills is a significant obstacle to their activity. STEP evidence suggests that worker skills and availability are more serious concerns for employers than labor market regulations and taxes. A majority of employers said that hiring new workers is a challenge either because of inadequate skills of job applicants (a skills gap), or because of a scarcity of workers in some occupations (an occupational skills shortage). The skills gap is particularly acute among applicants for jobs in technical, professional, and managerial occupations—jobs that are more likely to ask workers to conduct analytical, nonmanual, and nonroutine tasks. In contrast, a skills shortage, or a shortage in applicants in particular types of jobs, is common among more elementary occupations.

Skills in Demand Today and for the Next 10 Years

Defining Skills

A worker's skill set consists of different domains of skills: cognitive, social and behavioral, and technical. These domains cover technical skills that are relevant to particular occupations as well as cognitive abilities and the various personality traits that are crucial for success in the labor market. Cognitive skills include the use of logical, intuitive, and creative thinking and problem solving using acquired knowledge. They include literacy and numerical ability and extend to the ability to understand complex ideas, learn from experience, and analyze problems using logical processes. Social and behavioral skills capture personality traits that are linked to labor market success: openness to new experiences, conscientiousness, extraversion, agreeability, and emotional stability. Technical skills range from having the manual dexterity to use complex tools and instruments to occupation-specific knowledge and skills in areas such as engineering or medicine (figure O.4).

Figure O.4 The Three Dimensions of Skills Measured in the STEP Survey

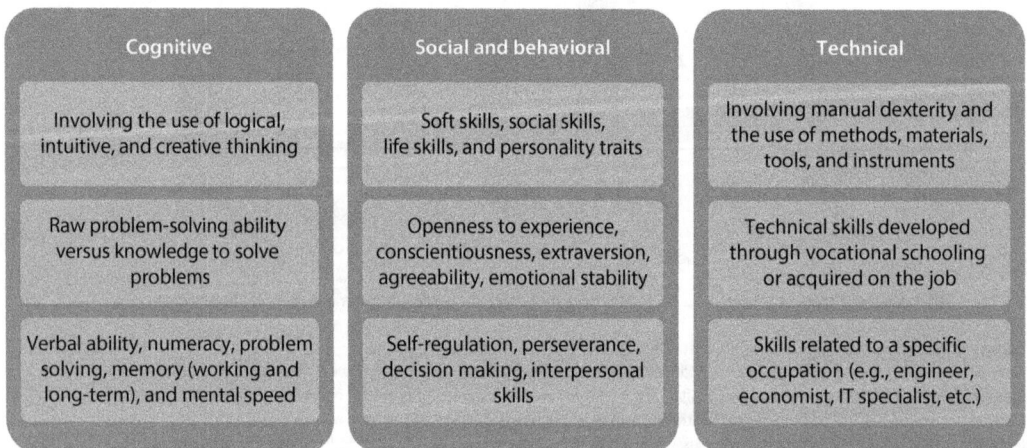

Cognitive	Social and behavioral	Technical
Involving the use of logical, intuitive, and creative thinking	Soft skills, social skills, life skills, and personality traits	Involving manual dexterity and the use of methods, materials, tools, and instruments
Raw problem-solving ability versus knowledge to solve problems	Openness to experience, conscientiousness, extraversion, agreeability, emotional stability	Technical skills developed through vocational schooling or acquired on the job
Verbal ability, numeracy, problem solving, memory (working and long-term), and mental speed	Self-regulation, perseverance, decision making, interpersonal skills	Skills related to a specific occupation (e.g., engineer, economist, IT specialist, etc.)

Source: Pierre, Sanchez Puerta, and Valerio, forthcoming.
Note: IT = information technology; STEP = Skills Toward Employment and Productivity.

Vietnamese employers are looking for a mix of high-quality cognitive, social and behavioral, and technical skills. Employers in greater Hanoi and HCMC surveyed for this book identified technical skills as the most important skills they are looking for when hiring both white- and blue-collar workers. Such technical skills may be the practical ability of an electrician to do the job. Like employers in more advanced middle- and high-income economies, however, Vietnam's employers report that they are also looking for employees with strong cognitive skills and social and behavioral skills. For example, next to technical skills, teamwork and problem-solving skills are considered important behavioral and cognitive skills for blue-collar workers. When they hire white-collar workers, employers expect that these workers are critical thinkers, can solve problems, and communicate well. Basic cognitive skills such as literacy and numeracy feature less prominently. That does not mean that they are not important—but it may mean they are simply taken for granted. In short, Vietnam's employers require that workers are not only good readers, but also good problem solvers (figure O.5).

How Cognitive, Social and Behavioral, and Technical Skills Are Formed

The skill profile of the Vietnamese workforce reflects investments made throughout their lifetimes. The foundations of cognitive and social and behavioral skills are formed early and are the platform upon which later skills are built. A skills strategy must take into account all of the points at which skills are formed and be built up from the early investments made during early childhood to on-the-job training in the labor market.

Figure O.6 provides a simplified summary of emerging evidence on the different points in childhood and early adulthood during which cognitive, social and behavioral, and technical skills may be formed. Four features of skill formation are worth noting for the development of a skills strategy.

1. *The most sensitive periods for building a skill vary across technical, cognitive, and social and behavioral skills.* These periods are indicated in dark shading in figure O.6; periods during which the skills are less sensitive to investment are indicated in light shading, and periods during which sensitivity is most limited are indicated in white. Research shows the critical importance of good early stimulation and early childhood development to be able to make the most of one's abilities. Children who fall behind early have a hard time catching up to their peers. Social and behavioral skills are beginning to be formed in the early years and continue to evolve throughout adult life.

2. *Skill formation benefits from previous investments and is cumulative.* A child who has learned to read fluently by second grade will be able to absorb more in third grade than a child who cannot yet read fluently. This implies that earlier investments are likely to have a greater long-term impact on skills because it is easier and less costly to build these skills at the moments when children are most receptive to learning.

Figure O.5 Employers' View of Importance of Job-Related Skills for Blue- and White-Collar Workers

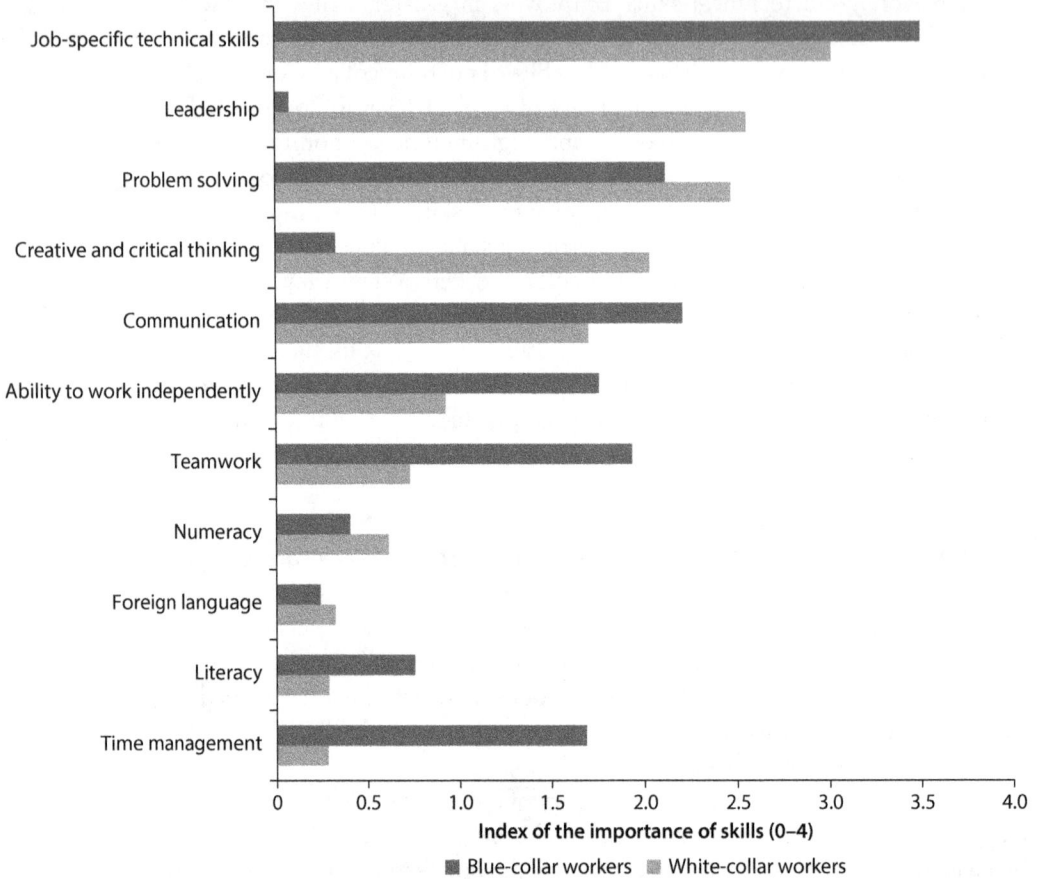

Index of the importance of skills (0–4)

■ Blue-collar workers ■ White-collar workers

Source: World Bank staff estimates using STEP employer survey data.
Note: STEP = Skills Toward Employment and Productivity. White-collar workers include the following: managers, professionals, technicians, and associated professionals. Blue-collar workers are classified as the following: clerical support; service; sales; skilled agriculture, craft, and related trades; plant and machine operators; and elementary occupations. This figure is based on the 328 and 329 businesses that reported having at least one worker in the white- and blue-collar category and were willing to respond about the skills used and needed by that worker in his or her work. The differences between blue- and white-collar occupations are all statistically significant with the exception of technical skills and communication skills.

3. *Social and behavioral skills are valuable early in a child's life because they support, and benefit from, cognitive skills development.* Children who display more openness to new experiences are more likely to be imaginative and creative and to apply themselves at school.

4. *Technical skills—often acquired last, through technical and vocational education and training (TVET), higher education, and on-the-job learning—will benefit from the stronger cognitive and behavioral skills acquired earlier in the education system.* The skills learned in formal education will help workers to continuously update their technical skills during their working lives. This ability will rise in

Figure O.6 The Process of Skill Formation: A Simplified Model

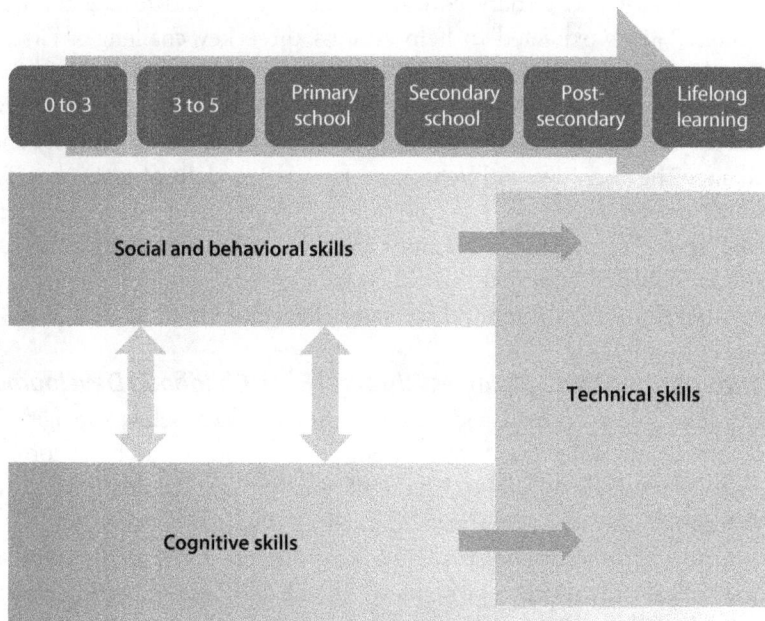

| 0 to 3 | 3 to 5 | Primary school | Secondary school | Post-secondary | Lifelong learning |

Social and behavioral skills

Technical skills

Cognitive skills

Source: Authors' illustration based on international evidence from a range of disciplines studying the development of abilities, including psychology, economics, and neuroscience.
Note: An overview of this literature can be found in Shonkoff and Phillips 2000; Almlund et al. 2011; Cunha, Heckman, and Schennach 2010; and Cunha and Heckman 2007.

importance as Vietnam's population ages, as production in Vietnam becomes more technically sophisticated, and as workers need to catch up with technological progress during their longer working lives.

Skills development starts at birth and continues through early childhood education and general primary and secondary education all the way to vocational and tertiary education and on-the-job training. Vietnam's skills development strategy should, therefore, take a holistic approach and look at how to better equip individuals with relevant skills and knowledge along an individual's life cycle. This book examines cognitive and behavioral skills acquisition in early childhood and general education and technical skill acquisition in vocational and tertiary education and on-the-job training.

Preparing the Workforce for a Modern Market Economy

Vietnam's general education system has undergone a remarkable transformation since đổi mới and is now entering a new phase. Enrollments have expanded dramatically at every level, and Vietnam's population has become increasingly well educated over the last decades. An initial successful focus on expanding primary education access and completion, as called for under the Millennium Development

Goals (MDGs), has made way to an increased emphasis on expanding pre-primary, secondary, and tertiary education enrollments and raising the quality of provision. This is expected to help address three key challenges. First, pre-primary education to promote school readiness provides the best chance to overcome remaining inequalities in education. Second, enhanced enrollments at the secondary level and improvements in teaching methods and quality should help enhance the cognitive and behavioral foundation skills of graduates. Third, overcoming disconnects among employers, universities and vocational training providers, and (prospective) students can help ensure that graduates come equipped with better technical skills. A holistic skills development strategy for Vietnam, therefore, should entail three steps (figure O.7).

Step 1: Promoting School Readiness through Early Childhood Development

Early childhood development and education for children below the age of 6 is the most important entry point for building their cognitive and behavioral skills and making them ready for school. The right nutrition and stimulation before the age of 3 through effective parenting and quality preschool between ages 3 and 6 contribute to children's school readiness. The concept of "school readiness" or "readiness to learn at school" represents whether a child entering primary school is able to succeed at school. School readiness is generally considered to be the product of a young child's cognitive, physical, and socioemotional development from an early age onward (Naudeau et al. 2011).

Figure O.7 Three Steps in Skills Development

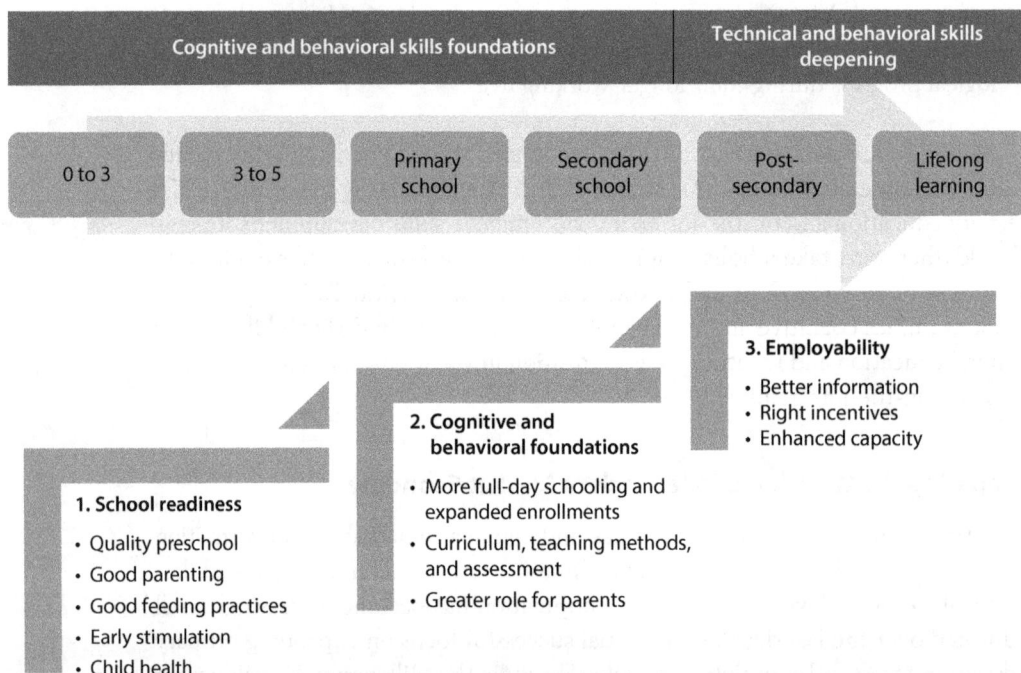

Vietnamese children from poor backgrounds are at a disadvantage in their readiness for school. In 2012 the Ministry of Education and Training (MOET) assessed school readiness among 5-year-old children in public preschools, using a survey that adapted the Early Development Instrument (EDI) to measure the development of children across five domains: physical health and well-being, social knowledge and competence, emotional health/maturity, language and cognitive development, and general knowledge and communication skills. The survey showed that children from poor households were significantly behind nonpoor children across these domains of school readiness (MOET 2012).

Malnutrition is a key driver of school "un-readiness." Almost a quarter of Vietnamese children below the age of 5 are stunted (GSO and UNICEF 2011; see figure O.8, panel a). Apart from poverty, child malnutrition can be explained by inadequate infant and young child feeding practices, including low rates of breastfeeding. In Vietnam and around the world, stunting has been found to have strong negative effects on cognitive skills development (Le Thuc Duc 2009).

Deficits in school readiness will persist throughout life. Much of the inequality in learning outcomes between different types of young Vietnamese observed in primary education and beyond is already established before the age of formal schooling. The government of Vietnam has placed increased focus on enhancing school readiness, a policy that is well motivated and addresses a key area of deficit. Vietnam's efforts at expanding access to preschool education for 3- to 5-year-olds are showing success, but more attention is needed for children aged 0–3, in particular on tackling malnutrition.

Children from poorer households often lack stimulation, which limits their development potential from an early age. The brain development of young children is highly sensitive to stimulation and interaction. The more parents and caregivers interact with a young child, by talking, singing, or reading, the better are the conditions for brain development. Evidence shows that in Vietnam,

Figure O.8 Adult Stimulation and Stunting among Children from Poorer and Wealthier Backgrounds

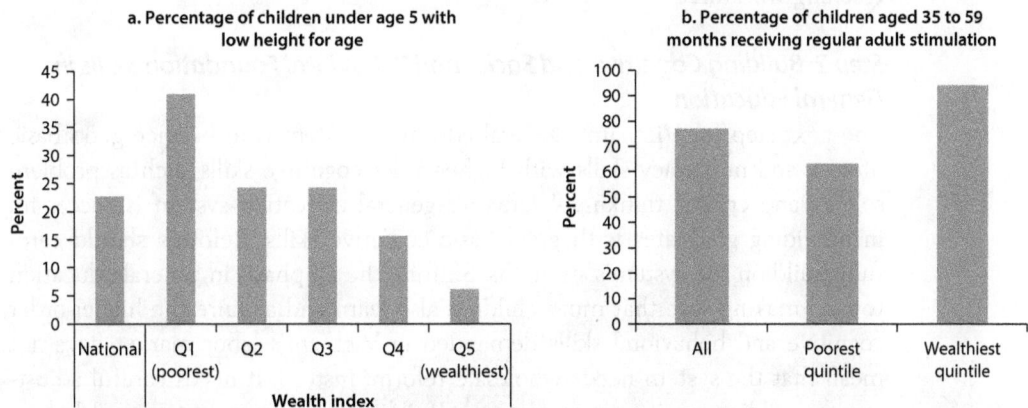

Source: GSO and UNICEF 2011.

young children from the poorest households receive less stimulation from their parents than children from the wealthiest families (figure O.8, panel b). This finding implies that during these early years, in which children's brains are the most sensitive to interactions and learning, children from poor households are not receiving the investments that they need and are already falling behind children from wealthier households.

The support for the development of children aged 0–3 remains weak in Vietnam. Considerable international and Vietnamese evidence presented in this report shows that targeted interventions can reduce stunting and mitigate its effect on a child's cognitive development. Despite high rates of stunting among children under the age of 5 and strong evidence of low and declining use of breastfeeding, the key policy interventions needed to curb the effects of malnutrition are not yet adequately prioritized in government policy. These interventions include a focus on child nutrition, particularly infant and young child feeding. There is significant scope for more systematic promotion of breastfeeding and child stimulation through family-based interventions in hospitals after birth, in local health stations, in communities, and through communication campaigns. These programs can be complemented by social safety nets to enable poor parents to make better choices for their children.

In contrast, the promotion of preschool for children aged 3–6 is currently the government's main policy lever to enhance school readiness. As a result of recent reforms, Vietnam's early childhood education system has many strengths, including a sound policy framework, child-focused curriculum, and rapidly expanding provision in the wake of the program to universalize full-day preschool for 5-year-old children (Program 239). Policies to promote access and quality at the national level, however, have not yet been fully translated into actual provision in the provinces, creating wide variations in quality and access that affect disadvantaged children. While promoting access remains a priority, particularly in underserved regions, the government's focus is now increasingly shifting toward translating its modern and child-centered curriculum into quality provision across all classrooms through upgrading the competence of the current teaching workforce.

Step 2: Building Cognitive and Social and Behavioral Foundation Skills in General Education

The next step for Vietnam's general education system is to balance good basic literacy and numeracy skills with higher-order cognitive skills such as problem solving and critical thinking. Vietnam's general education system is successful in providing graduates with good basic cognitive skills. Reforms should carefully build on the system's strengths. Shifting the emphasis in general education toward making sure that more children also learn and acquire the higher-order cognitive and behavioral skills demanded in Vietnam's labor market does not mean that the system needs wholesale reform. Instead, it needs careful adjustments, building on its strong features. Building stronger cognitive and behavioral skills will require (a) *more schooling for all*, with full-day instruction and expansion of access to secondary education; (b) *better schooling for all*, with a curriculum and teaching and assessment methods that foster the development of cognitive and behavioral skills in students; and (c) *greater involvement of parents and communities in schooling.*

More Schooling for All

Enhancing cognitive skills among Vietnam's next generation will require that they spend more time in school. First, enrollments in secondary education in Vietnam remain below potential. Enrollments are particularly low among children from less wealthy backgrounds. Education careers need to be extended through increasing progression rates from primary to lower secondary, from lower secondary to upper secondary, and then to postsecondary education. Accomplishing this goal will require easing the financial barriers to education affecting less well-off students through fee waivers and direct cash support. Second, tuition time in primary education with between 23 and 25 instruction periods over a school year of 36 weeks remains low compared to other countries. Better-off parents tend to make up for this by paying for their children to attend extra classes—regular, core academic lessons typically by their own teachers after school hours. Extra classes are not only a Vietnamese phenomenon; they are also encountered across several countries in East Asia. But they are prominent in Vietnam: in 2010 parents of 33 percent of primary students and 49 percent of lower secondary students reported some expenditure on coaching sessions for academic subjects.

Extra classes are problematic in multiple ways. First, if they focus on the same academic knowledge on a narrow part of the formal half-day curriculum (coaching sessions for compulsory subjects) as opposed to a wider curriculum and activities that help build behavioral skills, such as arts or sports, they risk consuming precious time that could be allocated for alternative activities. Second, extra classes are often informal and not regulated. They place teachers in an undue position of power in relation to parents. Parents are under pressure to pay for their children's participation in the extra classes if they want to avoid the risk that the teacher might otherwise not let the child pass the exam. There is evidence that many parents are asked to make unofficial payments to schools and teachers (World Bank 2012a; CECODES, VFF-CRT, and UNDP 2013). Receiving payments for extra classes may also undermine teachers' motivation to perform well during the formal hours of instruction. Third, richer households are able to spend much larger amounts on extra classes, and extra classes are mainly an urban phenomenon. There is, therefore, a risk that extra classes may deepen inequalities in learning.

Expanding formal full-day schooling can provide the space for a more varied curriculum and mix of instruction and may well be the best strategy to limit extra classes. MOET has attempted to regulate the provision of informal extra classes, but without much apparent effect. An alternative to regulating extra classes is to expand formal full-day schooling to reduce the time available for teachers to offer private tuition and help make up for their revenue loss related to forgone extra classes.

More schooling carries additional costs that need to be covered by the government or parents or both. Vietnam has adopted the policy of "socialization," which involves levying user charges from those who can pay, while using budget resources to subsidize access for those who cannot (usually the registered poor). This choice is appropriate so long as it is not creating new access barriers because of user charges, but getting the balance right between those who can pay and those who cannot is tricky. Well-off parents who currently finance extra classes for their children could be asked to provide formal cofinancing to schools for full-day schooling as opposed to informal payments to teachers who provide extra classes.

But there is also considerable potential to get more out of existing public expenditure because of Vietnam's demographic transition: According to Vietnamese census data, the size of the population cohort below the age of 15 declined by 17 percent between 1999 and 2009. A decline in student numbers in general education may open fiscal space to accommodate expanding full-day schooling and enrollments at secondary level. Falling student numbers due to declining age cohorts means that budget resources (fewer schools, fewer teachers) could be freed up to cover additional costs associated with expanding enrollments in secondary education and full-day schooling, including progressively abolishing tuition fees at secondary level.

Better Schooling for All

What matters is not just more schooling but more quality schooling with more creative curricula and teaching and assessment methods that foster the formation of higher-order cognitive and behavioral skills. More schooling should mean better schooling through a general education curriculum that balances competency-based and content-based learning, coupled with the right teaching methods to stimulate creative and critical thinking in primary and secondary school students and the right approach to student assessment. Vietnam can benefit from the experience of Singapore and Korea—two countries with leading education systems. These countries adopted curricula and student assessment systems that promote both knowledge acquisition and active learning and creative and critical thinking in schools. In Vietnam, steps toward modernizing the curriculum are getting under way: In response to a call from the XI Congress of the Communist Party in 2011, MOET launched an ambitious process of developing a new general education curriculum and new textbooks by 2015 with a definition of students' essential competencies, which will then form the basis of educational objectives, standards, learning content, teaching methods, and assessment.

Curriculum change and textbook reform are important steps, but what really matters is the resulting change in the teaching methods and instruction in the classroom with skilled teachers and school principals and parental involvement. Translating a new general education curriculum into concrete change in the classroom will require modernization of teacher professional development, both in-service and pre-service, and sustained investment in its rollout to all teachers. To inform its curriculum modernization, Vietnam has adapted a promising model from Colombia called *Escuela Nueva,* which features more group learning and problem solving than the predominant focus on memorization and copying often seen in Vietnamese primary school classrooms today. A Vietnam *Escuela Nueva* (VNEN) pilot under way in 1,500 schools across the country is already showing successes and holds lessons for broader reforms, and MOET intends to advance the pilot into lower secondary education.

Teacher quality matters most for better schooling, and Vietnam already has a strong teaching workforce. The primary education teacher workforce has become significantly better qualified in recent years. Nearly 60 percent of all primary school teachers now hold a college or university degree—almost double compared to 2006. Increased teacher qualification matters: evidence from a school survey conducted as part of the Young Lives research project on child poverty in Vietnam in 2012 suggests that high-performing schools have higher shares of teachers with a college or university degree. High teacher capacity is also evident in their ability to correctly assess their students' ability, which is critical to help them provide the support that their students need (Rolleston et al. 2013).

Higher-quality in-service professional development can help to better equip teachers with the skills to teach a modernized curriculum. Teacher training needs to focus not only on how to teach curriculum content but also on how to impart behavioral skills. There is a lot to improve: in-service professional development among primary teachers is limited, and the content and methods require modernization—away from the traditional cascading model (in which the MOET trains trainers who train other trainers to deliver training in the summer months) toward one in which capacities in provincial teacher training colleges are enhanced to provide more tailored programs all year round and with new teaching methods.

Beyond curriculum and teaching methods, student assessment needs to be aligned with the objective of fostering higher-order cognitive and behavioral skills. Vietnam makes heavy use of educational assessment: classroom assessments with written and oral tests and marked assignments and homework are used to provide real-time feedback on students' performance to inform teaching, and national examinations are used after grade 12 for making high-stakes decisions about students' progression to the next level in the education system. Once the curriculum and standards in general education are adjusted to better reflect higher-order cognitive and behavioral skills, the student assessment system needs to be equipped with the tools to help assess these skills (as opposed to just content knowledge that can be memorized) in students to see how schools perform in imparting these skills and to hold schools and local education authorities accountable for results. For example, the introduction of more open-ended questions would allow for greater emphasis on higher-order thinking and problem solving.

Schooling That Involves Parents and Communities

A prominent role for parents in school is important for several reasons. Parents have a strong interest in ensuring their children get a quality education. Providing them with information and a forum to voice views and advise the school can make the school more explicitly accountable to them for their children's learning progress. Much learning takes place at home, and the home environment is a critical contributor to learning success. Parents need to be aware of the school's learning process and academic content and how they can complement these by providing effective support to their children's learning at home—after school and during the long summer vacations. A greater involvement of parents and communities can also help make instruction more reflective of local needs, traditions, and contexts and can help build bridges where there are cultural and other gaps between school and home, for example, in the case of ethnic minority children who are taught by Kinh teachers.

The opportunities for formal parental involvement in schools, beyond making financial contributions, are limited in Vietnam. Schools can establish a parents' council for a class or the school as a whole but, where they exist, they have little formal powers. Such councils can channel parents' feedback to teachers on educational issues and bring their voice to the principal regarding educational activities and management of the school. Legally, however, the parents' council has only limited weight to influence the operation and monitor the performance of a public school, and in practice the role of the parents' council is often reduced to collecting parents' voluntary contributions to the school.

A greater role of parents in the school is possible even within the current system of central standards and predominant decision making at the province level. Provinces and districts could cede certain decisions to schools and involve parents. For example, schools could be entrusted with deciding on the arrangements for full-day schooling, and parents could contribute to this decision making. Parents could advise on how to incorporate extra classes into the formal program and how to arrange afternoon activities under formal full-day schooling. Greater parental involvement is already occurring in Vietnam: schools participating in the VNEN pilot have the freedom to bring parents into the learning process and contribute to learning content.

Step 3: Building Technical Skills through a More Connected System

Higher education, vocational training, and on-the-job training are the key avenues for acquiring technical skills that people need to work in their chosen profession. Higher education is booming in Vietnam and is viewed as the main avenue to raising the quality of human resources by the population, businesses, and the government alike. Returns to higher education in Vietnam are large, suggesting strong demand for university graduates. Employment prospects of graduates from a prestigious university in urban areas are good, but less so for those in rural and remote areas (World Bank 2013). In response to high returns to education, enrollments have expanded dramatically since 2002, though they remain low relative to comparable countries in East Asia (World Bank 2012c). Moreover, there are concerns about quality, particularly given the fast pace of expansion and the relevance of what students and trainees learn. Vocational training is less popular than higher education, and the share of 19- to 21-year-olds in vocational training has remained stagnant (figure O.9).

Figure O.9 Share of 19- to 21-Year-Olds in Postsecondary Education, by Type of Education Received, 1998–2010

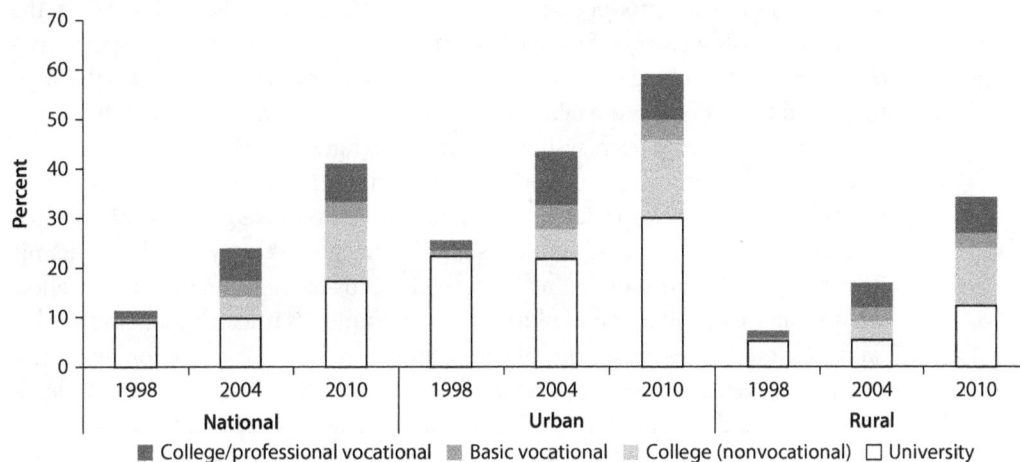

Source: World Bank staff estimates using the 1998, 2004, and 2010 VHLSS surveys.
Note: VHLSS = Vietnam Household Living Standards Survey. The figure shows the fraction of 19- to 21-year-olds enrolled in vocational training, college, or university. In 1998, it is not possible to separate out university and college; therefore, all college and university admissions are included in the university figure.

As they encounter skill gaps and shortages in the context of expanding enrollments in universities and in vocational schools, some employers choose to provide on-the-job training for their workers. The purpose of such training is to deepen the technical skills acquired in formal education and training and to adapt employees to the individual workplace. Many Vietnamese businesses report that they provide on-the-job training; however, most of this appears to be internal training, while external training is limited to few businesses and workers, often those that are already relatively well educated and trained.

Vietnam should not be concerned about the existence of skills gaps and occupational skill shortages, but about the ability of the skills development system to overcome them. Skills shortages and gaps are indicators of a dynamic economy that creates new, more skill-intensive jobs. The real concern is whether the education and training system is equally dynamic in adjusting quickly to supply graduates with the technical skills to keep up with a constant and accelerating evolution in the demand for technical skills. One indicator of responsiveness to expanding demand is the strong expansion in enrollments and in the supply of universities, colleges, and vocational training institutes. But gross enrollments in tertiary education remain lower than those in neighboring countries, suggesting that supply can and will need to expand further. Another indicator is whether the rising numbers of graduates and job applicants bring the skills that employers demand. And the evidence provided in this book suggests that they often do not.

Vietnam's skill development system today is not as responsive as it needs to be and is suffering from disconnects among employers, students, and universities and vocational schools. An unresponsive, underperforming skills development system is a disconnected system in which actors make choices and act in isolation and do not sufficiently interact with each other. Schools and universities may offer programs and produce graduates with skills that do not fully reflect the needs of the labor market. Students and parents may not be demanding the types of programs or teaching methods and content that would give graduates the skills they need to succeed in the labor market. Like many countries around the world, Vietnam suffers from such system disconnects (figure O.10).

Disconnects result from imperfect and asymmetric information among actors and their inadequate capacity and weak incentives to make good use of information. Information, incentive, and capacity deficits make the system less dynamic in responding to the evolving technical skill needs in the economy. They reflect what economists call market failures. The government's role in addressing market failures should shift away from planning and managing the education and training system centrally and top-down to an approach that empowers students, universities and schools, and businesses to make good decisions—by facilitating the flow of information, providing the right incentives to schools and universities to be responsive to information, and investing in raising their capacity. Interventions on these three drivers of system responsiveness are mutually reinforcing and should be conducted in parallel.

Better Information

Information is the oxygen of responsive skills development systems. First, without good information about employers' skill needs, conditions in the labor market, and returns to certain fields of study, education and training providers cannot make good choices on the programs to develop and offer. Second, without such information, students and parents cannot make good decisions on which school or university and which study program to choose. Third, without information

Figure O.10 Disconnects in Skills Development and Their Causes

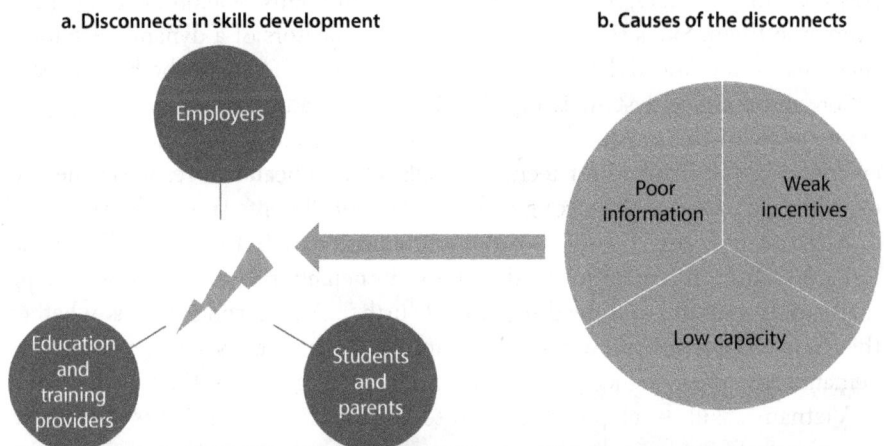

a. Disconnects in skills development

b. Causes of the disconnects

Source: Authors' illustration, adapted from World Bank 2012c.

on the quality of education programs and employment success of graduates, prospective students may not be able to make good choices.

Strengthened coordination and partnerships between businesses and universities and vocational schools can help to bridge many information gaps. Government at central and local levels can improve the flow and availability of information by using its convening power and using incentives to help initiate the establishment of formal and informal coordination mechanisms and partnerships between employers and training providers. Although institutional models and setups vary across countries, all successful skills development systems around the world have created such coordination mechanisms. They range from the highly formal and institutionalized dual system in Germany, which was built more than 100 years ago, to less formal and localized systems elsewhere. In Vietnam, partnerships already exist between leading businesses and universities, and the challenge is to learn from this experience and help spread them further. Today, however, the central government and local governments rarely act as a facilitator of such initiatives. International experience suggests they could and should.

Prospective students in urban Vietnam tend to have much better access to information to make education and career choices than their peers in rural areas have. In urban areas the market appears to provide adequate information to influence good decision making. Evidence shows that prospective students in urban areas choose those fields of study whose graduates earn the highest wages: business, information technology (IT), and sciences. Qualitative evidence suggests that prospective students in rural areas, by contrast, have fewer and less reliable information sources available than their urban peers. This finding suggests the need for more career advice in schools in rural areas and enhanced connectedness to the Internet in schools in these areas.

Better information on graduates' job placements through tracer studies can help future students choose the best schools, universities, and programs and provide an incentive to universities to focus on quality. Tracer studies can also provide useful information to hiring firms on the quality and relevance of education programs and providers. Such studies collect information on employment patterns of graduates after a certain period, usually six months. Some universities in Vietnam conduct such studies to demonstrate their graduates' labor market success, but the use of tracer studies is not systematic.

Improving the frequency and accessibility of labor market information can also help. Vietnam is collecting quarterly labor force data, but its record in publishing and disseminating this information is poor. It is usually limited to headline unemployment statistics. More disaggregated analysis and publication of returns to education, returns to occupations, and employment trends, for example, by levels of education and by occupations, can provide useful information to prospective students as well as to training providers.

Removing the scope for rent seeking and corruption in education also helps with improving information. Anticorruption surveys show that making unofficial payments in education is widespread (World Bank 2012a; CECODES, VFF-CRT, and UNDP 2013). Corruption and unofficial payments deepen the disconnects by undermining the quality of information. Paying for grades compromises the information value of grades. With such payments, grades do not fully reflect a student's real performance and therefore make diplomas less useful for students in their job search and for businesses in recruitment.

Right Incentives

Even in a world of perfect and symmetrical information, students and parents as well as education and training providers still may not be able to make the right choices if they face weak incentives. Universities that are not sufficiently autonomous in their decision making and that have to seek permission from the central government on whether to develop a new program or change any curriculum content will find it hard to respond to good information. A rigid curriculum that does not give space for vocational schools and universities to adjust their teaching methods and content to the changing and local needs expressed by employers may undermine their responsiveness.

Greater autonomy of decision making in education and training institutions, coupled with clear accountability for quality, is a critical precondition for enhanced linkages and partnership with industry. This is why the international trend in higher education and vocational training has been toward ensuring greater autonomy and accountability of institutions at the expense of central government control. In line with this international trend, Vietnam launched a comprehensive reform of the tertiary education sector that includes steps toward greater autonomy of higher education institutions. The recently adopted Law on Higher Education creates legal conditions for greater institutional autonomy for higher education institutions on many aspects such as planning, opening and closing units, new programs, financial management, and staffing. Vocational education and training institutions can choose up to 35 percent of curriculum content locally and can also introduce new study programs at their own initiative, though subject to approval by the Ministry of Labor, Invalids, and Social Affairs (MOLISA). Vocational schools also have autonomy to decide on matters such as staffing and financing.

Vietnam's principal challenge in higher education and vocational training now is to translate a legal framework for greater institutional autonomy into de facto autonomy. Despite expanded de jure autonomy of decision making on curriculum content and study programs in vocational training, many vocational institutions decide to follow directions from the government, and their main source of revenue remains government transfers, rather than proceeds from tuition fees and partnerships with enterprises (CIEM and World Bank 2013). Likewise, de facto autonomy of many higher education institutions for decision making in response to labor market needs is still limited, and university councils are not fully empowered to hold universities accountable. Although the two national universities in Hanoi and HCMC as well as regional universities are largely autonomous in decision making, public and private universities and colleges have to follow operational and academic policies set by MOET. The steps toward greater autonomy of national and regional institutions have demonstrated the benefits of a system in which MOET cedes more decision making to institutions; for example, one benefit is the establishment of partnerships with universities abroad and with local businesses.

Greater institutional autonomy for universities also means that the role of government needs to change from direct management to stewardship of the system. Despite the recent moves toward promoting greater institutional autonomy, the Vietnamese government still retains a strong say in managing the vocational and higher education systems, for example, by centrally setting enrollment quotas in higher education and regulating and approving curriculum content. In contrast, a more connected, responsive skills development system suggests a different role for government, with a shifting focus from controlling inputs (enrollment quotas, curriculum, teaching methods) to ensuring minimum quality levels (through accreditation) and incentivizing better outputs (qualifications and competencies of graduates).

Government can use regulative and financing tools to steer the system and promote accountability for results. Rather than approving the content of a training program to become an electrician, the government could invite employers and training providers to agree on occupational competency standards that an electrician should possess. Government could then focus on certifying electricians based on their competencies—whether they acquired them on the job, with a private or public training provider, or elsewhere. Other instances of partnership can be identified among the government, employers, and providers in Vietnam in determining occupational competencies. One example is the tourism sector. The government can use financing tools to incentivize excellence in universities (by allocating part of its financing based on results) or stimulate businesses to partner with training providers and expand on-the-job training (through tax breaks).

Enhanced Capacity

Even in a world of perfect and symmetrical information and appropriate incentives, students and parents as well as providers may still not be able to make the right choices if they face capacity constraints. Students from less wealthy backgrounds often drop out because they are unable to afford the tuition and nontuition as well as opportunity costs associated with education and training. Scholarship and tuition fee waivers are important tools to help students to overcome this barrier. Among schools and universities, capacity constraints may come in the form of insufficiently trained teaching staff or managers, inadequate curricula, or a simple lack of knowledge and experience on how to act on information. Financing capacity constraints can also prevent firms from investing in their workers' training.

Investments in the qualifications of staff and equipment will help universities and vocational schools to respond more effectively to the information on employer needs. At present, few staff in higher education have advanced academic degrees (figure O.11). Strengthening the graduate education and advanced training system as well as scholarships and programs to retain students in

Figure O.11 Staff Qualifications in Higher Education Institutions

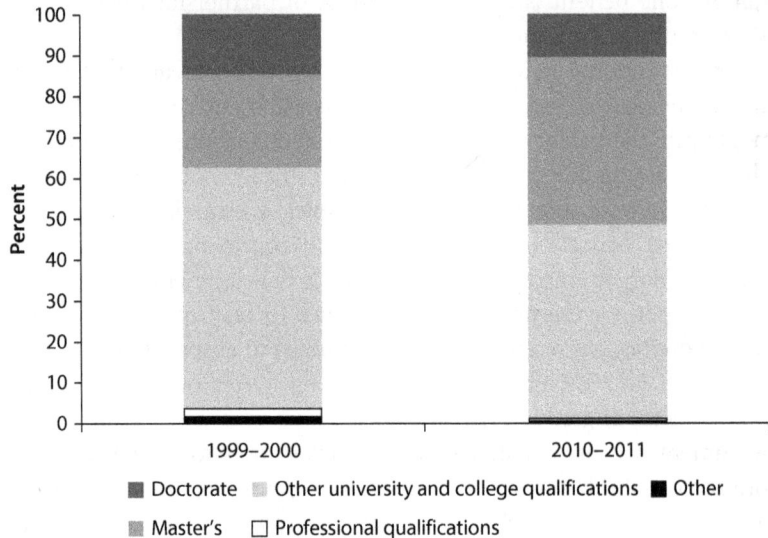

Source: MOET 2012.

universities and incentivize them to choose academic careers can help raise the overall qualification profile. Creating attractive conditions for research can help attract Vietnamese overseas PhDs back to Vietnam. Likewise, a strategic strengthening of the science, technology, and innovation system can create a better environment for attracting and retaining researchers and for promoting a growing, capable critical mass of international-level professors at higher education institutions. But capacity is not limited to teaching and research; investments in managerial capacity will enable university and vocational school leaders to take advantage of greater autonomy.

Better information, incentives, and capacity are mutually reinforcing. Government can use regulatory or financing incentives to promote partnerships between providers and industry and the generation and dissemination of better information on graduates' employment successes. In turn, better information makes providers more accountable. Ambitious and successful universities and vocational schools want to demonstrate that they have strong linkages with industry and that their graduates find good jobs quickly. Investments in their managerial and teaching capacity can enable them to do so.

Summary and Conclusion

Vietnam's continued transition toward a modern, industrial market economy is not automatic. Structural reforms in the enterprise and banking sectors and sound macroeconomic policies will matter in ensuring continued fast change, but so will the quality of Vietnam's workforce. Vietnam's return to strong economic

Table O.1 A Three-Step Agenda for Skills Development in Vietnam

Objective	Policies
Step 1: Promoting school readiness through early childhood development	
Early childhood development for children aged 0–3	More systematic promotion of breastfeeding and child stimulation through parallel family-based interventions in hospitals after birth, in local health stations, in communities, and through communication campaigns. Social assistance to enable poor parents financially to make better choices for their children.
Preschool for children aged 3–5	Universalize access to full-day preschool. Translate modern and child-centered curriculum into quality provision across all classrooms through upgrading of the competence of the current teaching workforce.
Step 2: Building cognitive and social and behavioral foundation skills in general education	
More schooling for all	Increase transition rates into secondary education through fee waivers and direct cash support for less well-off students. Expand formal full-day schooling to reduce informal extra classes and ensure more varied formal curriculum.
Better schooling for all	Modernize curriculum, teaching methods, and student assessment with stronger focus on critical thinking, problem solving, and behavioral skills. Equip teachers with tools to teach modernized curriculum through reformed in-service teacher professional development.
Schooling that involves parents and communities	Empower parents' councils in schools and involve them in decision making. Strengthen school-community linkages in disadvantaged contexts, such as through ethnic minority teaching assistants and greater involvement of parents.
Step 3: Building and updating technical skills in postsecondary education and training	
Better information	Initiate and incentivize formal or informal skills coordination and partnership forums at national, provincial, and local levels between businesses and education and training providers. Make more use of graduate tracer surveys. Address information barriers in rural and remote areas. Disseminate available labor market information. Tackle corruption in education.
Right incentives	Increase de facto autonomy of providers. Government to shift from management to stewardship of the system. Focus on outcomes, not inputs: stop setting enrollment quotas, define quality and occupational skills standards, and assess and certify graduates.
Adequate capacity	Invest in faculty/teacher training. Develop leadership and management capacity to exercise autonomy at institutional level retaining graduates in academia. Scholarships.

growth will come through increased labor productivity. Changes in education and training can take a generation to result in a workforce that is equipped with the right skills. To ensure that worker skills do not become a bottleneck over the coming decade and more, the time to modernize skills development is now. Table O.1 presents a list of key policy recommendations put forward in this book.

The nature of work in a modernizing market economy will continue to change and become more sophisticated. Vietnamese employers already are looking for a mix of higher-quality cognitive, social and behavioral, and technical skills. These skills are accumulated at various points along the life cycle from birth into adulthood, suggesting that a smart skill development strategy for Vietnam should encompass reforms and investments from early childhood development to on-the-job training. Views by Vietnamese employers are very similar to those of employers in more advanced middle- and high-income economies where, as in Vietnam, employers report that critical thinking and communication skills

Skilling Up Vietnam · http://dx.doi.org/10.1596/978-1-4648-0231-7

among workers are also in high demand but lacking. By reorienting its education system to focus more on teaching these types of skills, Vietnam can prepare itself to deliver skills that will never go out of fashion and are important in almost any industry. Vietnam's challenge, therefore, is to turn graduates from good readers into critical thinkers and problem solvers who are well equipped to acquire technical skills in universities, vocational training, and throughout their working lives.

Preparing the workforce for a modern market economy is not just the government's job. It requires a change in behavior by all actors in skills development—employers, schools and universities, and students and their parents. Businesses and universities need to build close partnerships. Parents need to become involved in their children's schooling. Students need to have work experience before they graduate.

The government's role should be as steward, not manager, of the system. It can facilitate necessary changes in behavior by helping to ensure a better information flow between all the actors; to address capacity constraints, including financing capacity; and to set the right incentives by freeing up universities to partner more effectively with businesses. Pockets of excellence in the system of cognitive, social and behavioral, and technical skills development exist already; as the system's steward the challenge for the government is to translate these pockets into system-wide change.

References

Almlund, M., A. L. Duckworth, J. Heckman, and T. Kautz. 2011. "Personality Psychology and Economics." In *Handbook of the Economics of Education*, edited by E. A. Hanushek, S. Machin, and L. Woessmann, 1–181. Amsterdam: Elsevier.

CECODES (Centre for Community Support Development Studies), VFF-CRT (Centre for Research and Training of the Viet Nam Fatherland Front), and UNDP (United Nations Development Programme). 2013. "The Viet Nam Governance and Public Administration Performance Index (PAPI) 2012: Measuring Citizens' Experiences." Joint Policy Research Paper, Hanoi.

CIEM (Central Institute for Economic Management) and World Bank. 2013. "Workforce Development." Vietnam SABER [Systems Approach for Better Education Results] Country Report 2012.

Cunha, F., and J. J. Heckman. 2007. "The Technology of Skill Formation." *American Economic Association Papers and Proceedings* 97 (2): 31–47.

Cunha, F., J. J. Heckman, and S. M. Schennach. 2010. "Estimating the Technology of Cognitive and Noncognitive Skill Formation." *Econometrica* 78 (3): 883–931.

GSO (General Statistics Office—Viet Nam) and UNICEF (United Nations Children's Fund). 2011. *Monitoring the Situation of Children and Women: Vietnam Multiple Indicator Cluster Survey 2011.* Hanoi.

Le Thuc Duc 2009. "The Effect of Early Age Stunting on Cognitive Achievement among Children in Vietnam." Young Lives Working Paper 45, Department of International Development, University of Oxford, Oxford, U.K.

MOET (Ministry of Education and Training of Vietnam). 2012. *Early Development Instrument (EDI) in Vietnam.*

Naudeau, S., N. Kataoka, A. Valerio, M. J. Neuman, and L. K. Elder. 2011. *Investing in Young Children: An Early Childhood Development Guide for Policy Dialogue and Project Preparation.* Directions in Development. Washington, DC: World Bank.

OECD (Organisation for Economic Co-operation and Development). 2013a. *OECD Skills Outlook 2013: First Results from the Survey of Adult Skills.* Paris: OECD Publishing.

————. 2013b. *PISA* [Program for International Student Assessment] *2012 Results: What Students Know and Can Do: Student Performance in Mathematics, Reading and Science.* Vol. 1, PISA. Paris: OECD Publishing.

Pierre, G., M. L. Sanchez Puerta, and A. Valerio. Forthcoming. *STEP Skills Measurement Surveys: Innovative Tools for Assessing Skills.* Washington, DC: World Bank.

Rolleston, C., Z. James, L. Pasquier-Doumer, and Tran Ngo Thi Minh Tam. 2013. "Making Progress: Report of the Young Lives School Survey in Vietnam." Young Lives Working Paper 100, Department of International Development, University of Oxford, Oxford, U.K.

Shonkoff, J. P., and D. A. Phillips, eds. 2000. *From Neurons to Neighborhoods: The Science of Early Childhood Development.* Washington, DC: National Academy Press.

World Bank. 2012a. *Corruption from the Perspective of Citizens, Firms, and Public Officials: Results of Sociological Surveys.* 2nd ed. Hanoi: National Political Publishing House.

————. 2012b. *Market Economy for a Middle-Income Vietnam.* Washington, DC: World Bank.

————. 2012c. *Putting Higher Education to Work: Skills and Research for Growth in East Asia.* Washington, DC: World Bank.

————. 2012d. *Well Begun, Not Yet Done: Vietnam's Remarkable Progress on Poverty Reduction and the Emerging Challenges.* Washington, DC: World Bank.

————. 2013. *Vietnam Higher Education Project 2 Implementation Completion Report.* Washington, DC: World Bank.

CHAPTER 1

Vietnam's Economic Transformation and the Role of Education

Vietnam is a global economic development success story. Since the launch of the đổi mới reforms in the late 1980s, Vietnam has seen rapid economic growth, which catapulted it to middle-income country (MIC) status in 2010 and contributed to one of the fastest declines in poverty ever recorded. This economic miracle was associated with substantial productivity increases and a rapid movement of labor out of agriculture and into wage employment. In large part, this structural transformation was driven by rising levels of education and an influx of foreign and domestic capital investment. Vietnam's focused investments over the last decades into universalizing primary education completion and expanding access at all levels have paid off and allowed larger shares of the population to take advantage of expanding economic opportunities.

Vietnam's development story is entering a new chapter, one that will shift the focus from factor accumulation to productivity growth.[1] Despite the success, labor productivity remains low relative to competitors in the region. Unlike in the early period of Vietnam's transition, growth in recent years has been entirely driven by factor accumulation rather than by productivity growth. Economic growth has slowed in recent years in the wake of domestic macroeconomic and structural challenges. The slower growth had an effect on the labor market, with evidence of a bifurcation that is associated with educational attainment. Well-educated workers are taking advantage of expanding opportunities in the private sector, especially in urban areas. But less-educated workers and youth from rural areas have more difficulty transitioning into the expanding private sector and are often left in the agricultural sector or in small informal enterprises such as street vending. With relatively flexible formal labor markets and still widespread informality, even in wage employment (World Bank 2014), the main barriers to labor mobility in Vietnam today are skills gaps and shortages and the lack of information about vacancies and job opportunities.

Strengthening the skills development system is an important element of Vietnam's restructuring needs to ensure that the structural transformation proceeds apace and Vietnam succeeds as a MIC. The experience from Vietnam's more advanced neighbors shows that a continued structural transformation over the coming decade and beyond will trigger a skills-biased occupational transition with growing importance of the types of jobs that require strong cognitive and behavioral skills. The pace of this change will depend on many things, most prominently on the scope of economic restructuring and on the soundness of macroeconomic policy. Taking decisive steps to modernize skills development now can help to accelerate the structural transformation, to improve productivity and growth, to boost living standards, and to ensure that skills will not become a bottleneck.

Trends in Vietnam's Labor Market since Đổi Mới

The đổi mới reforms and the transition from central planning to a market economy with a socialist orientation triggered a period of remarkable growth in the 1990s and throughout much of the first decade of the 21st century. As shown in figure 1.1, real gross domestic product (GDP) growth averaged 7.5 percent from 1995 to 2007, slightly below China's average of 10 percent. Compared to other countries in the region, Vietnam's economic growth has been remarkably robust in spite of the 1998 Asian financial crisis and the 2008–09 global economic crisis. Growth dipped to about 5 percent in 1998, but then quickly rebounded to 7 percent in 2000. Since 2008 Vietnam has experienced a growth

Figure 1.1 Real GDP Growth in Vietnam and Its Neighbors, 1995–2010

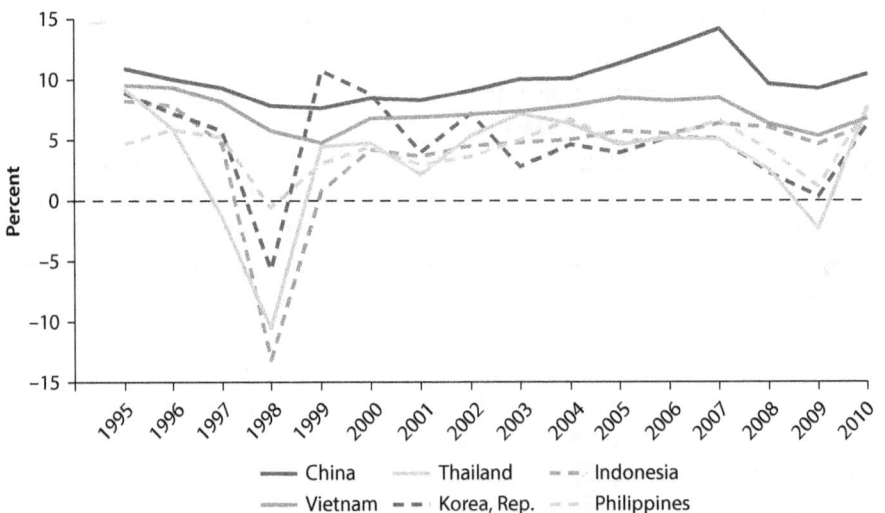

Source: IMF 2012.
Note: GDP = gross domestic product.

slowdown, which, in most recent years, has been driven by domestic macroeconomic and structural challenges. Real GDP growth fell to 5 percent in 2008, temporarily rebounded to 7 percent in 2010, and fell again to 6 percent in 2011 and to 5.2 percent in 2012.

Fast economic growth has helped millions of Vietnamese to escape poverty. Rising incomes have helped to boost living standards in urban and rural Vietnam alike. Poverty has fallen from 58 percent (1993) to 14.5 percent (2008) to under 10 percent (2010), using comparable series of Vietnam Household Living Standards Surveys (VHLSS), consumption aggregates, and the poverty line (World Bank 2012c). Changes in employment, including improvements in human capital and increases in the employment share of the export sector, accounted for more than 60 percent of the probability of households escaping poverty in rural Vietnam in the 1990s (Inchauste 2012).

Fast increases in labor productivity have been the key to Vietnam's impressive growth performance. Figure 1.2 indicates that Vietnam has seen the second-fastest growth in labor productivity in the region since 1990 after China, albeit from a very low base. The reallocation of labor across sectors, most notably from low-productivity agriculture into nonagricultural wage employment, has been a particularly important component, accounting for 2.6 percent of the 4.2 percent of labor productivity growth. Despite this fast growth, labor productivity remains low relative to Vietnam's peers, with GDP per person (at constant 1990 GDP) at 10 percent of the U.S. level.

Although productivity growth was the main driver of GDP growth in the early years of Vietnam's transition, capital investment has become more important in recent years. In the early period after the đổi mới reforms, much of the fast GDP growth was driven by increases in total factor productivity (TFP), largely in the wake of liberalization in the agricultural sector and improvements in education, which triggered the reallocation of labor across sectors. Over the years, productivity gradually gave way to factor accumulation, in particular to increases in the capital stock, as the main driver of economic growth (figure 1.3). The contribution of TFP to GDP growth since 2007 appears to have declined to nearly zero. This trend is concerning because relying on factor accumulation as the sole source of economic growth is not a sustainable strategy for Vietnam if it wants to succeed as a MIC. Rather, a return to sustained strong economic growth will require productivity improvements through structural reforms and investments in human capital (World Bank 2012b). This is why it is appropriate that Vietnam's "Socio-Economic Development Strategy 2011–2020" places the strengthening of human resources as one of the key breakthrough objectives.

Productivity growth was intrinsically linked with a transformation in the structure of the labor market. Reforms under đổi mới have had far-reaching effects on the labor market, pulling large numbers of workers out of less productive agriculture and into more productive wage jobs. In developing countries, jobs in the agricultural sector tend to be the least productive and worst paid. As countries develop, workers first shift into nonfarm self-employment and then into wage work. In Vietnam the strong growth during the 1990s was associated with

Figure 1.2 Growth of Labor Productivity in Vietnam Compared with Peers, 1990–2010

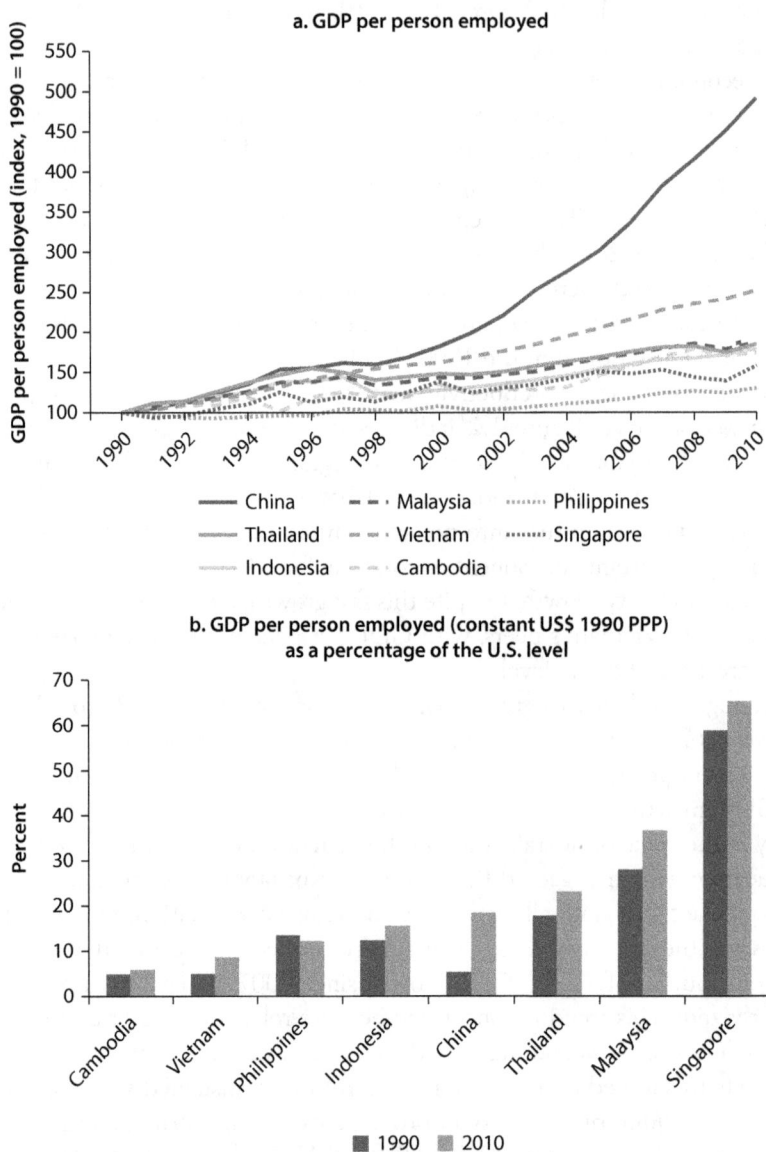

a. GDP per person employed

China — Malaysia ········ Philippines
Thailand — Vietnam ········ Singapore
Indonesia — Cambodia

b. GDP per person employed (constant US$ 1990 PPP) as a percentage of the U.S. level

■ 1990 ■ 2010

Source: World Bank staff estimates using ILO 2011.
Note: GDP = gross domestic product; PPP = purchasing power parity.

a substantial reduction in agricultural employment, driven by the dramatic decline in collective farming and a jump in the share of workers in salaried jobs (figure 1.4). More than half of Vietnam's workforce is now working outside of agriculture and is increasingly focused on wage employment. Vietnam's economy is modernizing, but the path from agriculture to wage employment is not without bumps.

Figure 1.3 Decomposition of GDP Growth in Contributions from Capital, Labor, and TFP, 1990–2010

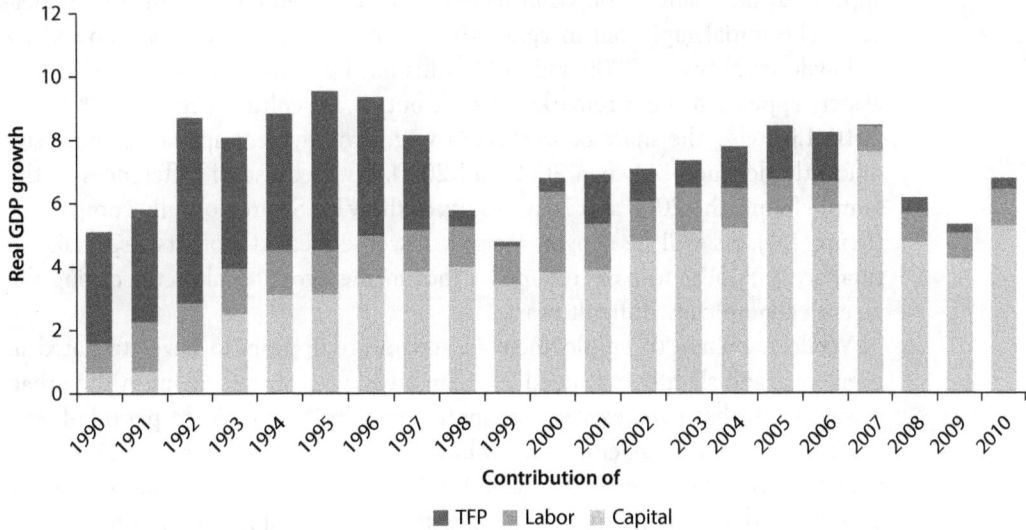

Contribution of

■ TFP ■ Labor ▨ Capital

Source: World Bank 2012b.
Note: GDP = gross domestic product; TFP = total factor productivity.

Figure 1.4 Share of Vietnam's Workforce in Agricultural and Nonagricultural Wage Employment, 1993–2010

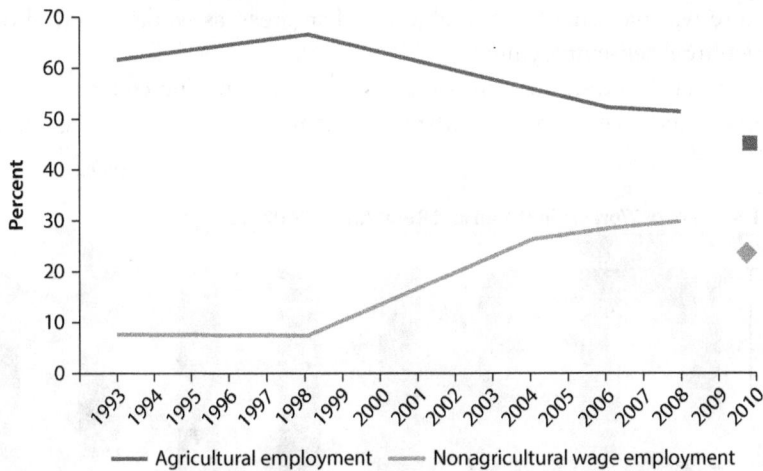

—— Agricultural employment   —— Nonagricultural wage employment

Source: World Bank staff estimates using the Vietnam Household Living Standards Survey (VHLSS).
Note: The 2010 VHLSS used a new sample frame based on the 2009 census. The new sampling frame and 2010 VHLSS are more likely to include peri-urban areas and areas with migrant populations than the sampling frame used for the 2008 survey.

The reallocation of labor out of agriculture and into wage employment appears to have slowed down in recent years as economic growth has decelerated. The initial rapid fall in agriculture from 1998 to 2006 was followed by a slowdown between 2006 and 2008. This has been followed by what, at first glance, appears to be a remarkable shift out of agriculture between 2008 and 2010. Likewise, the share of workers in wage employment appears to have significantly declined between 2008 and 2010, but because of differences in the sample frame, the 2008 and 2010 results of the VHLSS are not fully comparable (figure 1.4). As will be shown, many less well-educated workers, especially in rural areas, appear to have retained a foot in the agricultural sector during the recent economically difficult years.

While the share of employment in agriculture appears to have stagnated in rural areas and slightly expanded in urban areas, wage employment in the urban private sector has been expanding rapidly even during the recent period of economic slowdown. Wage employment in the private sector rose from 6 percent to over 8 percent between 2007 and 2010. This growth in the private sector has been more than enough to absorb a slight decline in public sector employment, which fell from 12 percent to just under 11 percent of the population. In urban areas, the share of private sector wage jobs outside of agriculture rose five percentage points in four years, reflecting a remarkable shift from public to private employment in a relatively brief period (see figure 1.5). In rural areas, the growth in private sector employment was much smaller. Meanwhile, consistent with a slowdown in the overall economy, more workers pursued agriculture. Growth in agriculture was particularly noticeable in urban areas, as workers moved out of nonagricultural self-employment.

Most nonagricultural jobs in Vietnam today are in blue-collar occupations and service and sales. Jobs as craftsmen, machine operators, or in elementary

Figure 1.5 Share of Workers in Urban and Rural Areas, 2007–10

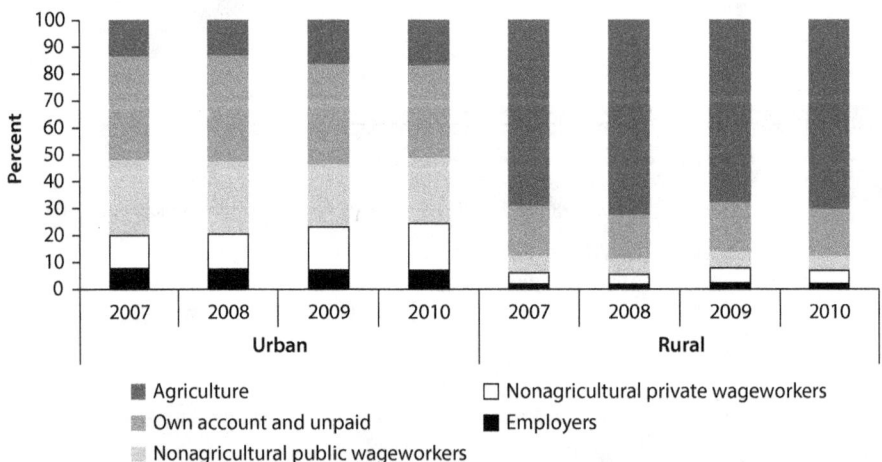

Agriculture
Own account and unpaid
Nonagricultural public wageworkers
Nonagricultural private wageworkers
Employers

Source: World Bank staff estimates using Vietnam's labor force surveys for 2007, 2008, 2009, and 2010.

Figure 1.6 Employment Shares in Nonagricultural Occupations of Workers Aged 15–64 Years, 2010

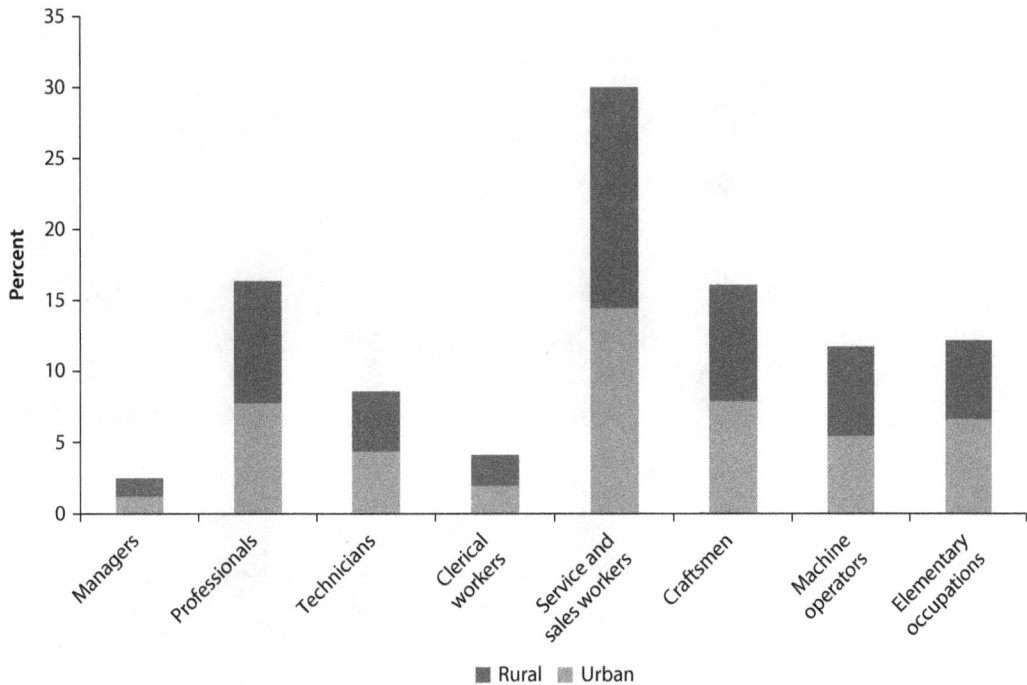

Source: World Bank staff estimates using VHLSS 2010 data.
Note: VHLSS = Vietnam Household Living Standards Survey.

occupations jointly make up 40 percent of nonagricultural employment—much more than technicians. Another 30 percent of nonfarm workers have service or sales jobs. Professionals make up 16 percent of the nonagricultural workforce (figure 1.6). Jobs across all these occupations are divided almost equally between rural and urban areas, suggesting that rural areas remain an important part of the nonagricultural economy.

Despite the rapid structural change since the mid-1990s, Vietnam's labor market development still trails that of many of its neighbors. Vietnam's share of workers in agriculture remains higher than that in China, Indonesia, and the Philippines (see figure 1.7). Similarly, despite the rapid progress in creating wage jobs that has seen it catch up to Indonesia, Vietnam still lags behind Thailand, the Philippines, and especially the Republic of Korea in terms of the share of the workforce in a salaried job. What will Vietnam need to do to catch up? What will be drivers of Vietnam's continued structural transformation in the labor market?

The pace of Vietnam's continued economic modernization will depend on the success of its economic restructuring efforts. The skills of the workforce are a critical part of that. Continued economic growth, expansion of the nonagricultural sector, and its move up along the value chain will be contingent on sound macroeconomic policy, well-planned and executed public investment, and reforms in the enterprise and banking sectors (World Bank 2012b). But worker skills matter, too. This book shows that equipping Vietnamese workers with the

Figure 1.7 Employment Patterns in Vietnam and Its Neighbors, 2008

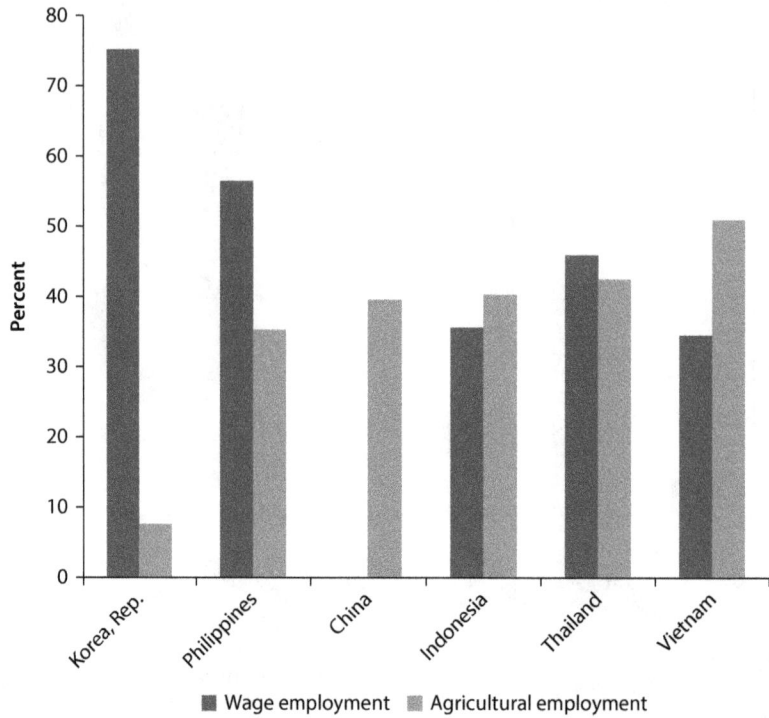

■ Wage employment   ■ Agricultural employment

Source: World Bank 2012a.
Note: Wage employment data for China not available.

right skills will enable them to continue to take advantage of expanding opportunities in a growing, nonagricultural private sector. The remainder of this chapter first examines the role of education in the urban and rural labor market since the economic slowdown and then looks ahead to its likely evolution of labor demand over the coming decade.

The Role of Education in Vietnam's Labor Market

Expanding educational attainment of Vietnam's workforce has contributed to the shifts in the labor market. Over the last few decades, the share of Vietnamese without primary education has declined significantly, and many workers, especially in professional and technical occupations, now have secondary and higher degrees. Figure 1.8 presents educational attainment by birth year for those born between 1920 and 1988. Educational attainment increased rapidly for those born before the 1960s: the share of the population with primary education or higher rose from 10 percent to over 70 percent for those born after 1960. This rapid rise in educational attainment stalled, and even reversed in the case of lower secondary attainment, for the generation born during the turbulent war period. But the rapid rise in educational attainment continued for those born after 1980 with a particularly sharp increase for those with upper secondary education or higher.

Skilling Up Vietnam • http://dx.doi.org/10.1596/978-1-4648-0231-7

Figure 1.8 Educational Attainment of Population by Age Cohort

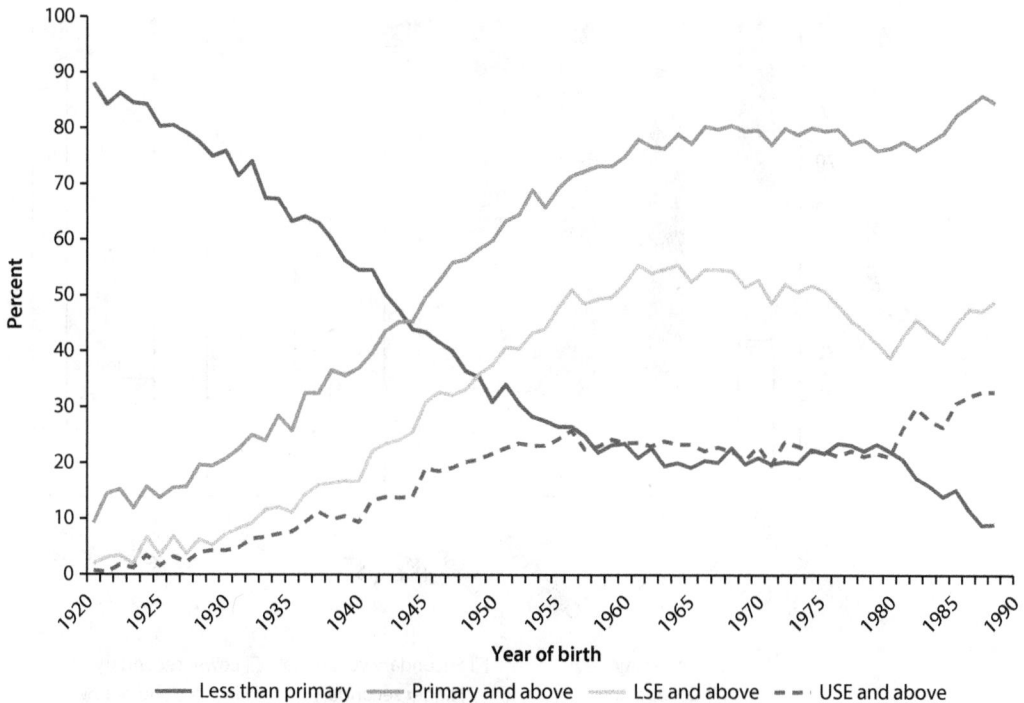

Sources: World Bank staff estimates using the Vietnam Living Standards Survey (VLSS) 1998 data and the Vietnam Household Living Standards Survey (VHLSS) 2004, 2006, 2008, and 2010 data.
Note: Year of birth was estimated based on age and year of survey. To capture those who have completed their education, only individuals older than 22 were included. The sample consists of 103,320 individuals from repeated VHLSS rounds. LSE = lower secondary education; USE = upper secondary education.

The education profile of today's workforce varies considerably across occupations. Basic general education at a primary level and below or at a lower secondary level continues to dominate the education profile of the bulk of Vietnam's workforce today—workers in agriculture, in elementary occupations, sales and services, and among craftsmen (figure 1.9). In fact, few craftsmen have even basic vocational training, and only 30 percent of machine operators have completed any level of vocational training. Vocational education and training is predominant among technicians: almost half of technicians hold a professional vocational education and training degree and another 30 percent a higher education degree. Apart from technicians, the best educated are professionals, with almost 80 percent holding a university degree and another 10 percent a college degree. There is an important demographic aspect to this: younger workers are not only better educated than older workers, but they are also significantly more likely to work in professional and technical occupations.

Despite the large increase in educational attainment in recent years, demand for well-educated workers remains high, and the economy continues to reward them. The rapid increase in educational attainment shown in figure 1.8 is partly

Figure 1.9 Highest Level of Educational Attainment by Occupation, 2010

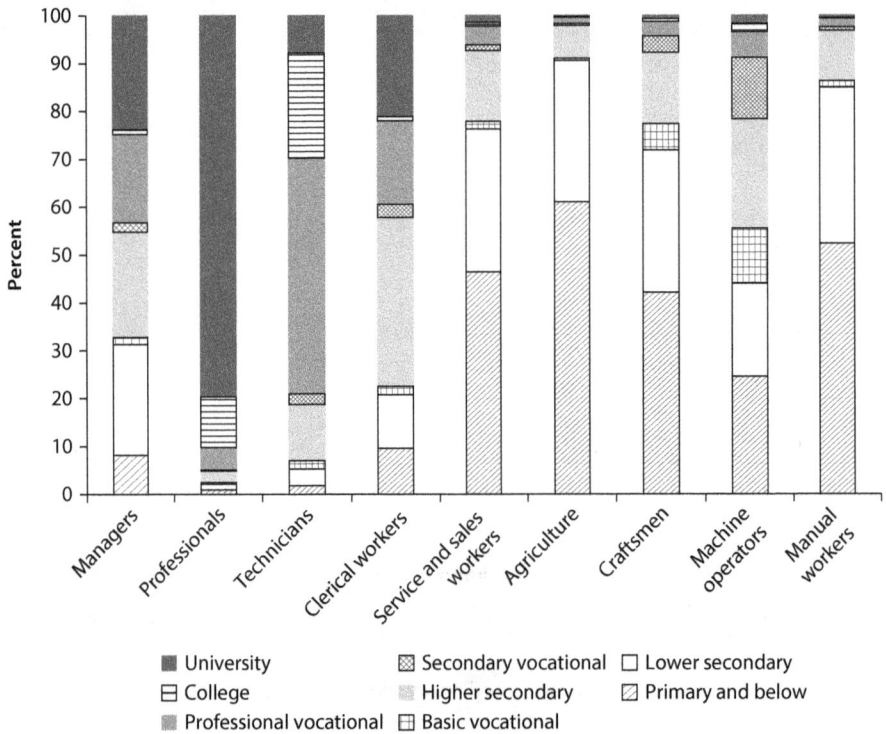

Source: World Bank staff estimates using Vietnam Household Living Standards Survey 2010 data.

a response to expanding demand for workers with higher degrees, which has been growing even faster than the supply. This is particularly noticeable at the top end of the education distribution, where the number of college graduates has not kept up with demand. Among wageworkers, the returns to college and university education surged to 80 percent in 2008 (figure 1.10). The large increase in the number of lower and upper secondary graduates has helped moderate the increase in returns at these lower levels, but upper secondary graduates in wage work could still expect to earn more than 30 percent more than primary school graduates.

Strong demand for secondary and higher education graduates has remained robust during the recent years of economic slowdown, but the demand for poorly educated workers has been declining. As shown in figure 1.11, poorly educated workers in wage jobs were earning much less in 2010 than they were in 2007, suggesting a decline in the demand for workers with primary education or less. Meanwhile, returns appear to have hardly changed for graduates from secondary education and above during this period. Graduates with vocational education and training degrees are particularly attractive: earnings premiums for workers with elementary and secondary vocational education were higher than for workers with general lower and upper secondary degrees, respectively. The high rate of return for tertiary education can help to explain

Figure 1.10 Estimated Education Earnings Premium among Wageworkers, 1993–2008

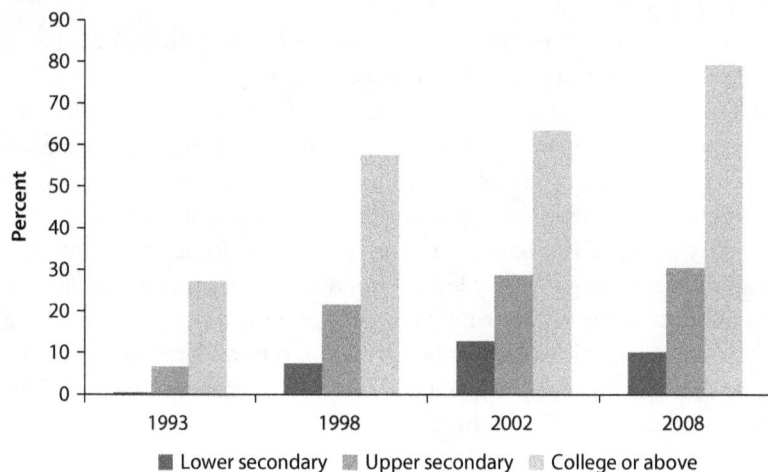

Source: Coxhead and Phan 2012.

Figure 1.11 Estimated Returns to Education among Wageworkers Relative to Lower Secondary Education, 2007 and 2010

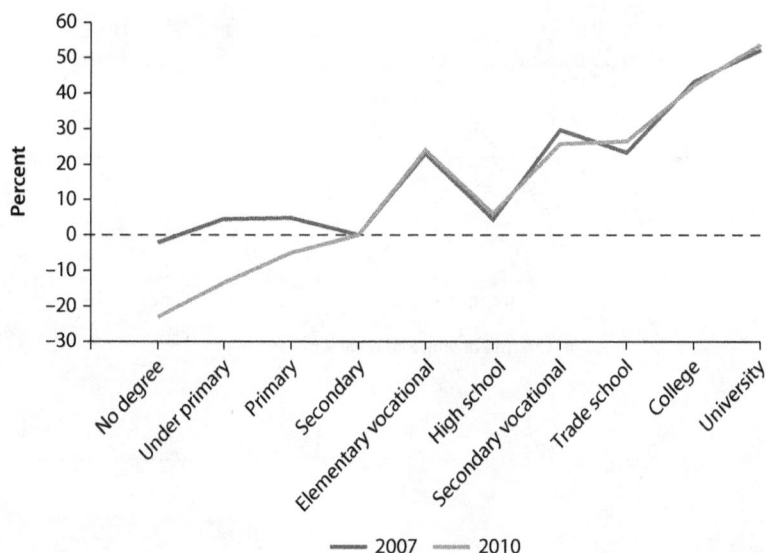

Source: World Bank staff calculations using Vietnam labor force survey data.
Note: The returns are estimated using a Mincerian wage regression in which the logarithm of hourly wages is regressed against education, sex, and experience. Various robustness checks were performed to examine whether the relative returns profile is robust to controlling for sector and occupation.

the substantial rise in the share of youth acquiring a tertiary education but also signals the need to continue to expand the fraction of workers with these sought-after qualifications.

The urban private sector is a strong source of good jobs in Vietnam, and a secondary or tertiary education degree is increasingly a predictor of employment chances. Vietnam's labor market appears to have become more bifurcated as public sector employment is declining and the structural transformation has slowed. Many well-educated workers in urban areas, in particular the young, are able to obtain wage work in the growing private sector. But many urban workers with primary or secondary education appear not to be attractive to private sector employers and are forced to take less productive jobs in agriculture (figure 1.12). The situation is starker still in rural areas, where even tertiary-educated workers struggle to obtain employment in the private sector and have to rely on agricultural employment. In short, the demand for well-educated workers in Vietnam is high and has remained robust during the recent economic slowdown.

Figure 1.12 Change in Share of Employment by Education Group and Urban/Rural, 2007–10

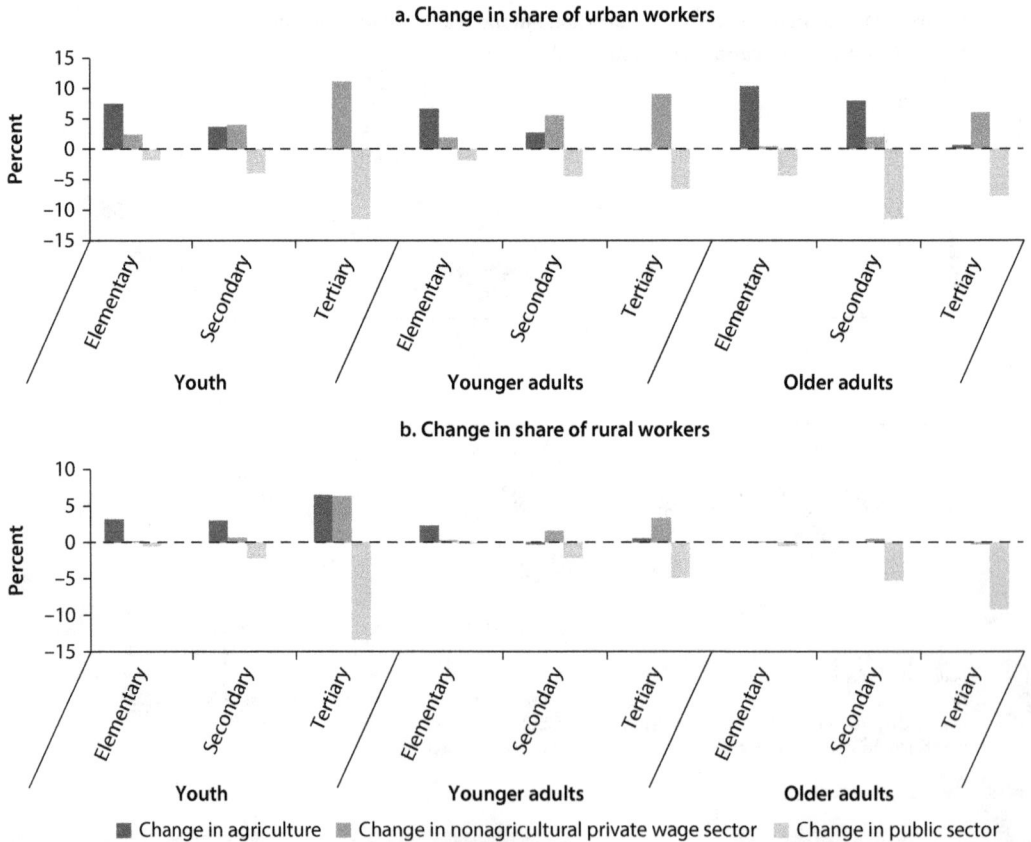

a. Change in share of urban workers

b. Change in share of rural workers

■ Change in agriculture   ■ Change in nonagricultural private wage sector   ■ Change in public sector

Source: World Bank staff calculations using Vietnam labor force survey data.

Education and skills are a predictor of labor market success more than ever before (see also box 1.1). How can the demand be expected to evolve over the coming decade and beyond?

Looking Ahead: Skill Needs for an Industrializing Vietnam

The transformation in the structure of Vietnam's economy since đổi mới has changed the type of work in Vietnam. The labor market that young Vietnamese job seekers face in 2014 is quite different from the labor market they would have entered in the early 1990s. The differences are evident not just in the employment patterns we described, but also in the sources of household income: in 1998 the majority of household income came from agricultural production; by 2010 the majority of household income came from household enterprises and wage employment.[2] Through the eyes of recent labor market entrants, the expansion of the nonagricultural sector has changed the type of jobs they pursue, the careers they can aspire to, and the education and skills they need for these careers.

Box 1.1 What Are the Barriers to Labor Mobility in Vietnam?

Labor market regulations set the legal parameters for employment through, for example, a minimum wage or hiring and firing restrictions. These regulations are often considered protective in nature and are designed to address labor market imperfections, such as unequal power between job seekers and providers. However, they may come at an efficiency cost by affecting employment, unemployment, and earnings.

Employment protection legislation (EPL) does not appear to be particularly severe in Vietnam compared to other countries. The EPL index displayed in figure B1.1.1 compares some of the most critical EPL costs faced by employers across Organisation for Economic Co-operation and Development (OECD) and East Asia and Pacific countries. In de jure terms, Vietnam's EPL is not particularly stringent for dismissals or regulation on temporary employment. Moreover, in de facto terms the impacts of regulations are likely to be relatively small because informal employment remains widespread, even among the wage employed.

This book argues that skills gaps, skills shortages, and information barriers represent the main barriers to labor mobility in Vietnam today and that labor market regulations play a subsidiary role compared with these other issues. Employers surveyed for this book stated that they consider workforce skills and experience bigger obstacles to their business operation and growth than EPL, (minimum) wage levels, or payroll taxes (figure B1.2.2).

Meanwhile, workers report that their main avenue for finding a job is their social network consisting of friends and family and not other, more formal, sources of vacancy and labor market information. People with limited networks—for example those living in rural areas far away from centers of economic agglomeration—have fewer chances to make good labor market (and education) choices. (See chapter 5 for further discussion of information barriers.)

---

box continues next page

Box 1.1 What Are the Barriers to Labor Mobility in Vietnam? *(continued)*

Figure B1.1.1 Employment Protection Legislation in Vietnam Compared with Other Countries, 2008–10

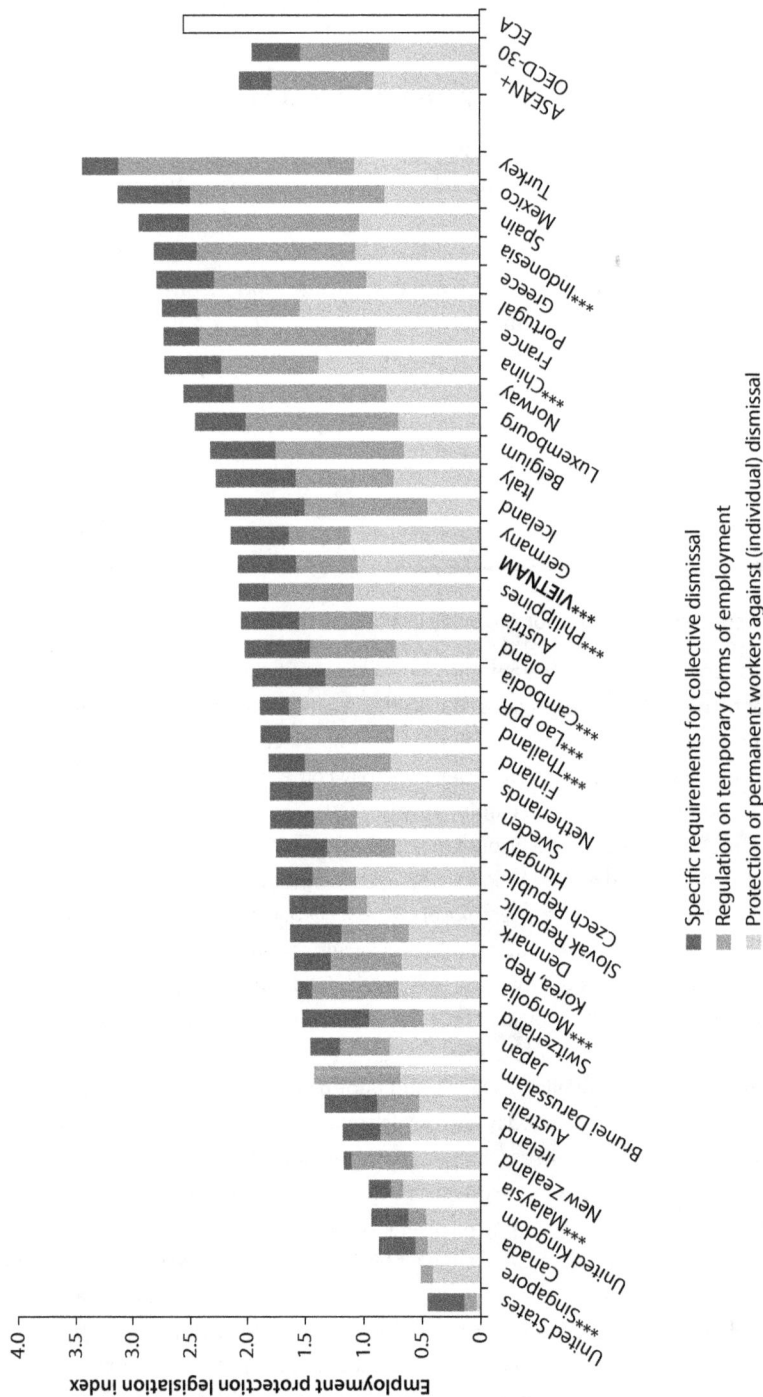

Legend:
- Specific requirements for collective dismissal
- Regulation on temporary forms of employment
- Protection of permanent workers against (individual) dismissal

Source: World Bank 2014.

Note: Scores range from 0 (least stringent) to 6 (most restrictive). OECD (Organisation for Economic Co-operation and Development) and ASEAN (Association of Southeast Asian Nations) unweighted average. OECD average includes a sample of 30 countries. OECD figures are for 2010. ECA (Europe and Central Asia) figures are for 2007 and only reflect a total (with no breakdown by category). *** = ASEAN+ countries.

box continues next page

Box 1.1 **What Are the Barriers to Labor Mobility in Vietnam?** *(continued)*

Figure B1.1.2 Labor Market Issues Affecting Businesses' Operations and Growth

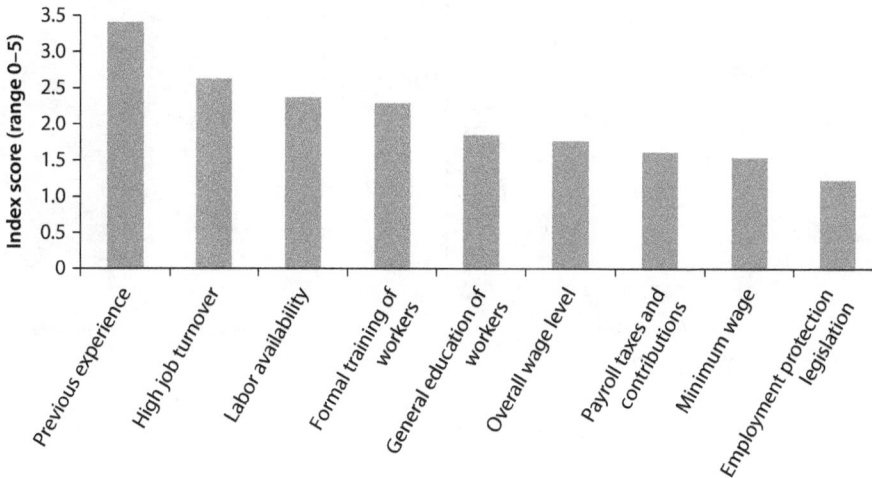

Source: World Bank staff estimates using STEP employer survey data.
Note: STEP = Skills Toward Employment and Productivity; index score range from 0 (least problematic) to 5 (most problematic). *N* = 330.

What will Vietnam's future labor market look like, and what are the implications for skill needs? A look at Vietnam's neighbors is suggestive of the direction that Vietnam might take in the coming decades and of the transformations in the type of work that will be conducted in the next stage of Vietnam's development. The share of the workforce employed in agriculture in Korea, Thailand, Malaysia, and Vietnam has seen a long-term decline (figure 1.13, panel a). While approximately 50 percent of Korea's workforce was employed in the agricultural sector in 1970, this figure had halved to 25 percent by the mid-1980s. Likewise, in Thailand the share of agricultural employment dropped from nearly 80 percent in 1970 to approximately 40 percent in 2008. The decline in agricultural employment was accompanied by an increase in employment in the manufacturing sector, from 13 percent of employment in Korea in 1971 to approximately 25 percent by the mid-1980s.

The sectoral transformation that occurred in more industrialized countries has been accompanied by a shift to more skill-intensive jobs. In Korea, Malaysia, and Thailand, the share of white-collar workers expanded over time. Figure 1.13, panel b, shows the fraction of professional and technical workers in the labor force between 1971 and 2008. Professional and technical occupations include chemists, doctors, lawyers, technicians in information technology and science, teachers, accountants, and mechanical, civil, and other engineers. Similar, but less pronounced, increases were seen in the fraction of clerical (pink-collar) workers, such as receptionists and librarians.

Figure 1.13 Percentage Employed in Agriculture and Professional and Technical Occupations in Vietnam and Comparator Countries

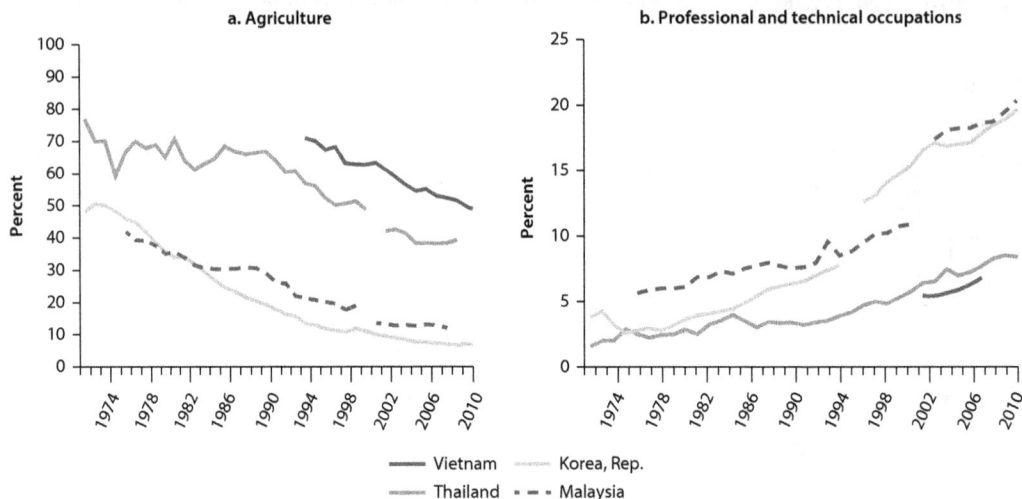

a. Agriculture

b. Professional and technical occupations

—— Vietnam   ······ Korea, Rep.
══ Thailand   – – Malaysia

Source: World Bank 2012a.

Skilled white- and blue-collar occupations dominate the manufacturing sector employment in these more developed East Asian economies today. In Thailand in 2010, approximately 10 percent of workers in manufacturing conducted elementary unskilled work, while 27 percent were machinery operators, and 45 percent were craftsmen.[3]

Placing Vietnam's economic transformation in the context of its neighbors' development paths suggests that its economy is at a transitional juncture. In Vietnam the labor force employed in agriculture has declined from more than 60 percent in 1993 to 45 percent in 2010, and the share of the workforce in manufacturing has risen by 50 percent from 10 percent to 15 percent of the labor force. These numbers put Vietnam in a comparable moment to Korea's economic transformation in 1975, a point at which the economy was transitioning away from low value-added manufacturing activities toward heavy manufacturing (Kim and Hong 1997).

The skill-biased occupational transition that has taken place in more advanced economies in East and Southeast Asia is already under way in Vietnam. The demand for analytical and interpersonal skills has been growing in urban Vietnam since the early 1990s, while the demand for manual skills has been declining. Jobs that are nonrepetitive or nonroutine in nature—in other words, jobs that involve conducting different tasks on a regular basis—expanded between 1998 and 2010. At the same time, the jobs that require the worker to do the same tasks or movements all the time have been contracting (figure 1.14). Box 1.2 explains in greater detail how the measure of the skill content of the urban workforce has been constructed.

Figure 1.14 Trends in the Nature of Tasks in Vietnam's Urban Labor Market, 1998–2010

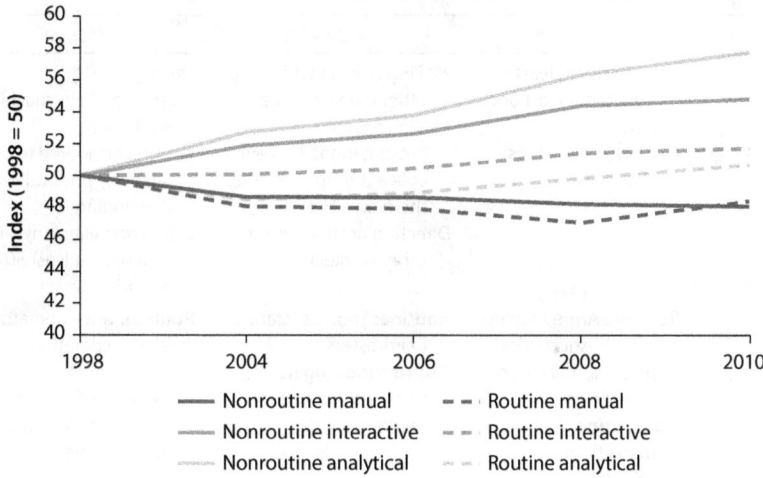

Sources: World Bank staff estimates using STEP and VHLSS survey data.
Note: STEP = Skills Toward Employment and Productivity; VHLSS = Vietnam Household Living Standards Survey. See also box 1.2.

Box 1.2 Vietnam's Occupational Changes through the Lens of Skills

The occupational changes that have occurred in Vietnam since the đổi mới reforms have changed the type of work that people do and the skills they use in the workplace. The analysis presented here uses the framework of Autor, Levy, and Murnane (2003) to examine the changes in the skills content of jobs. Jobs can be thought of as a series of tasks or activities, such as moving an object, presenting information, or conducting a calculation. A worker conducting a job needs to make overarching decisions on what tasks and activities to do next, through prioritizing tasks and making trade-offs in the face of unknown or partial information. For example, an engineer may be required to conduct and choose between multiple tasks, including complex analysis, to solve problems, to supervise members of a team, and to make presentations about their work. Classifying jobs into the skills they require allows researchers to consider the types of skills that are needed to conduct different types of work and to examine how the skills used in the workforce in Vietnam have evolved over time.

The Skills Toward Employment and Productivity (STEP) household survey conducted in 2012 and covering Vietnam's urban working-age population asks individuals about the tasks that they conduct in their jobs. For example, workers are asked how often they have to think for at least 30 minutes about a problem or how often they learn new things in their workplace. Activities or tasks conducted in different occupations are separated into four main categories: routine or nonroutine activities, analytical work, interactive work, and manual work. Routine and nonroutine is used as a primary classification because it allows a separation of jobs into those that are predictable and repetitive (routine tasks, such as those conducted by assembly-line workers in factories) and those that require workers to be adaptive to changes in their

box continues next page

Box 1.2 Vietnam's Occupational Changes through the Lens of Skills *(continued)*

Table B1.2.1 Tasks and Types of Occupations Conducted in Different Skill Brackets

	Analytical	*Interpersonal*	*Manual*
Routine: Conducting short repetitive tasks all the time **Nonroutine**: Conducting short repetitive tasks less than half the time	Thinking for at least 30 minutes at least once a week Learning new things every day	Making contact with people other than coworkers Making formal presentations to clients/colleagues to persuade them on a topic Directing or supervising other workers	Driving a car Operating heavy machines or equipment Work is considered to be relatively physically demanding Lifting or pulling anything weighing at least 50 pounds
Examples of jobs	**Routine:** Armed forces officers, shop sales persons, machinery mechanics **Nonroutine:** Architects, marketing professionals, finance professionals, teachers	**Routine:** Shop assistants, hairdressers **Nonroutine:** Engineers, sales and marketing assistants and professionals	**Routine:** Truck operators, food preparation workers, craftspeople **Nonroutine:** Shop sales persons, transport clerks, repairpeople

environment and not repeat the same processes on a regular basis (nonroutine tasks, such as those conducted by architects, engineers, and salespersons) (table B1.2.1).

Using the information in the STEP household survey on the task content of jobs and data from the VHLSS, it is possible to estimate the fraction of the urban workforce that are in jobs using analytical, interpersonal, and manual skills between 1998 and 2010. The average skill used in occupations (at a one-digit level) can be calculated using the STEP survey, and then the average skill usage can be applied to the fraction of the urban population in that one-digit occupation, as captured in the VHLSS. An increase in the fraction of the population with, for example, nonroutine analytical skills implies that occupations that are relatively intensive in the use of these skills are expanding over time.

Figure 1.14 shows the evolution of these skills in the workforce over time, using the fraction of the workforce using those skills in 1998 as the benchmark. In absolute terms, the fraction of the population doing routine tasks and using manual skills continues to be high. However, the fraction of the population in jobs that use analytical and interpersonal skill sets has increased over time in urban Vietnam, while the fraction of the population in jobs that use manual skills has declined over time. Therefore, although work using manual skills continues to be in demand, there has been a gradual shift in the fraction of jobs that use analytical and interpersonal skill sets.

Analytical and interpersonal skills are in high demand and highly valued, as signaled by high wage returns to these skills relative to manual skills. It is not just that the use of analytical and interactive tasks has expanded over the last decade. These tasks also carry high wage returns. Figure 1.15 shows the return to conducting analytical, interactive, and manual skills, broken down by whether these skills are used in repetitive or nonrepetitive tasks.

Figure 1.15 Percentage Return to Different Task Combinations, Controlling for Education and Demographics

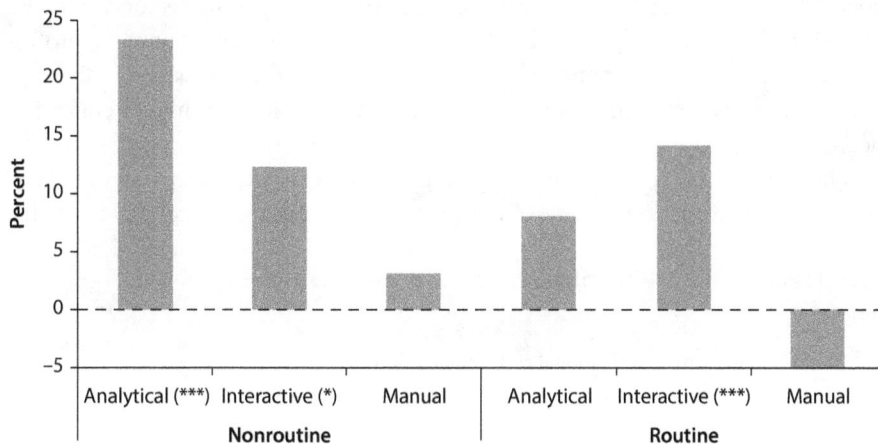

Source: World Bank staff estimates using STEP household survey data.
Note: STEP = Skills Toward Employment and Productivity. Jobs are divided into categories based on the type of tasks that people in the jobs are reported to do. In particular, a job is first divided into routine or nonroutine tasks, and is further classified into those that are analytical (require continuous thinking and problem solving), interactive (that require interacting with others), and manual. Jobs can be classified into more than one category; for example, jobs can be nonroutine analytical and interactive. The return displayed is the return of being in a job in which a task is performed relative to being in a job that is nonanalytical, noninteractive, and nonmanual, such as office clerks. The returns are estimated using a Mincerian wage regression that controls for education, sex, experience, and one-digit sector as well as the task content of jobs. See box 1.2 for more information on the evidence used to generate this figure.
Significance level: * = 10 percent, ** = 5 percent, *** = 1 percent.

The transition into jobs requiring more advanced cognitive and behavioral skills has already begun with the youngest generation of labor market entrants. Figure 1.16, panel a, shows the fraction of workers employed in professional and technical occupations, by location and age cohort. Among labor market participants aged 25–34, there appears to have been a sharp increase in the fraction employed in professional and technical occupations in urban areas. These occupations have also been on the rise among other age cohorts in urban areas, albeit less rapidly, and have also expanded to account for 7 percent of jobs among younger rural workers. In rural areas, as shown in panel b of figure 1.16, the expansion of the manufacturing sector has increased the demand for craftsmen and machine operators. The fraction of 25- to 34-year-olds working in skilled blue-collar occupations in manufacturing has more than doubled, from 7 percent of the rural workforce in 1998 to 18 percent in 2010.

Summary and Conclusion

The expanding educational attainment of its workforce has been an important driver of the rapid modernization of the Vietnamese economy since the launch of the đổi mới reforms. Universal primary education and expanding secondary education have helped workers make the transition out of agriculture into nonagricultural wage employment and from the rural sector to the urban sector. Education has become an ever more important predictor of success in finding a good job in the expanding occupations and in the urban private sector. While the majority of jobs are in skilled blue-collar occupations, employment in professional and technical occupations has grown rapidly in urban areas and with it the demand for workers with a secondary general and vocational or higher education degree.

The experience of Vietnam's neighbors suggests that the sectoral and occupational transformations witnessed over the last 20 years are likely to continue.

Figure 1.16 Growth of Employment in Technical and Professional Occupations among Different Age Cohorts

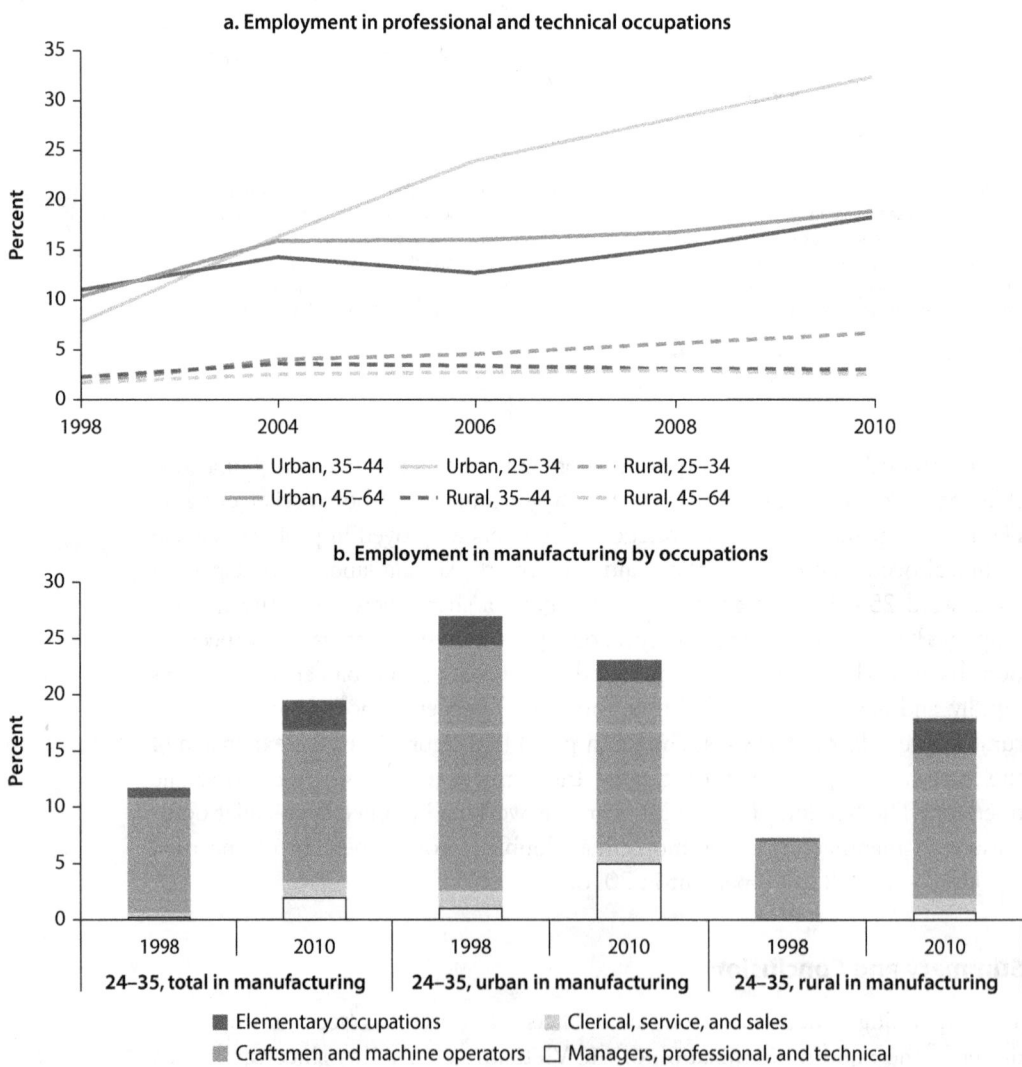

a. Employment in professional and technical occupations

Legend: Urban, 35–44 — Urban, 25–34 — Rural, 25–34 — Urban, 45–64 — Rural, 35–44 — Rural, 45–64

b. Employment in manufacturing by occupations

Legend: Elementary occupations — Clerical, service, and sales — Craftsmen and machine operators — Managers, professional, and technical

Sources: World Bank staff estimates using the Vietnam Living Standards Survey (VLSS) 1998 data and Vietnam Household Living Standards Survey (VHLSS) 2004, 2006, 2008, and 2010 data.

This transformation is not automatic, however, and the question to be answered is how fast its pace will be. Structural reforms and sound macroeconomic policies will matter in ensuring continued fast change, but so will the quality of Vietnam's workforce. With changes in education and training taking a generation to result in a workforce equipped with the right skills, now is the right time to modernize skills development to ensure worker skills do not become a bottleneck.

Jobs that are likely to grow in Vietnam—in professional and technical occupations—require workers to have more advanced skills than those working in jobs that are likely to decline in demand over the next 20 years. Traditional jobs in agricultural and elementary occupations require routine and manual work. The jobs of the future involve performing increasingly complex tasks that require workers to be able to solve problems, learn on the job, and be responsive to shifting needs. The jobs of the future also require workers to have strong social and behavioral skills because they will require workers to conduct tasks such as working in teams and supervising others. These more complex tasks command higher wages, commensurate with the more advanced skill sets they demand. The next chapter will review the demand for skills by Vietnamese employers today and assess to what extent the education system is providing graduates with these skills.

Notes

1. Factor accumulation is an increase in the basic factors used to produce goods and services in the economy: labor and capital.

2. In 1993, 60 percent of rural household income came from agriculture and sideline activities (McCaig, Benjamin, and Brandt 2009). In 2010 approximately 34 percent of rural household income came from these activities (Badiani and Brandt 2013).

3. Due to changes in occupational codes over time, it is difficult to examine the change in the share of skilled blue-collar occupations in the manufacturing sector over time.

References

Autor, D., F. Levy, and R. Murnane. 2003. "The Skill Content of Recent Technological Change: An Empirical Exploration." *Quarterly Journal of Economics* 118 (4): 1279–1334.

Badiani, R., and L. Brandt. 2013. "Inequality in Vietnam: Explanations of Changes in Disparities." Working Paper, World Bank, Washington, DC.

Coxhead, I., and D. Phan. 2012. "Long-Run Costs of Piecemeal Reform: Wage Inequality and Returns to Education in Vietnam." Staff Paper Series 566, University of Wisconsin, Agricultural and Applied Economics.

ILO (International Labour Organization). 2011. *Key Indicators of the Labour Market.* 7th ed. Geneva, Switzerland: International Labour Organization.

IMF (International Monetary Fund). 2012 (October). *World Economic Outlook: Coping with High Debt and Sluggish Growth.* Washington, DC: International Monetary Fund.

Inchauste, G. 2012. "Jobs and Transitions Out of Poverty: A Literature Review." Background Paper for the World Development Report 2013, World Bank, Washington, DC.

Kim, K. S., and S. D. Hong. 1997. *Accounting for Rapid Economic Growth in Korea, 1963–1995*. Seoul: Korea Development Institute.

McCaig, B., D. Benjamin, and L. Brandt. 2009. *The Evolution of Income Inequality in Vietnam between 1993 and 2006*. University of Toronto.

VHLSS (Vietnam Household Living Standards Survey). Multiple years. National Statistics Organization, Hanoi.

Vietnam Labour Force Survey. Multiple years. General Statistics Office of Vietnam, Hanoi.

World Bank. 2012a. *World Development Indicators 2011*. Washington, DC: World Bank.

———. 2012b. *Market Economy for a Middle-Income Vietnam*. Washington, DC: World Bank.

———. 2012c. *Well Begun, Not Yet Done: Vietnam's Remarkable Progress on Poverty Reduction and the Emerging Challenges*. Washington, DC: World Bank.

———. 2014. *East Asia Pacific at Work: Employment, Enterprise, and Well-Being*. East Asia and Pacific Regional Report. Washington, DC: World Bank.

CHAPTER 2

Skills for Current and Future Jobs

The shift away from agriculture seen since the đổi mới reforms has changed the type of work that Vietnamese people do and the skills they need to do their jobs. Jobs can be thought of as a series of activities, such as harvesting rice, sewing clothes, checking the temperature of a patient, calculating profits, and presenting analysis. A worker conducting a job needs to make overarching decisions on what tasks and activities to do next, through prioritization and recognizing trade-offs. Making these choices and conducting these activities require a set of skills for the person to perform them well, from physical strength and manual dexterity to numerical skills and the self-confidence to put forward new ideas. Vietnam is gradually moving away from the type of jobs that consist mainly of manual and repetitive activities and is moving toward jobs that require workers to solve problems and to use more modern technology.

Although the shift in the demand for skills in Vietnam has been gradual, it has been transformative. The change in the type of jobs that Vietnamese people do over time has implications for the skills that the education system needs to build. A young urban labor market entrant in Vietnam faces not only a more diversified choice of career paths than ever before, but also a more demanding set of employers. Rural households that were previously focused on agricultural activities have moved in large numbers into nonfarm enterprise activities that require choosing products and suppliers, interacting with customers, setting prices, and calculating profits. Although this book focuses on data from urban areas, the rise in nonagricultural activity in rural areas implies that similar, if not as fast-paced, transitions are under way there. These changes to what people across rural and urban Vietnam do on a daily basis imply that the way that they use their education has changed over time.

Both employers and employees in urban areas report that the education system does not provide all the skills needed in the current Vietnamese labor market. The skill shortages are reported to be greatest for businesses with international links and among employees expected to do complex tasks. Although education has improved over the last 30 years, employers and employees recognize that the education system today does not provide graduates with all the needed skills for their enterprises, workplaces, and career aspirations. Reports from employers suggest that the economy suffers from a skills shortage and that the shortage is a substantial obstacle to the operation and growth of their businesses. "International" firms—foreign direct investment (FDI) firms, firms that are engaged in international trade, and firms that have international links—are affected by the skills shortage more than "local" businesses. This means that the skills shortage, if not addressed, may become a binding constraint to the modernization and growth of the Vietnamese economy. Workers of all education levels report that their literacy and information technology (IT) skills are a constraint to their career growth.[1]

Although technical skills are in high demand, employers value a broader skill set. There is a strong return to education in urban Vietnam, and the return to education has increased over time (Coxhead and Phan 2012). One reason that people with upper secondary or university education earn more than those with primary education is that they have better technical, cognitive, social, and behavioral skills. Employers value and pay for cognitive and technical skills, such as being able to solve problems and think critically. Employers also value social and behavioral skills, such as being able to communicate well, work in teams, and have positive job attitudes. This chapter discusses the type of skills that employers in urban Vietnam demand and examines the importance of skills in Vietnam's economy. It shows that to serve the emerging needs of the labor market, it is necessary to look beyond educational attainment to focus on the underlying skills that are produced by the education system.

Shifting the Dialogue: From Education to Skills

Vietnam has made impressive strides in raising education levels and in reducing inequalities in education access over the past two decades. Among young adults between 20 and 24 years of age, 90 percent had completed primary education in 2010 compared to 85 percent in 2004 (figure 2.1, panel a). The rise in primary school completion among this age cohort has been dominated by poorer households, and primary completion rates among the rural and urban population are nearly identical among individuals transitioning into the labor market in 2010. More important, these gains in education and narrowing disparities across income groups are also seen at lower and upper secondary levels. The share of 20- to 24-year-olds who have completed at least lower secondary education has increased across all expenditure quintiles, most notably among the poorest households (figure 2.1, panel b). In urban Vietnam, 6 in 10 workers have attained a higher level of education than their parents, and the youngest cohort of labor market participants is more likely to have graduated from tertiary education than older workers. Enrollment rates reported by the United Nations Educational, Scientific, and Cultural Organization's (UNESCO) Institute for Statistics reveal a rapid increase in tertiary enrollment from 10 percent in 2000 to 24 percent in 2011 (UNESCO 2013).

Figure 2.1 Educational Achievement of the Population Aged 20–24 Years, 2004–10

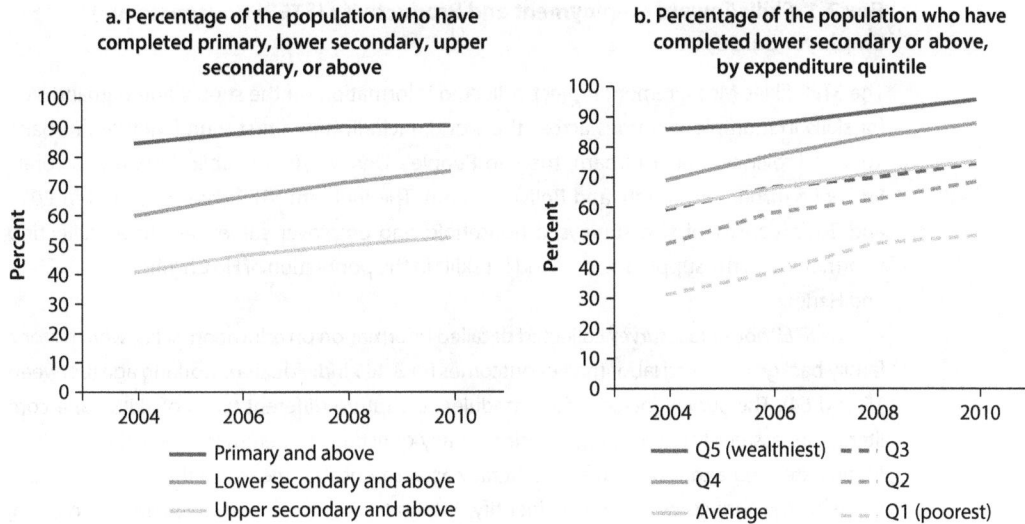

a. Percentage of the population who have completed primary, lower secondary, upper secondary, or above

— Primary and above
—— Lower secondary and above
—— Upper secondary and above

b. Percentage of the population who have completed lower secondary or above, by expenditure quintile

—— Q5 (wealthiest)   - - Q3
—— Q4   - - Q2
—— Average   - - Q1 (poorest)

Source: World Bank staff estimates using VHLSS survey data, 2004–10.
Note: VHLSS = Vietnam Household Living Standards Survey.

Despite the impressive rise in education acquisition, many Vietnamese businesses report a shortage of workers with adequate skills as a significant obstacle to their activity. A majority of employers surveyed under the Skills Toward Employment and Productivity (STEP) employer survey (see box 2.1) report that hiring new workers is difficult either because of inadequate skills of job applicants (a skills gap) or because of a scarcity of workers in some occupations (skills shortage) (see box 2.2 for a definition of these terms).[2] STEP evidence suggests that worker skills and availability are more binding concerns for employers than labor market regulations and taxes. Over 60 percent of international firms view the shortage of labor with the right skills as an obstacle to their activity, and nearly half of these firms view it as a major obstacle (figure 2.2). Nearly 40 percent of international firms see the general education of workers as an obstacle, and 46 percent see vocational education as an obstacle. Employers from international firms estimate that approximately 14 percent of their employees are not fully qualified to do their jobs, which suggests that despite expanding attainment, the educational system does not respond to labor market needs and that improving the quality of education will remove an important barrier to productivity and growth of Vietnamese firms.

Vietnamese employers are highly critical of the quality of the education system. Almost half of the employers in the STEP survey complain that graduates do not have the level of skills needed in their workplace. International firms complain about the quality of education more often than local businesses do. Two-thirds of all international firms claim that both the general and vocational education systems do not meet the skill needs of their workplace. In the eyes of

Box 2.1 Skills Toward Employment and Productivity (STEP) Household and Employer Surveys

The STEP Skills Measurement Project collected information on the supply and demand side for skills in multiple countries across the world, including in a first round Vietnam (urban), Yunnan Province, China (urban), the Lao People's Democratic Republic (urban and rural), Sri Lanka (urban and rural), and Bolivia (urban). The Vietnam STEP data, collected in 2011 and 2012, consist of two surveys, a household and employer survey, aimed at collecting information on the supply and demand for skills in the population of Ho Chi Minh City (HCMC) and Hanoi.

The *STEP household survey* collected detailed information on education, skills, work history, family background, and labor market outcomes for 3,405 individuals of working age (between 15 and 64). The survey includes four modules to capture different types of skills: (a) a core literacy assessment that asks eight easier literacy questions to determine basic literacy skills; (b) an extended and more advanced literacy assessment that measures the level of competence of the individual to access, identify, integrate, interpret, and evaluate information; (c) a battery of self-reported information on personality and behavior; and (d) a series of questions on task-specific skills that the respondent possesses or uses in his or her work. The same questions were asked in all countries participating in the survey, thereby allowing for international comparisons of skills and skill development.

The literacy assessment in the STEP household survey and the Survey of Adult Skills (a product of the Programme for the International Assessment of Adult Competencies, or PIAAC) conducted by the Organisation for Economic Co-operation and Development (OECD) in 24 OECD and partner countries (OECD 2013) were linked and their results can be placed on the same scale. Comparisons should be interpreted with caution given differences in the surveys' target population, assessment areas, and technical standards. More detail on this can be found in annex 2A.

The skill profile of older workers reflects a lifetime of accumulation at work and school, while the skill profile of younger individuals reflects accumulation during earlier stages. Skills depend on innate abilities, learning at home and school during early childhood and subsequently, and on acquisition on the job. More discussion on the measurement of skills can be found in annex 2A.

The *STEP employer survey* was conducted in HCMC and Hanoi and immediately surrounding provinces; it can therefore be considered to be representative of these two major urban conglomerations. The employer survey gathers information on hiring, compensation, termination, and training practices as well as enterprise productivity. The survey includes questions to identify: (a) employers' skill needs and utilization; (b) the types of skills that are considered of most value; and (c) the tools used to screen prospective job applicants.

Throughout the text, "international firms" are defined as businesses that have international business contacts with entities in other countries. International firms are considered as modern firms, while businesses that do not have international business contacts are considered as traditional firms. International firms represent 35 percent of all firms, but account for 93 percent of total employment in the survey. International firms are therefore much larger than local

box continues next page

Box 2.1 Skills Toward Employment and Productivity (STEP) Household and Employer Surveys *(continued)*

businesses: on average they employ 490 workers compared with 29 workers employed by local businesses. International firms are more likely to report good economic performance than local firms and more frequently introduce innovations. The share of blue-collar occupations is significantly higher in international firms, while the share of white-collar occupations (including professionals and technicians) is lower. There are no significant locational differences between international and local firms.

The employer and household surveys use the same skills concepts and definitions, which enables the analysis of skills constraints from demand- and supply-side perspectives. On the person or worker side, the household survey measures the human capital stock of skills—the skill supply. On the employer side, the employer survey captures the types of skills demanded and potential shortages—the demand for skills. The simultaneous measurement of skills stocks and demands allows an in-depth analysis of skill needs and the skill profile of the population of HCMC and Hanoi.

Box 2.2 Defining Skill Gaps and Occupational Skill Shortages

Businesses report that hiring workers is difficult. Although the explanation for this difficulty varies by occupation, two explanations stand out. First, applicants lack required skills—*a skills gap*. Second, there are no or few applicants—*an occupational skills shortage*. Other reasons, such as excessive wage expectations or unsatisfactory working conditions (meaning that the applicants turn down the job offer), are usually secondary.

An occupational shortage occurs when, given the prevailing wage level, the demand for workers with certain technical skills exceeds their supply. When businesses are not able to fill vacancies in a certain occupation because there are too few applicants, this is an indication of an occupational shortage. For example, when the job vacancy rate for electricians is high, it indicates a shortage of electricians. An occupational shortage tends to be associated with a growth in relative wages for the workers in the occupation that is in short supply. In a competitive labor market, the growing relative wages induce an increase in the supply of workers in the given occupation; this eventually leads to an equilibrium whereby demand and supply match.

A skills gap occurs when workers lack the skills required by employers. They may lack technical skills, cognitive skills, or social and behavioral skills (or some combination of them). An indication of a skills gap is employers finding it difficult to hire workers with the required skills despite the fact that there are numerous job applicants. For example, there are many applicants for a position of an office clerk, but employers are not satisfied with the applicants' skills. A skills gap points to weaknesses in the educational system in the sense that it does not equip workers with the skills demanded by employers. Accordingly, a skills gap should be addressed by reforms to the education and training systems.

box continues next page

Box 2.2 Defining Skill Gaps and Occupational Skill Shortages *(continued)*

Figure B2.2.1 illustrates the difference between these two concepts. If there is an occu-pational shortage, job vacancies are difficult to fill because there are few applicants. Craftsmen are the case in point. Many employers found it hard to hire craftsmen because there were no or few applicants, meaning that the supply of craftsmen fell short of the demand, which may point to an underdeveloped vocational education and training system. This is in sharp contrast to the case of technicians (as well as professionals) where it is the lack of adequate skills among the job applicants, rather than the lack of applicants, that is the main problem. This is a clear case of a skills gap. Workers have the diplomas (formal qualifications) required for the jobs that they apply for, but they lack the actual skills they need to do their jobs, which may indicate that the quality of tertiary education does not keep up with employers' expectations.

Figure B2.2.1 Problems Businesses Encountered When Trying to Hire

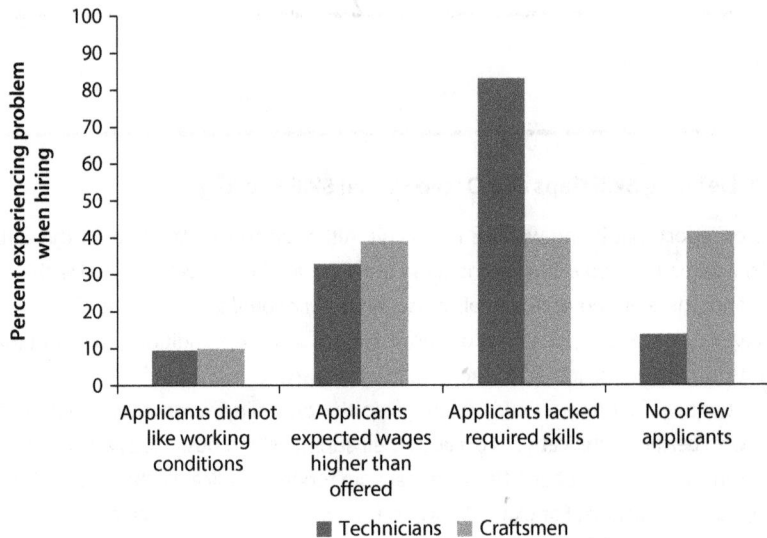

Source: World Bank staff estimates using STEP employer survey data.
Note: STEP = Skills Toward Employment and Productivity. Employers were asked if they had tried to hire workers for various positions during the previous 12 months and what problems they encountered. The data cover reports from 132 businesses that hired craftsmen and 34 businesses that hired technicians. Because the number related to technicians is small, care should be taken in interpreting this figure. The displayed differences between technicians and craftsmen are statistically significant at a 5 percent level for two responses: applicants lacking required skills and too few applicants.

the employers, school leavers are equipped neither with the appropriate skills acquired through the school and university system nor with the appropriate vocational skills.

Concern about missing skills is particularly pronounced among white-collar workers, such as professionals and technicians. A lack of required skills among job

Figure 2.2 Reported Obstacles to Business Activity

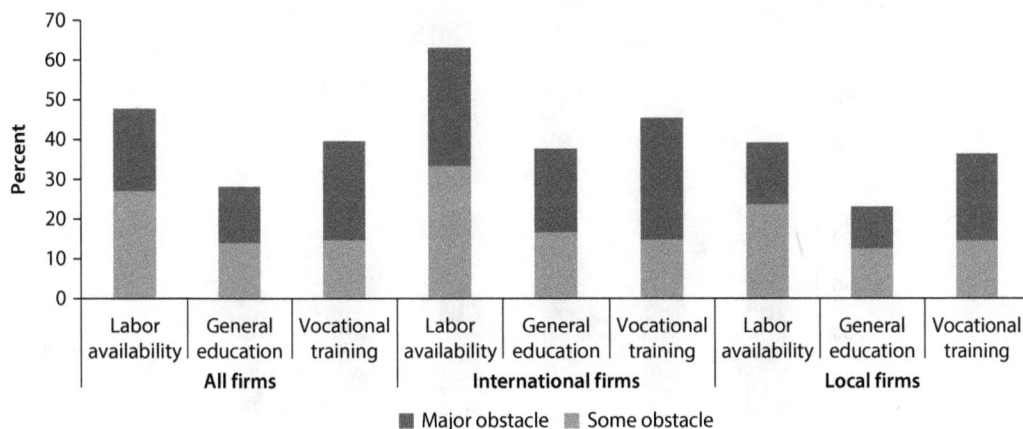

Source: World Bank staff estimates using STEP employer survey data, *n* = 305.
Note: STEP = Skills Toward Employment and Productivity. Employers were asked to report whether any of the following was an obstacle to the operation and growth of their businesses: labor availability; general education of workers; or formal training of workers.

applicants is cited by approximately 80 percent of employers who were trying to hire professionals and technicians. By comparison, a lack of required skills is cited by only 40 percent of employers who were hiring craftsmen.[3] The severity of the skills gap among blue-collar workers should not, however, be underestimated. The percentage of employers who complain that blue-collar workers lack required skills is substantial: 25 percent of businesses claim that workers applying for a position as a machine operator lack the required skills (figure 2.3). There is substantial room to improve the skills of blue-collar workers in order to match the job requirements.

Employers' concerns on skill constraints are mirrored by workers' views that their skills limit their ability to advance in the workplace. Although workers value their education, they report that their skills constrain their workplace development. Approximately half of workers report that their education was either moderately or very useful for their current work. More highly educated workers and those working in skilled occupations are more likely to report this to be the case. The majority of workers, however, report that their writing and reading skills—core analytical skills—are a constraint to their career advancement (figure 2.4). Highly educated workers and those who are required to read and write lengthy documents as part of their work are the most likely to report that they do not have all the literacy skills needed to advance. Although these workers have strong basic literacy skills—they score very well on the literacy assessment and have the highest self-reported literacy and writing skills—they may not have the full set of written analytical skills and argument foundation skills they need for their workplace development.[4] Similarly, these individuals report that their IT skills are not as advanced as they would need for their careers.

Figure 2.3 Percentage of Employers Claiming that Job Applicants Lacked Skills Required for the Job

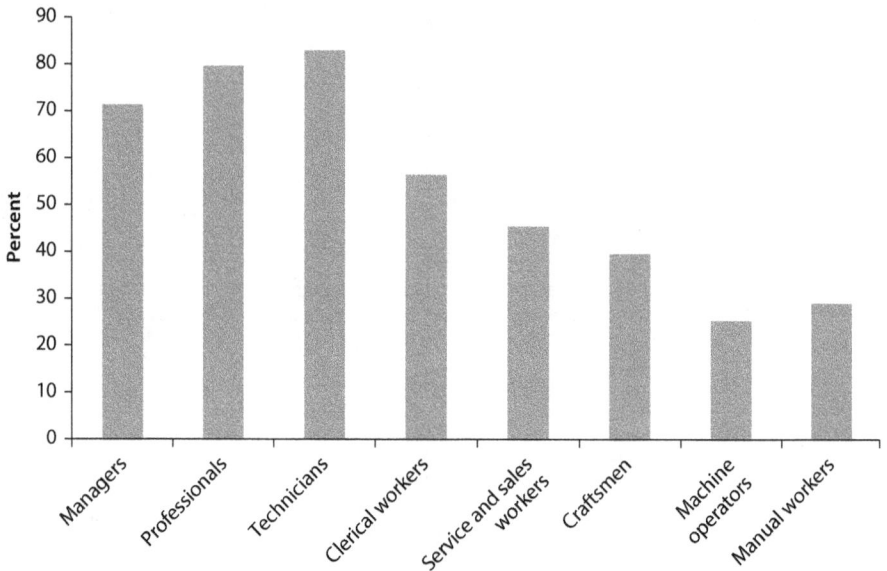

Source: World Bank staff estimates using STEP employer survey data.
Note: STEP = Skills Toward Employment and Productivity. Employers were asked if they had tried to hire workers in various positions during the last 12 months and if the applicants for the positions lacked the required skills. The data came from 350 firms that were asked about hiring. The figure covers the following number of employers hiring a given position: managers, 36 businesses; professionals, 18; technicians, 34; clerks, 98; service and sales workers, 114; craftsmen, 132; machine operators, 87; and laborers, 78.

Figure 2.4 Percentage of Individuals Reporting that the Lack of Literacy or Computer Skills Has Prevented Obtaining a Job or Advancement

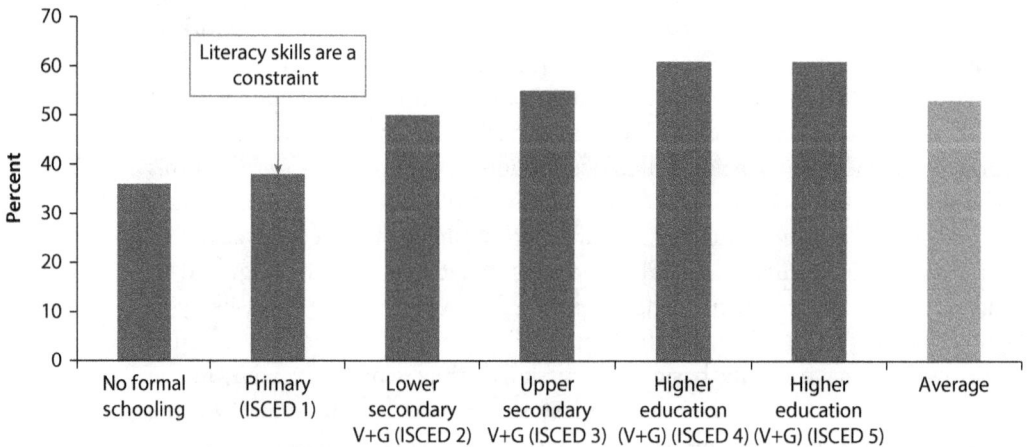

Source: World Bank staff estimates using STEP household survey data.
Note: N = 3,316. The data displayed reflect responses to the question: "Has a lack of reading or writing skills in Vietnamese ever kept you from getting a job, a promotion, a pay rise, or held you back from advancing your career?" A similar question was repeated for business/own activity. G = general education; ISCED = International Standard Classification of Education; STEP = Skills Toward Employment and Productivity; V = vocational education.

What Do We Mean by Skills?

This book focuses on three domains of skills: cognitive skills, social and behavioral skills, and technical skills. These domains cover the technical skills that are directly applicable to particular occupations, the various personality traits that are crucial to labor market outcomes, and the cognitive ability generally believed to underpin human capital.[5] Figure 2.5 puts forward the definition of skills used in this book. Annex 2A, "What Are Cognitive, Social and Behavioral, and Technical Skills and How Are They Measured?" explains in greater detail what these skill domains capture and how they are measured in the STEP surveys.

Basic cognitive skills are separated from more advanced cognitive skills. Cognitive skills include the use of logical, intuitive, and creative thinking as well as problem solving using acquired knowledge. They include literacy and numerical ability as basic or foundational cognitive skills and extend to the ability to understand complex ideas, learn from experience, and analyze problems using logical processes.

The fast expansion of education in Vietnam has meant that basic cognitive skills are widespread in urban areas. The STEP household survey conducted in Hanoi and Ho Chi Minh City (HCMC) in 2012 tested the literacy skills of working-age individuals (see annex 2A). This survey revealed solid achievement by urban Vietnamese in important basic literacy ability. Figure 2.6 presents the percentage of individuals who passed a "core" literacy assessment in the five countries in which the STEP household survey was administered—Bolivia, the Lao People's Democratic Republic, Sri Lanka, Yunnan province of China, and Vietnam. The core literacy assessment assesses basic literacy skills

Figure 2.5 Skills Measured in the STEP Survey

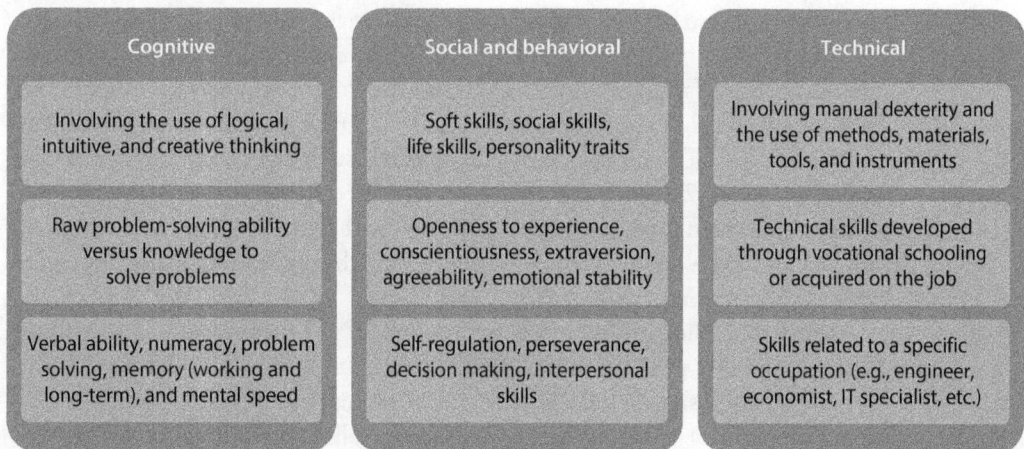

Cognitive	Social and behavioral	Technical
Involving the use of logical, intuitive, and creative thinking	Soft skills, social skills, life skills, personality traits	Involving manual dexterity and the use of methods, materials, tools, and instruments
Raw problem-solving ability versus knowledge to solve problems	Openness to experience, conscientiousness, extraversion, agreeability, emotional stability	Technical skills developed through vocational schooling or acquired on the job
Verbal ability, numeracy, problem solving, memory (working and long-term), and mental speed	Self-regulation, perseverance, decision making, interpersonal skills	Skills related to a specific occupation (e.g., engineer, economist, IT specialist, etc.)

Source: Pierre, Sanchez Puerta, and Valerio, forthcoming.
Note: IT = information technology; STEP = Skills Toward Employment and Productivity.

Figure 2.6 Percentage of Individuals, by Literacy Assessment Score

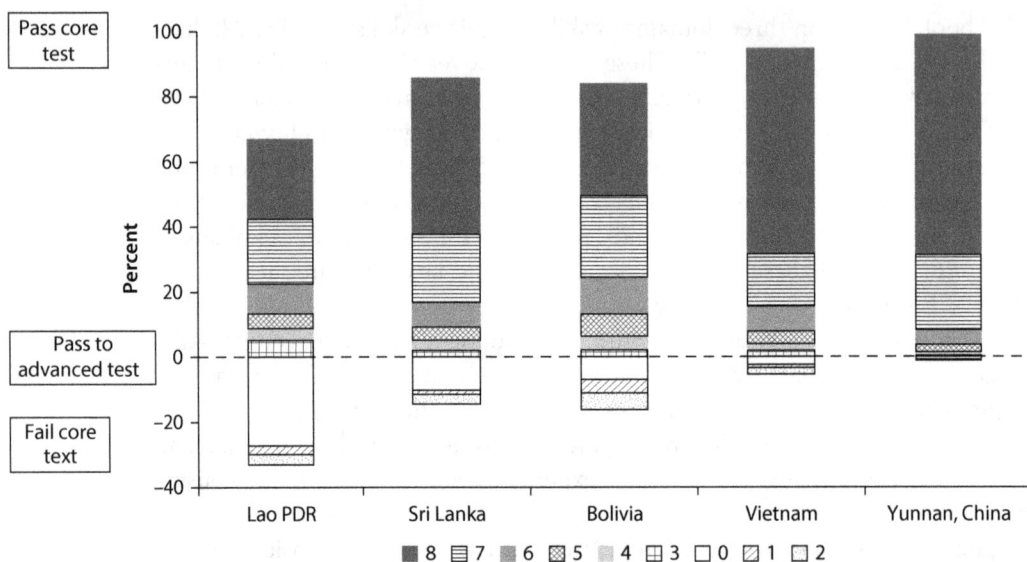

Source: World Bank staff calculations using STEP household survey data.
Note: N = 3,328. STEP = Skills Toward Employment and Productivity. All country samples are restricted to urban only for comparison reasons. The scores reflect performance of individuals on a reading literacy test; individuals who score 3 or higher on the test are considered sufficiently skilled to be able to continue on to the next level of the test, and those who score below 3 are considered to have failed the test of basic literacy skills. Greater information on the measurement of literacy skills is given in annex 2A.

and sorts the most literate from those with lower levels of literacy skills.[6] Vietnam came second to Yunnan in the share of respondents who passed the literacy assessment. Nearly two-thirds of the sample obtained full marks on the test, suggesting strong average basic literacy skills among the Vietnamese urban population.

Although Vietnamese workers are well equipped with basic literacy skills, the urban workforce is lacking more advanced skills. The literacy proficiency of urban Vietnamese lies below the levels seen in many Organisation for Economic Co-operation and Development (OECD) countries. The extended literacy module in the STEP household survey and the Programme for the International Assessment of Adult Competencies (PIAAC) literacy proficiency test conducted in multiple OECD countries were linked and results can be placed on the same scale (see annex 2A for further details). As figure 2.7 shows, the literacy proficiency of Vietnam's urban workforce lies below the proficiency level seen among urban and rural workforces in the countries in which the PIAAC literacy assessment has been conducted.

More urban Vietnamese workers than urban and rural workers in wealthier OECD countries perform at the lowest competency level, but Vietnam also has a relatively high share of urban workers at the highest competency level. More than a quarter of workers in urban Vietnam fall into the two lowest competency levels (figure 2.8). Such individuals are able to locate basic information in simple texts but do not have the literacy proficiency to deal with more

Figure 2.7 PIAAC and STEP Literacy Proficiency Scores

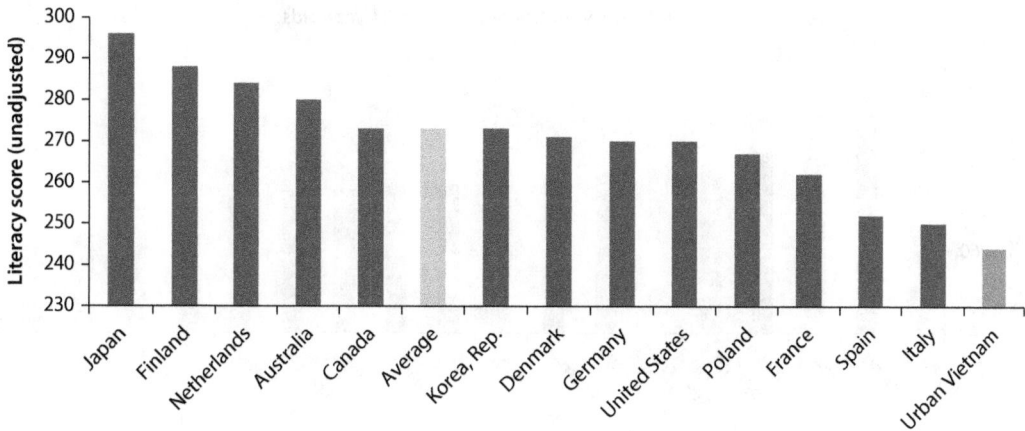

Sources: OECD 2013. Vietnam estimates from World Bank staff estimates using STEP household data.
Note: PIAAC = Programme for the International Assessment of Adult Competencies; STEP = Skills Toward Employment and Productivity. Literacy scores from other countries were measured as part of the PIAAC, and the unadjusted scores are taken from table A2.2a in OECD 2013.

Figure 2.8 Literacy Competency Levels

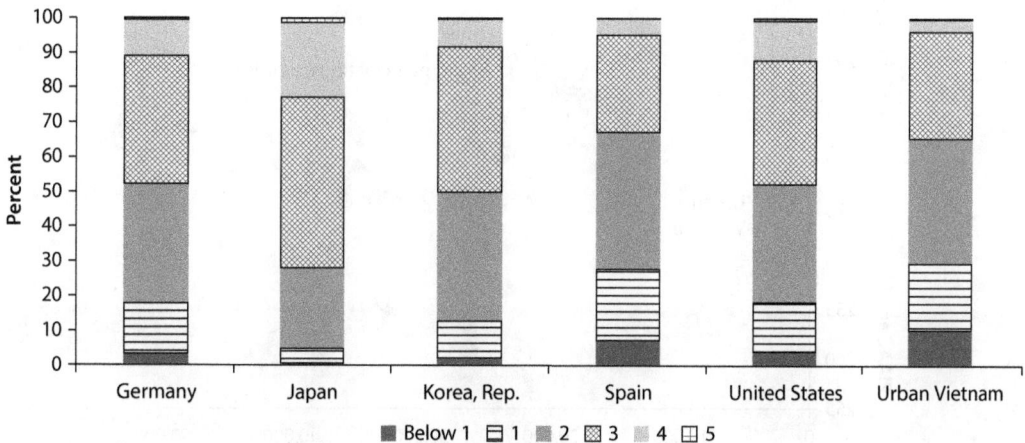

Sources: OECD 2013. Vietnam estimates from World Bank staff estimates using STEP household data.
Note: STEP = Skills Toward Employment and Productivity. Literacy scores from other countries were measured as part of the Programme for the International Assessment of Adult Competencies, and the unadjusted scores are taken from table A2.2a in OECD 2013.

complex texts (see annex 2A for further details on the proficiency levels). Despite the substantial number of individuals who fall into the lowest categories, urban Vietnam also has a similar share of individuals in the top three competency levels as Spain has.

Although the literacy skills of older urban workers in Vietnam lie below those seen in many OECD countries, the skills of younger urban adults are

Figure 2.9 Literacy Proficiency of Vietnamese Adults

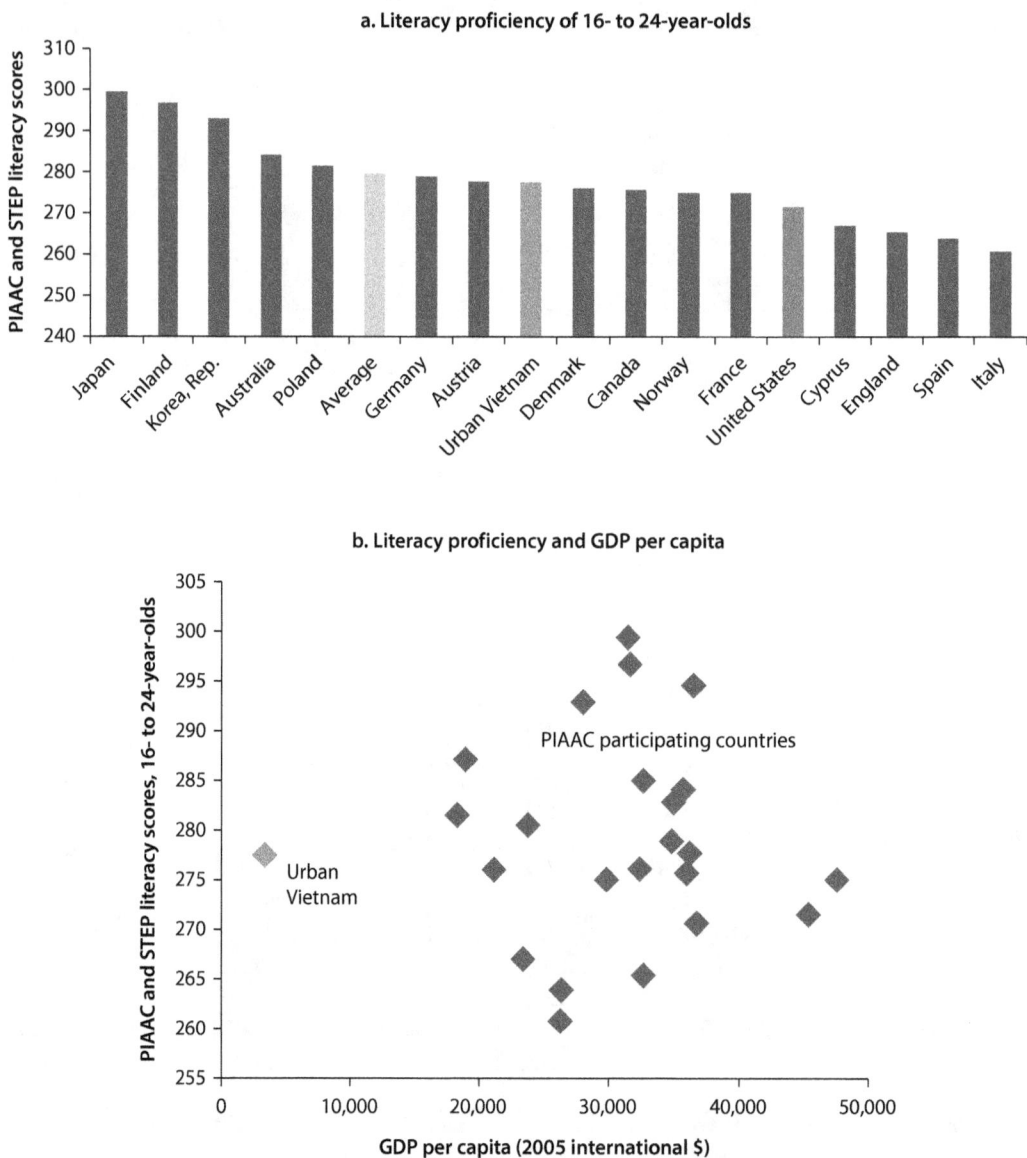

a. Literacy proficiency of 16- to 24-year-olds

b. Literacy proficiency and GDP per capita

Sources: Vietnam estimates from World Bank staff analysis using STEP household survey data. Literacy scores from other countries were measured as part of the PIAAC (Programme for the International Assessment of Adult Competencies), and the unadjusted scores are taken from table A2.2a in OECD 2013. GDP per capita are based on 2005 purchasing power parity and were obtained from World Bank 2012.
Note: GDP = gross domestic product; STEP = Skills Toward Employment and Productivity.

comparable to their urban and rural peers in many wealthier countries. Figure 2.9 presents the literacy proficiency scores of 16- to 24-year-olds in urban Vietnam and other PIAAC countries. Younger respondents score better on the literacy assessments overall in Vietnam. The same is true in most countries where the PIAAC has been administered, which might be attributable to younger respondents' higher levels of education. But even after taking into account their higher education levels, younger respondents perform better than older respondents.[7] The literacy levels of younger adults in urban Vietnam are comparable to the levels of their peers in many richer OECD countries and have similar literacy levels to those in Austria, Canada, Denmark, France, Germany, and Norway.

The difference between the literacy skills of older and younger workers in urban Vietnam is substantial. Figure 2.10 shows the difference in the average literacy score between 55- to 64- and 16- to 24-year-olds. The difference in scores in urban Vietnam is substantial, and second only to Korea in size. This suggests that the education system has done an impressive job in imparting key literacy skills to the young urban workforce, taking Vietnamese worker skills from below those seen in OECD countries for the oldest generation to levels on a par with wealthier OECD countries.

Although basic and midlevel cognitive skills are widely used in urban Vietnam, more advanced skills are less likely to be used.[8] Figure 2.11 shows the use of numeracy skills in urban Vietnam, where numerical tasks are split by the complexity of operations conducted. Approximately 90 percent of individuals conduct at least basic numerical operations, such as estimating weights and distances or calculating prices or costs. Moving to the next level of complexity, three-quarters of the population do more complicated operations such as using decimals, percentages, multiplication, or division. Similarly, although over 80 percent of the urban working-age population reports reading or writing either at home or at work, the majority of workers make only basic use of their literacy and writing skills.

Figure 2.10 Difference between Literacy Proficiency of Older and Younger Adults

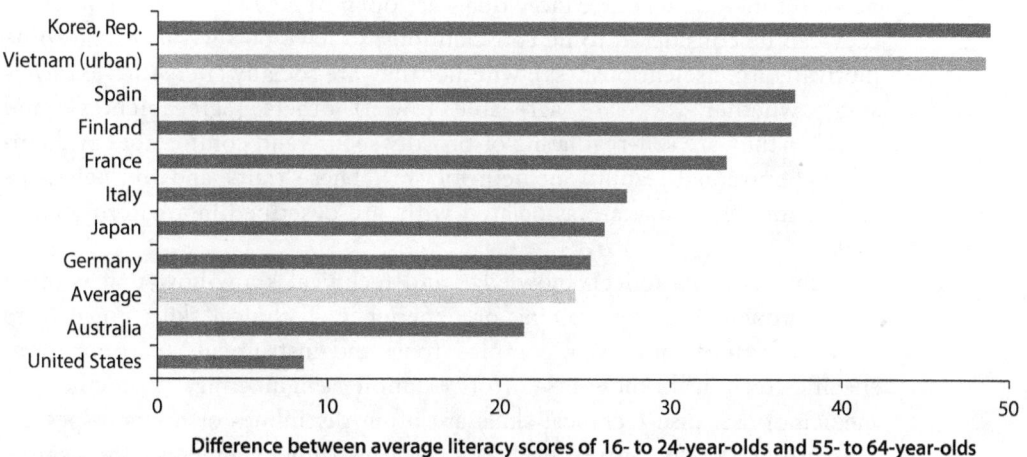

Difference between average literacy scores of 16- to 24-year-olds and 55- to 64-year-olds

Sources: Vietnam estimates from World Bank staff analysis using STEP household survey data. Literacy scores from other countries were measured as part of PIAAC (Programme for the International Assessment of Adult Competencies) and are taken from table A3.1 (L) in OECD 2013. Older adults are defined as aged 55 to 64 years and younger workers as aged 16 to 24 years.
Note: STEP = Skills Toward Employment and Productivity.

Figure 2.11 Use of Numeracy Skills

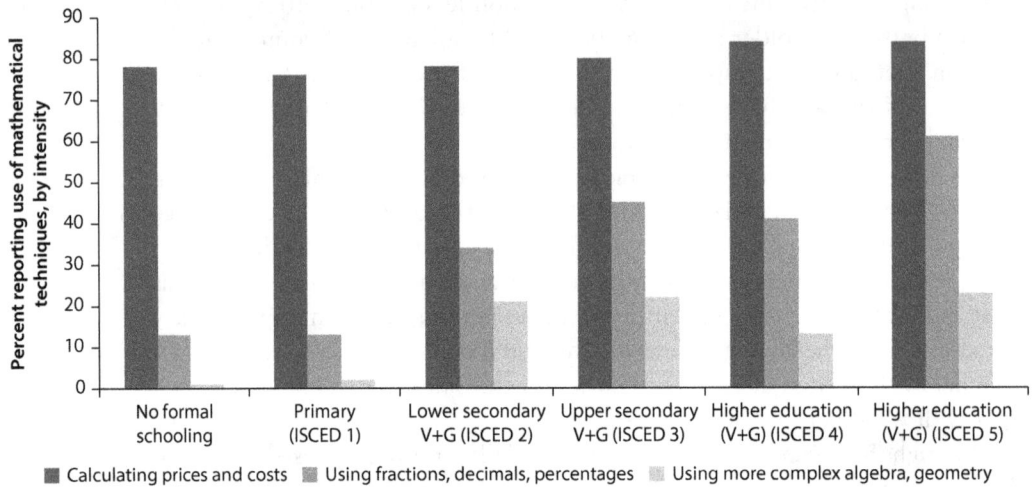

Source: World Bank staff estimates using STEP household survey data.
Note: G = general education; ISCED = International Standard Classification of Education; STEP = Skills Toward Employment and Productivity; V = vocational education.

Social and behavioral skills refer to the social ability and personality traits that have been found to be strongly linked to success in life, including doing well in school and at work. These skills are captured in the STEP household survey using the "Big Five" taxonomy of personality traits, which are viewed as high-order *proxies* of behaviors or actions that are a manifestation of personality and that are associated with a myriad of socioemotional skills. The measures include whether individuals are open to new experiences; whether they can be considered to be conscientious, to have perseverance, and to be motivated (conscientiousness); whether they are socially energetic (extraversion); whether they are agreeable toward others (agreeableness); and whether they are self-regulating or broadly secure and comfortable in themselves (emotional stability or neuroticism). These traits, and the behaviors and actions that they are associated with, are described in greater detail in table 2.1.

Technical skills reflect knowledge and technical know-how that is often built through in-depth training or experience. Technical skills range from manual dexterity for using complex tools and instruments to occupation-specific technical know-how (for example, engineering, economics, or medicine). Because technical skills are often discipline- or domain-specific, they are harder to capture using a survey instrument aimed at the general population. The technical skills that are measured in the STEP skill survey therefore reflect specialized abilities that are relevant to perform tasks that can be found in multiple jobs.

Table 2.1 Social and Behavioral Skills: The Big Five Personality and Motivational Traits

Personality trait	Characterization of individual[a]	What is it associated with?
Openness to experience	Openness to experience is a personality dimension that characterizes someone who is intellectually curious and who tends to seek new experiences and explore novel ideas. Someone who scores high on openness can be described as creative, innovative, imaginative, reflective, and untraditional. Someone low on openness could be seen as conventional, narrow in interests, and unanalytical.	Openness is positively associated with intelligence, especially aspects of intelligence related to creativity, such as divergent thinking (McCrae and Costa 1987).
Conscientiousness	Conscientiousness indicates an individual's degree of organization, persistence, hard work, and motivation in the pursuit of goal accomplishment. This personality dimension may be an indicator of the desire or ability to work hard (Barrick and Mount 1991).	Conscientiousness has been the most consistent personality predictor of job performance across all types of work and occupations (Barrick, Mount, and Judge 2001).
Emotional stability	An individual who scores low on an emotional stability scale can be thought of as self-confident, calm, even-tempered, and relaxed. Individuals who score high on the emotional stability scale tend to experience a number of negative emotions, including anxiety, hostility, depression, self-consciousness, impulsiveness, and vulnerability (Costa and McCrae 1992).	Emotional stability has been linked to education and labor market outcomes, although the trait is not as robust or consistent as conscientiousness. Traits related to emotional stability (for example, the locus of control and self-esteem) predict a variety of labor market outcomes, including job search effort (Almlund et al. 2011).
Extraversion	Extraversion describes the extent to which people are assertive, dominant, energetic, active, talkative, and enthusiastic (Costa and McCrae 1992). People who score high on extraversion tend to be cheerful, like people and large groups, and seek excitement and stimulation. People who score low on extraversion prefer to spend more time alone and are characterized as reserved, quiet, and independent.	Traits related to extraversion have been found to be linked to wages, but the relationship differs by occupation (Cattan 2010). For example, adolescent sociability has been found to increase the wages of managers, sales workers, and clerical workers, but to decrease the wages of professionals and technicians.
Agreeableness	Individuals who score high on the agreeableness scale can be thought of as having cooperative values and a preference for positive interpersonal relationships. Those at the low end of the dimension can be characterized as manipulative, self-centered, suspicious, and ruthless (Costa and McCrae 1992; Digman 1990).	Agreeableness has been found to be negatively related to salary levels and career performance (McClelland and Boyatzis 1982; Seibert and Kraimer 2001).

a. These characterizations draw heavily on Zhao and Seibert 2006.

What Skills Are in Demand and Used in the Urban Labor Market?

Employers in urban Vietnam place the heaviest emphasis on job-related skills, including technical skills and the ability to solve problems and think critically. Employers were asked what types of skills or characteristics they considered to be most important when deciding to keep an employee after a probation period. Figure 2.12 shows the relative importance placed on job-related skills, social and behavioral skills, and personal characteristics among employers at international and local firms. Job-related skills were valued most highly, but social and

Figure 2.12 Importance of Job-Related Skills versus Social and Behavioral Skills or Personal Characteristics

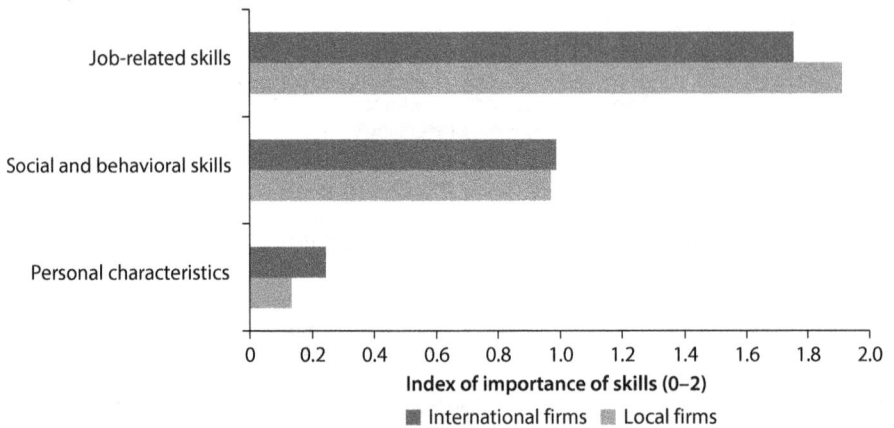

Index of importance of skills (0–2)

■ International firms ▨ Local firms

Source: World Bank staff estimates using STEP employer survey data.
Note: STEP = Skills Toward Employment and Productivity. Employers were asked to indicate which attributes—job-related skills, social and behavioral skills, and personal characteristics—were the first and second most important when deciding which workers should be retained after a probation period. *N* = 330, of which 149 firms have international links and 181 do not. Job-related skills were defined to include: job-specific technical skills, being able to communicate well, displaying leadership abilities, working well in teams, being able to engage in creative and critical thinking, being able to solve problems, being able to work independently, and being able to manage one's time. Personal characteristics include age, appearance, gender, family relations, and personal ties. Social and behavioral skills include measured personality traits, notably whether an individual is conscientious, emotionally stable, agreeable, extraverted, and open to new experiences. The differences between international and local firms that are displayed are not statistically significant at a 10 percent level.

behavioral skills are also important. In contrast, personal characteristics (such as age, sex, and appearance) have little impact on hiring decisions. The relative importance of these three broad skill groups is the same for both white- and blue-collar workers, and across international and local firms.

Among job-related skills, employers consider strong technical competencies as the most important attribute a worker can have. Employers were asked to define which job-related skills were most important in determining whether an employee on probation should be retained. Job-specific technical skills were ranked highest by employers among both blue- and white-collar workers (figure 2.13). International firms value job-specific technical skills more than local businesses do. They also attach a somewhat higher value to the ability to work independently, to whether workers are open to new experiences, and to teamwork skills. Local businesses value leadership and communication skills more than international firms do. The reason may lie in the different production profiles of both types of businesses or it may be that local businesses find it more difficult to attract workers with these skills, perhaps because they offer lower remuneration.[9] Employers value employees who are able to think critically and creatively and who are able to solve problems. These employee attributes are typically associated with having advanced cognitive skills. Being able to solve problems and think creatively and critically were highly valued

Figure 2.13 Importance of Job-Related Skills among White- and Blue-Collar Workers

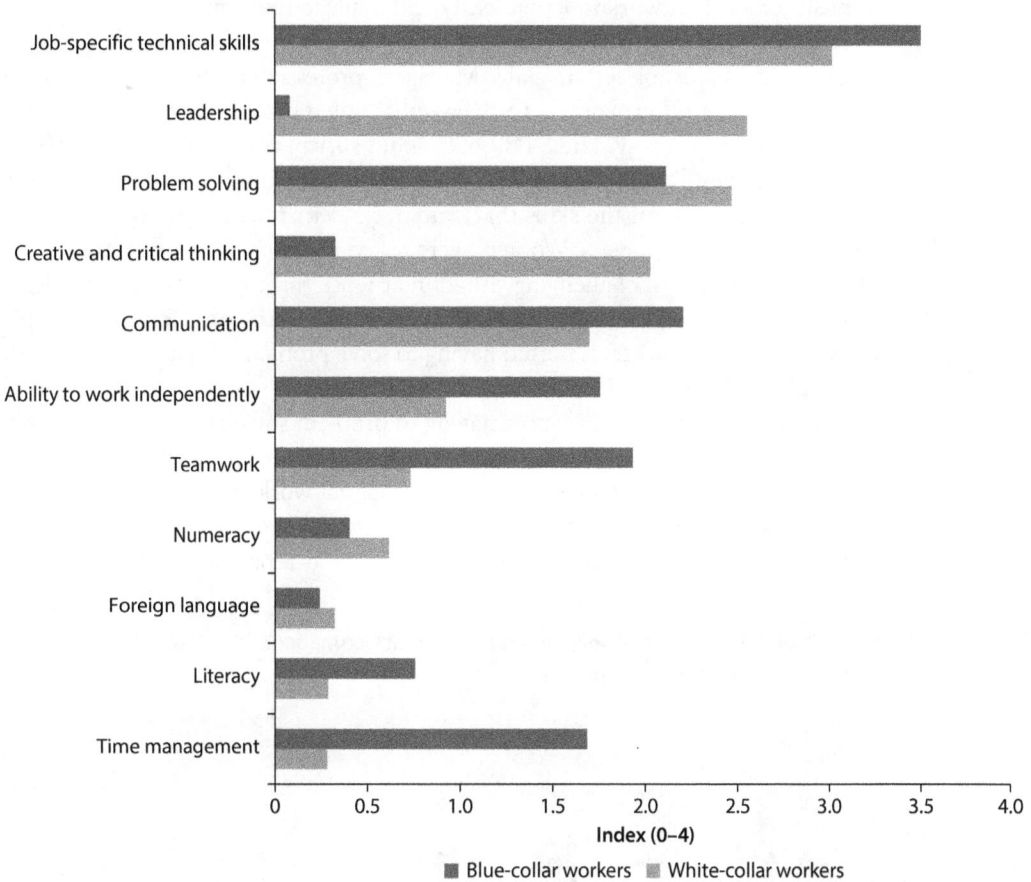

Index (0–4)

■ Blue-collar workers ▨ White-collar workers

Source: World Bank staff estimates using STEP employer survey data.
Note: STEP = Skills Toward Employment and Productivity. White-collar workers include the following worker types: managers; professionals, technicians, and associated professionals. Blue-collar workers are classified as the following workers: clerical support; service; sales; skilled agriculture, craft, and related trades; plant and machine operators; and elementary occupations. This figure is based on the 328 and 329 firms that reported having at least one worker in the white- and blue-collar category and were willing to respond about the skills used and needed by that worker in his or her work. The differences between blue- and white-collar occupations are all statistically significant with the exception of job-specific technical skills and communication skills.

attributes for both blue- and white-collar workers—they were considered the third and fourth most valuable job-related skills for white-collar workers, while problem solving was ranked third most important for blue-collar workers. Creative and critical thinking was, however, not viewed by employers as an important skill for blue-collar workers.

Employers value workers who display strong leadership abilities, are able to work in teams as well as independently, are able to manage their time, and communicate well. Employers valued employees who displayed leadership competencies as the second most valuable trait among white-collar workers, while being able to communicate well and work in a team were among the most valued attributes for blue-collar workers. These workplace skills draw upon workers' social and behavioral abilities. For example, conscientious workers are more likely to push forward on work independently and manage their time.

Employee reports of what they are asked to do in their jobs often mirror employer demands for certain skills. Managers, professionals, and technicians are more likely than other workers to be asked to solve problems and to think in a creative and critical way. The STEP household survey complemented the STEP employer survey by asking workers what they do in their jobs. This question allows a comparison of the skills that employers demand with the skills that are actually used by employees. Workers were asked to report how often they need to find a solution to a challenging situation at work through thinking for at least half an hour. Approximately three-quarters of managers, professionals, technicians, and clerical workers reported having to solve problems as part of their work (figure 2.14). The intensity with which these skills are used is also high—nearly one in two of these workers report having to problem solve at least once a week.

Although employers indicate that they value problem-solving skills in all their workers, craftsmen, machine operators, and manual workers are much less likely than professional and technical workers to report having to solve problems as part of their jobs. Craftsmen and machine operators also report a lower intensity of

Figure 2.14 Percentage of Wageworkers in Different Occupations Who Report Having to Problem Solve at Work, by Frequency

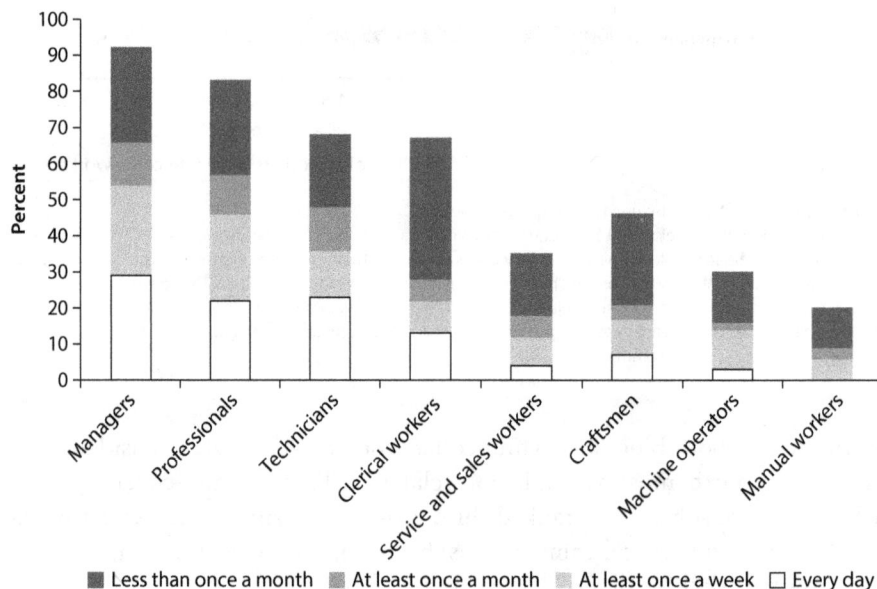

■ Less than once a month   ▨ At least once a month   ▨ At least once a week   ☐ Every day

Source: World Bank staff estimates using STEP household survey data.
Note: STEP = Skills Toward Employment and Productivity. The figure shows responses to the following question: "Some tasks are pretty easy and can be done right away or after getting a little help from others. Other tasks require more thinking to figure out how they should be done. As part of this work as [occupation], how often do you have to undertake tasks that require at least 30 minutes of thinking (examples: mechanic figuring out a car problem, budgeting for a business, teacher making a lesson plan, restaurant owner creating a new menu/dish for restaurant, dressmaker designing a new dress)." Respondents were asked to indicate how often they conducted a task of this kind. The sample includes only wage employees (*n* = 1,313).

problem solving. Approximately 45 percent of craftsmen and 30 percent of machine operators report having to solve problems in their work, although half of these workers report using these skills less than once a month. Worker reports of problem solving contrast with the importance and value placed on these skills by employers—as shown in figure 2.13, employers place almost as much value on these skills for white-collar workers as they do for blue-collar workers. The discrepancies between these reports may reflect a shortage of problem-solving skills among certain types of workers.

Nearly all wageworkers report that their job requires them to be adaptive to changes in their work environment since they are continuously learning on the job. Learning new skills requires workers to have strong core cognitive skills to build off. Workers were asked how often their work involved learning new things (figure 2.15). Nine in ten managers, professionals, and technicians report continuous learning as part of their work, and of these, more than half report learning every day. The incidence of learning among craftsmen and machine operators is also high and relatively intensive—70 percent of craftsmen report learning on the job, and 26 percent of them report having to learn new things every day. Workers who carry out manual tasks are the only category of workers for whom learning does not appear to be an important component.

Among social and behavioral skills, employers value conscientiousness most highly for all types of workers, while openness to experience is highly valued for

Figure 2.15 Percentage of Wageworkers in Different Occupations Who Report Having to Learn New Things, by Frequency

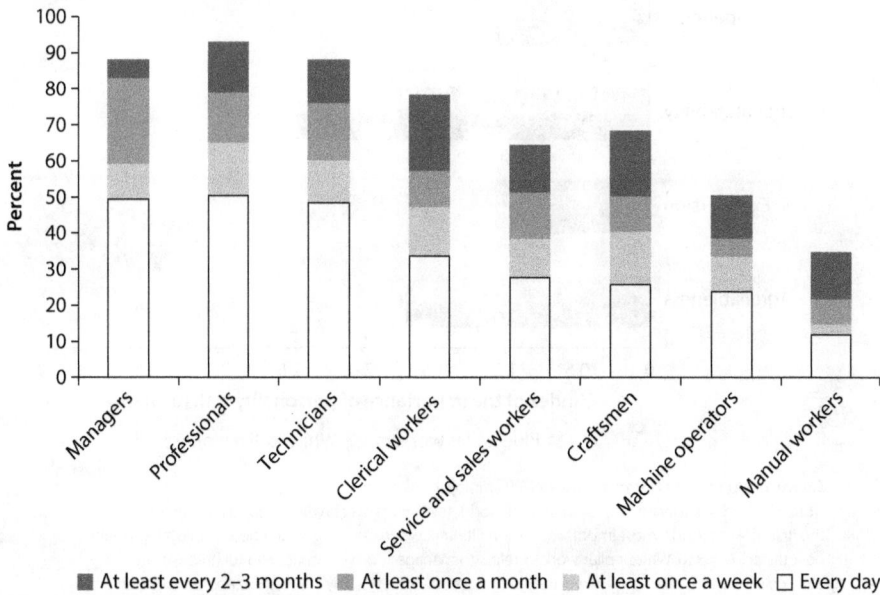

At least every 2–3 months   At least once a month   At least once a week   Every day

Source: World Bank staff estimates using STEP household survey data.
Note: STEP = Skills Toward Employment and Productivity. The figure shows responses to the following question: "How often does (did) this work involve learning new things?" Respondents were asked to indicate how often they conducted a task of this kind. The sample includes only wage employees (*n* = 1,313).

white-collar workers. Conscientiousness emerges as a key employability skill in virtually all countries where the demand for skills has been studied (for example, the former Yugoslav Republic of Macedonia, Poland, the Russian Federation, and the United Kingdom). Conscientiousness includes elements such as responsibility, self-discipline, carefulness, thoroughness, self-organization, and the need for achievement (motivation). Workers who do a thorough job are hard-working and do things efficiently, and they are more likely to be hired and retained than workers who lack these traits. In addition, employers deem openness to new experiences to be important traits for managers, professionals, and technicians, while being emotionally stable is considered to be important for blue-collar workers (figure 2.16).

The high value placed on workers who are conscientious and open to experience is mirrored in earnings: workers with these types of skills earn more. There are, however, substantial differences across jobs in the types of social and behavioral skills that are most valued, likely reflecting differences in the types of tasks conducted in different jobs (figure 2.17). Among managers, professionals, and technicians, people who display higher levels of openness

Figure 2.16 Importance of Social and Behavioral Skills for White- and Blue-Collar Workers

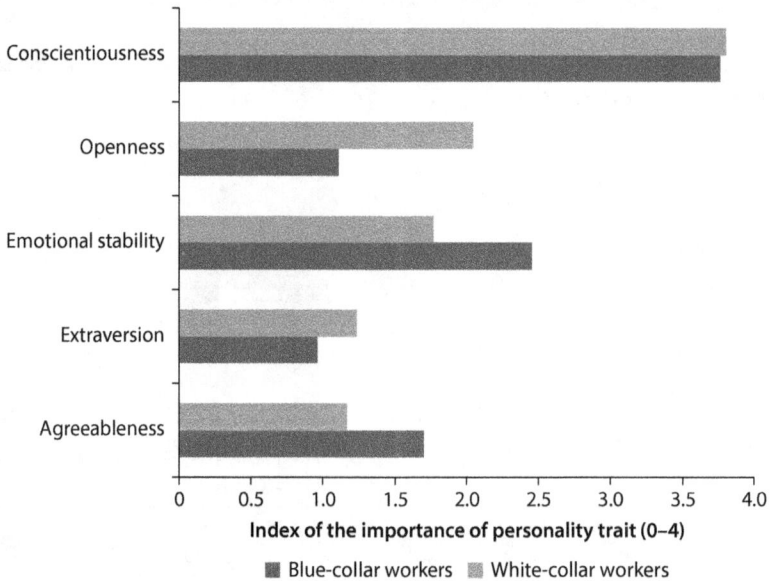

Index of the importance of personality trait (0–4)

■ Blue-collar workers ▨ White-collar workers

Source: World Bank staff estimates using STEP employer survey data.
Note: STEP = Skills Toward Employment and Productivity. Employers were asked to indicate which was the first most to fourth most important personality trait when deciding which new employees should be retained. $N = 330$. White-collar workers refers to managers, professionals, and technicians, and blue-collar workers refers to workers in all other occupations, notably clerks, sales and service workers, craftsmen, machine operators, and manual laborers. Differences in emotional stability, agreeableness, and openness to new experiences are statistically significant at a 5 percent level. Among white-collar workers, conscientiousness and openness to new experiences are statistically different from zero at a 5 percent level; among blue-collar workers, emotional stability is statistically different from zero at a 5 percent level; and conscientiousness and agreeableness are statistically different from zero at a 10 percent level.

Figure 2.17 Returns to Social and Behavioral Skills, by Occupation Type

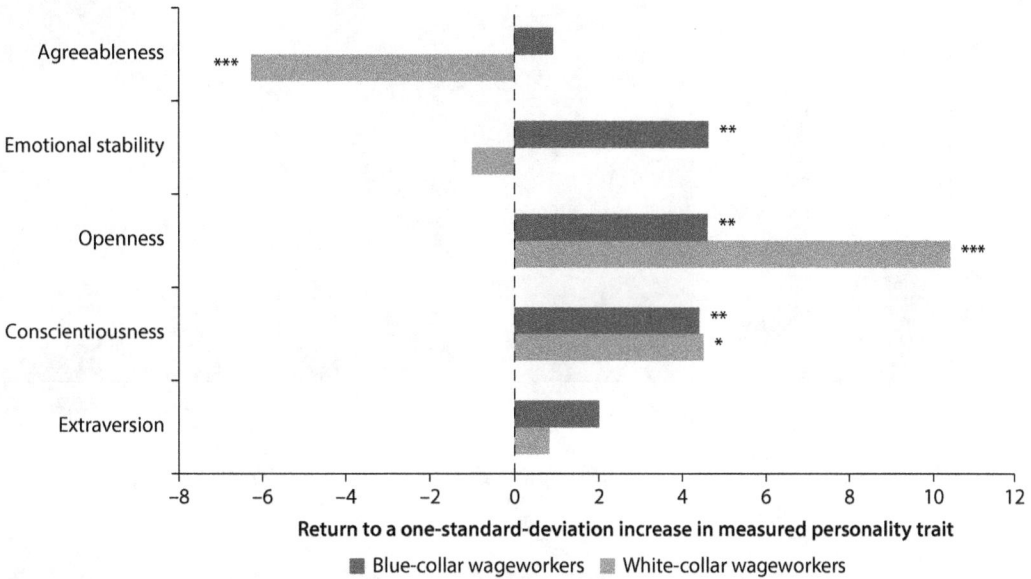

Return to a one-standard-deviation increase in measured personality trait

■ Blue-collar wageworkers   ■ White-collar wageworkers

Source: World Bank staff estimates of returns to monthly incomes among white-collar (managers, professionals, and technicians) and blue-collar (clerical, service and sales, craftsmen, machine operators, and elementary) wageworkers, STEP household survey data (*n* = 1,244).
Note: The reported results are from a Mincerian earnings regression that controls for demographics, cognitive skills, and education. Reported standard errors are jackknifed bootstrapped, and outliers are eliminated using a robust regression technique based on Cook's distance measure. Significance level: * = 10 percent, ** = 5 percent, *** = 1 percent.

and conscientiousness earn more. Those who are more agreeable actually earn less—this is a finding that reflects patterns in the international literature. More disagreeable people have been found in multiple contexts to have higher incomes and wages (Diaz, Arias, and Tudela 2012; Seibert and Kraimer 2001). Among pink- and blue-collar workers, social and behavioral skills appear to play a greater role in wage setting. Workers who are more open and conscientious again earn more (figure 2.17, blue bars). Among these workers more emotionally stable workers earn more.

Wageworkers need strong social and behavioral skills because they are often required to persuade others of their ideas and work with and supervise others. Workers in multiple occupations report needing to be persuasive through providing information to clients or having to convince colleagues of their point of view (figure 2.18). These attributes are most needed in occupations that require direct contact with workers outside of their enterprises—70 percent of sales and service sector workers report that they regularly have to sell ideas, inform others, or persuade others of their opinion. Tasks that involve interaction with others and persuasion require workers with strong social and behavioral skills such as self-esteem and agreeableness—these workers will be required to pick up on social cues to change their strategies according to the personality of the person with whom they are interacting.

Figure 2.18 Percentage of Wageworkers Who Report Having to Interact with Others, Present Ideas to Others, or Supervise Others at Work

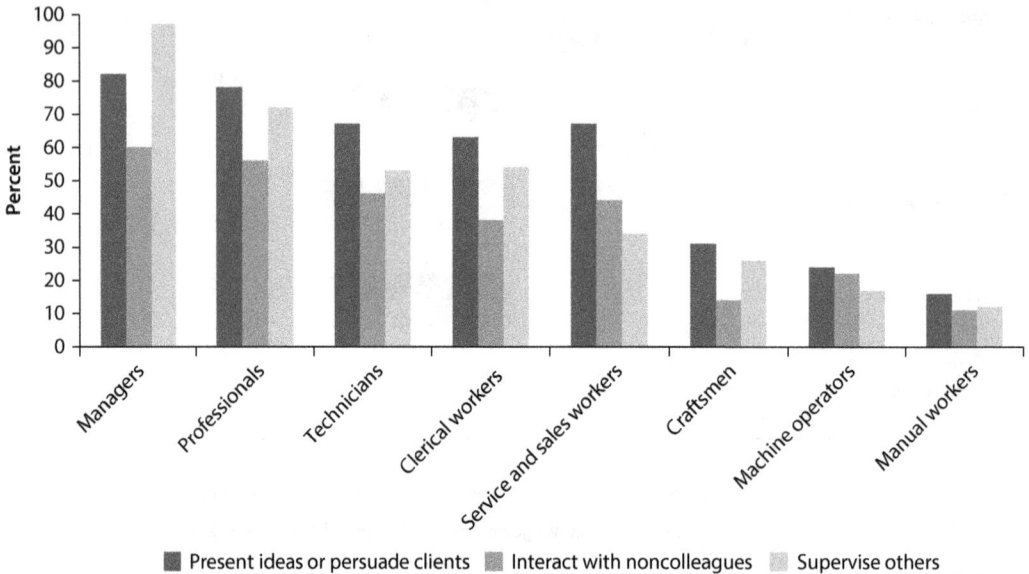

■ Present ideas or persuade clients   ■ Interact with noncolleagues   ■ Supervise others

Source: World Bank staff estimates using STEP household survey data.
Note: STEP = Skills Toward Employment and Productivity. The figure shows responses to the following questions: (a) "As part of this work, do you (did you) have to make formal presentations to clients or colleagues to provide information or persuade them of your point of view?" (b) "As a normal part of this work do you direct and check the work of other workers (supervise)?" (c) "As part of this work, do you (did you) have any contact with people other than coworkers, for example, with customers, clients, students, or the public?" The sample includes only wage employees (*n* = 1,313).

Skills are not a formal sector phenomenon: strong social skills are most highly valued in the informal sector. The earnings premium to being more open to new experiences and conscientious is higher for self-employed people than for wageworkers (figure 2.19).[10] This may reflect the observation that more educated workers cluster into wage employment and that openness to experience and conscientiousness are both highly associated with education. In studies in other countries, entrepreneurs have been found to be more conscientious and open to experience than managers (Zhao and Seibert 2006). There is, however, no clear evidence in Vietnam that the average self-employed person is more open or conscientious than the average wageworker or manager.

One reason that openness and conscientiousness are more highly rewarded in self-employment is that the work of entrepreneurs—engaging with clients, needing to be self-motivated—is more intensive in the use of these skills. Entrepreneurs are more likely to report doing interactive tasks, such as talking to and assisting individuals outside of their business. In addition, they are more likely to have to supervise others or make formal presentations. Their work is less likely to involve technology such as computers, more likely to afford a higher level of freedom, and more likely to be nonroutine and manual in nature, implying that their work involves readjustment. Although self-employed work is less analytical than the work reported by wageworkers, many self-employed workers report needing to think for at least 30 minutes on a regular basis.

Figure 2.19 Returns to Social and Behavioral Skills for Wage Employment and Self-Employment

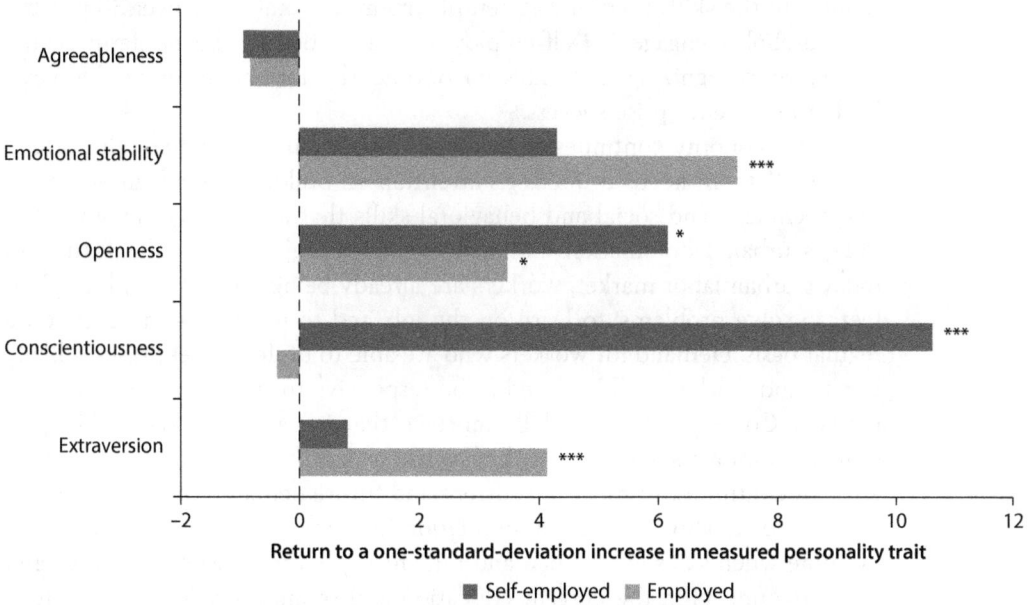

Return to a one-standard-deviation increase in measured personality trait

■ Self-employed   ▨ Employed

Source: World Bank staff estimates of monthly income returns among wageworkers and self-employed workers, STEP household survey data (*n* = 2,058).
Note: The reported results are from a Mincerian earnings regression that controls for demographics, cognitive skills, and education. Reported standard errors are jackknifed bootstrapped, and outliers are eliminated using a robust regression technique based on Cook's distance measure. Significance level: * = 10 percent, ** = 5 percent, *** = 1 percent.

Summary and Conclusion

Vietnam's education system is producing strong basic cognitive skills, an important asset that enhances the country's competitiveness in the global economy. There are, however, signals that the education system is not building all the skills needed by employers and the workforce. The STEP household survey data suggest that the education system is producing workers with strong basic cognitive skills. Higher-level cognitive skills are highly valued by employers but are less likely to be used in the workforce. Employers are concerned that the education system is not providing all the skills they need of their workers, and these concerns are mirrored among workers. The good news for Vietnam is that it will be investing in the missing skills from a strong base—the urban workforce has strong basic literacy and numeracy skills, a necessary requirement for building more advanced cognitive and job-relevant skills.

The diversity of skills used in the urban labor market has implications for the education system, which is expected by employers to develop the whole range of employability skills in addition to technical skills. The need to have strong cognitive, technical, and social and behavioral skills is not a formal sector phenomenon or limited to certain professional or technical occupations. Cognitive, behavioral, and technical skills are required in all types of wage employment and are strongly predictive of labor market outcomes and enterprise success.

The informal and enterprise sector appears to use a different but overlapping skill set to the skills used in wage employment. In rural areas, over 30 percent of households engage in self-employment activities in the nonfarm sector. Therefore, recognizing that skills go beyond the formal sector workforce is likely to raise enterprise success.

As its economy continues to grow and transition into higher value-added sectors, Vietnam needs to focus its attention on building the advanced cognitive, technical, and social and behavioral skills that are already being used in today's urban labor market and will be increasingly used in the future. In today's urban labor market, workers are already being asked to think on their feet, to solve problems, to learn on the job, and to interact with others on a regular basis. Demand for workers who are able to perform these tasks is likely to rise, and workers will be asked to be responsive to shifting needs and labor markets. Consequently, the skills shortage that is reported today is likely to grow as employers ask more of their workers and the transition toward modern jobs continues. To meet the current and future demands of employers, the focus needs to shift to laying a foundation for strong skills. The next chapters examine when skills are formed and puts forward a framework to understand how disconnects in the current education and training system may result in underinvestment in the skills needed for a modern industrialized Vietnam.

Annex 2A: In Depth

What Are Cognitive, Social and Behavioral, and Technical Skills and How Are They Measured?

The STEP household data focus on three domains of skills: cognitive, social and behavioral, and technical. Cognitive skills can be defined as "the ability to understand complex ideas, to adapt effectively to the environment, to learn from experience, to engage in various forms of reasoning, to overcome obstacles by taking thought" (Neisser et al. 1996). The literature on intelligence has separated cognitive skills into a general intelligence factor (g factor) and multiple second-order factors, which display different paths over an individual's life cycle (Carroll 1993). Two seminal and widely discussed factors are fluid intelligence and crystallized intelligence. Fluid intelligence reflects the capacity to perceive and act upon complex problems under novel conditions, independent of acquired knowledge (Cattell 1971). In contrast, crystallized intelligence reflects learned skills and knowledge and is therefore dependent on education and the formation and learning of knowledge (Horn and Cattell 1967).

Cognitive skills are typically measured using achievement or assessment tests that capture, to different degrees, fluid and crystallized intelligence. Broadly speaking, aptitude tests are designed to measure differences in the rates at which individuals learn (fluid intelligence), whereas achievement tests are designed to measure acquired knowledge (crystallized intelligence). The relative weight of fluid versus crystallized intelligence captured by a test depends on the amount of prior knowledge or experience that is required to perform well on the test.

In the STEP household survey, cognitive skills are measured in two ways. First, respondents are asked to report whether and how often they read, write, and do numerical tasks both at work and at home. The questions were designed to capture both overall use of reading, writing, and numeracy skills as well as the intensity of their use. These measures are likely to capture a combination of the person's actual ability to conduct tasks involving these skills and their motivation/opportunity to do so. In this case, they may represent a lower-bound estimate of these skills in the population. For example, an individual may be able to write long documents but have no recourse to do so in his or her work or home life. On the other hand, individuals may claim to read on a regular basis but may actually not be able to do so. This miscategorization would result in overestimates of the skill stock. The survey asks respondents the following questions on the three skill categories:

Self-reported reading: "Do you read anything [*in daily life/at this work*], including very short notes or instructions that are only a few sentences long?" "Among the things that you normally read [*in daily life/at this work*], what is the size of the longest document that you read?"

Self-reported writing: "Do you ever have to write anything (else) [*in daily life/ at work*], including very short notes, lists, or instructions that are only a few sentences long?" "Thinking about all the things you normally write (wrote) [*in daily life/at work*], what is the longest document that you write (wrote)?"

Self-reported numeracy: "[*As a normal part of this work/in daily life*], do you do any of the following . . . ?"

A second measure of cognitive ability captures an individual's literacy by testing their reading competency. The STEP literacy assessment is aligned with and draws from other large-scale international surveys, which have included the International Adult Literacy Survey (IALS), Adult Literacy and Life Skills Survey (ALL), and the PIAAC. STEP is based on the same conception of literacy used in other large-scale assessments, notably "understanding, evaluating, using and engaging with written texts to participate in society, to achieve one's goals, and to develop one's knowledge and potential" (PIAAC Literacy Framework).

The STEP household survey restricts the target population to all urban adults aged 15–64, while in the PIAAC survey the target population includes all rural and urban adults aged 16–65. Both surveys define the target population to include all residents, regardless of citizenship, nationality, or language, and to exclude all individuals living in institutions (e.g., prisons, hospitals, nursing homes). STEP's target population excludes adults living at school in a student group quarter, but PIAAC includes this group. The sampling frames in both surveys require at least 95 percent of the target population to be included.

As urban populations tend to be better educated and belong to higher socio-economic groups than rural residents and are also more likely to hold jobs requiring advanced skills, they are expected to perform better on the reading literacy assessment when compared to the rest of the population. The STEP household survey in Vietnam focused on Hanoi and HCMC. Both cities account for close to 35 percent of the country's urban population and close to 16 percent of the overall population. Results from the STEP survey should not be interpreted as providing an estimate of the reading proficiency of Vietnam's adult population as a whole. Rather, they provide an estimate of the proficiency of a specifically defined subgroup of that population (adults in Hanoi and HCMC) whose reading proficiency may differ considerably from that of the 15- to 64-year-old population as a whole.

The STEP survey concentrates narrowly on the measurement of reading literacy, whereas PIAAC measures reading literacy, numeracy, and problem solving in technology-rich environments. The design for the STEP literacy assessment has two primary goals: to provide items that target the lower end of the literacy scales and to link results to the literacy scale used in PIAAC. The selection of items for any assessment requires meeting certain constraints. To meet the psychometric linking requirements, the pool of items used in STEP is limited to items used in PIAAC as well as some items from the Adult Literacy and Life Skills Survey.

The literacy items selected for STEP were all developed based on the same literacy frameworks developed for PIAAC. The assessment design for STEP specifies a Core block with the easiest items, a reading components block, and four additional blocks of literacy items. Respondents who pass the Core are administered two of the four booklets of literacy items at random. Findings from PIAAC included in this report all refer to its reading literacy assessment section.

The sample size requirement for STEP usually ranges between 2,400 and 3,000 observations per reporting language using a paper-and-pencil approach. In PIAAC, which assesses four different cognitive areas and uses both paper-and-pencil and computer-based instruments, the sample size requires at least 5,000 observations per reporting language.

Although the translation and adaptation of the survey instruments follow the same methodology in both surveys, STEP's field test requirements call for testing in-depth about 20–30 cases. In the case of PIAAC, however, field test requirements require about 1,500 cases to test all items and in all of its administration modalities.

Although STEP and PIAAC field team composition and size differ slightly due to smaller sample sizes in STEP, training requirements and supervision standards during data collection are very similar. Finally, the weighting process is different, as PIAAC uses replicate weights and STEP uses probability weights. Whenever reliable data were available, STEP weights were adjusted using benchmark variables for age and gender.

The literacy proficiency score for urban Vietnam that was generated can be separated into six different proficiency levels (taken from OECD 2013, pages 68 and 69):

- **Proficiency at Level 5 (scores equal to or higher than 376 points)**
  Level 5 is the highest proficiency level on the literacy scale. Adults reaching this level can perform, among others, tasks that involve searching for and

integrating information across multiple, dense texts; constructing syntheses of similar and contrasting ideas or points of view, or evaluating evidence and arguments.

- **Proficiency at Level 4 (scores from 326 points to less than 376 points)**
  At Level 4, adults can perform multiple-step operations to integrate, interpret, or synthesize information from complex or lengthy continuous, noncontinuous, mixed, or multiple-type texts that involve conditional and/or competing information.
- **Proficiency at Level 3 (scores from 276 points to less than 326 points)**
  Adults performing at Level 3 can understand and respond appropriately to dense or lengthy texts, including continuous, noncontinuous, mixed, or multiple pages. They understand text structures and rhetorical devices and can identify, interpret, or evaluate one or more pieces of information and make appropriate inferences.
- **Proficiency at Level 2 (scores from 226 points to less than 276 points)**
  At Level 2, adults can integrate two or more pieces of information based on criteria, compare and contrast or reason about information, and make low-level inferences.
- **Proficiency at Level 1 (scores from 176 points to less than 226 points)**
  At Level 1, adults can read relatively short continuous, noncontinuous, or mixed texts to locate a single piece of information, which is identical to or synonymous with the information given in the question or directive. They can complete simple forms, understand basic vocabulary, and read texts with a degree of fluency.
- **Proficiency below Level 1 (scores below 176 points)**
  Individuals at this level can read brief texts on familiar topics and locate a single piece of specific information identical in form to information in the question or directive. They are not required to understand the structure of sentences or paragraphs and only basic vocabulary knowledge is required.

The literacy items cover a range of areas, notably:

- Material types, focusing on non-school-based materials in adult contexts (example 1);
- Task types, including tasks that require respondents to access and identify information (in both text-based and nonprose materials such as tables, graphs, and forms), to integrate and interpret information, and to evaluate information by assessing the relevance, credibility, or appropriateness of the material for a particular task (example 2); and
- Difficulty, with tasks ranging from locating a single piece of information in a very short advertisement to summarizing reasons for using generic drugs as presented in a newspaper article. Tasks are reported along a scale divided into five levels, with Level 1 characterized by the least demanding tasks and Level 5 the most demanding.

Example 1

Example 2

STAR SAND GLASS

Circle the correct word.

Does the following sentence make sense?
THE MAN WAS TOO TIRED TO BRUSH HIS PLANT SO HE WENT STRAIGHT TO SLEEP.

Circle the correct word:
IT STARTED RAINING, SO I PUT UP MY UMBRELLA/MUSHROOM.

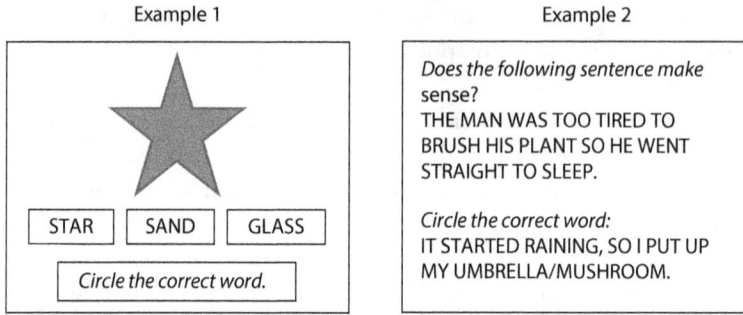

The self-reported reading, writing, and numeracy questions capture a concept of cognitive skills different from the literacy assessment. The literacy assessment captures an objective assessment of an individual's literacy that can be compared to the literacy of others in the survey. In comparison, the self-reported questions capture the *use* of reading and writing skills; because these measures are self-reported, they may well differ from an individual's actual ability to read or write. Figure 2A.1 displays the fraction of correct responses in

Figure 2A.1 Self-Reported Reading Length and Fraction of Correct Responses in Literacy Assessment

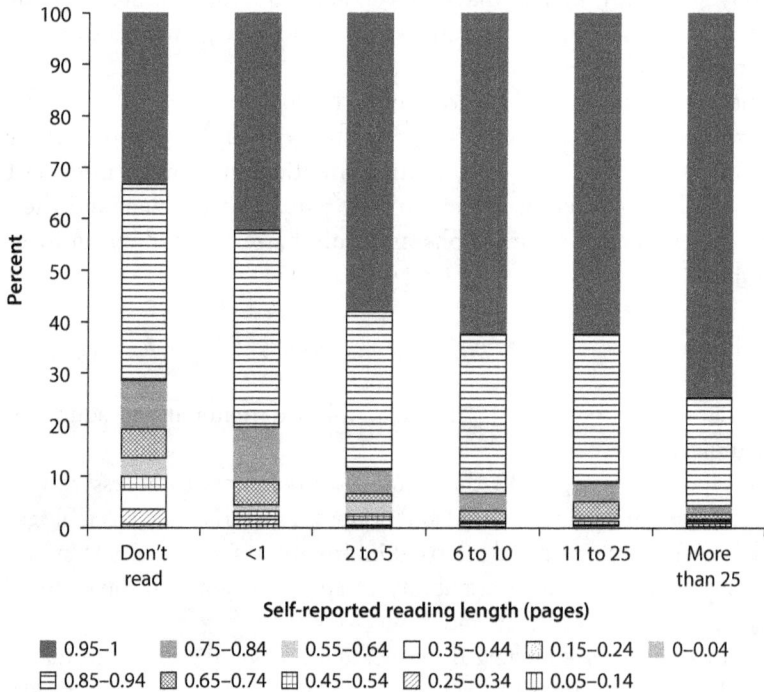

Legend:
0.95–1 0.75–0.84 0.55–0.64 0.35–0.44 0.15–0.24 0–0.04
0.85–0.94 0.65–0.74 0.45–0.54 0.25–0.34 0.05–0.14

Source: World Bank staff estimates using STEP household survey data.
Note: STEP = Skills Toward Employment and Productivity. The literacy scores reflect performance of individuals on a literacy assessment, and the self-reported reading length reflects how much the person reports reading.

the literacy assessment by self-reported reading category. The average number of correct responses increases as self-reported reading intensity rises—among those who read more than 25 pages, 75 percent got over 95 percent of the questions correct on sections A and B of the reading assessment compared to approximately 40 percent correct by those who read less than a page. However, nearly 33 percent of those who do not read anything on a regular basis also scored in the highest category. It is therefore clear that although self-reported skills are related to reading ability as captured in the literacy assessment, they do not fully capture a person's actual skills.

Technical skills reflect learned knowledge in particular domains and are therefore more likely to reflect crystallized intelligence than fluid intelligence. As such, technical skills can be strengthened later in life, but are likely to be most responsive to investment earlier in life. Because technical skills are often discipline specific, they are harder to capture using a survey instrument aimed at the general population. The technical skills that are measured in the STEP skill survey reflect specialized types of skills that are relevant to perform tasks that are specific to multiple jobs.

Behavioral skills refer to academically or occupationally relevant skills and traits that are not directly related to intelligence but are otherwise associated with personality or motivational traits. These skills include self-regulation, perseverance, motivation, and effort (Borghans et al. 2008). The measures used to capture behavioral attributes are less well established than those used to capture cognitive skills, a reflection in part that there is less consensus regarding the structure and evolution of personality.[11] The most common and widely accepted taxonomy for capturing personality traits is the Big Five. The Big Five includes conscientiousness, openness to experience, extraversion, agreeableness, and emotional stability, and within each of these five factors lie lower-order facets (John and Srivastava 1999). This taxonomy has been found to be replicable across cultures and can capture the evolution of personality over the life course (John and Srivastava 1999).

Gender and Skills in Vietnam

There are few differences between men and women in terms of their measured cognitive skills. Men and women performed equally well on the literacy assessment, suggesting that no gender gaps in basic literacy skills exist in Vietnam. Women, however, are slightly less likely to report reading or writing and do so in a lower intensity. The differences between men and women are substantially reduced once education is considered, suggesting that these differences are likely to reflect gender gaps in education. Gender differences in cognitive skills are smaller for the population under 40, for whom gender gaps in educational investment are less marked. The exception to this is the fraction reporting conducting complex numerical tasks, which is higher for men than for women even among the population under the age of 40.

Several gender differences can be found in social and behavioral skills, mirroring patterns seen internationally. Women in the sample are more risk averse, are less open to new experiences, and have lower levels of self-esteem, but similar levels of other social and behavioral traits, such as extraversion, agreeableness, and grit (figure 2A.2).[12] Studies in OECD countries have found that female students have higher levels of social and behavioral skills, which has contributed to women performing relatively well at school (Cornwell, Mustard, and Van Parys 2013; Jacob 2002). There is little evidence of this finding in urban Vietnam—no differences in social and behavioral skills can be seen between male and female students at upper secondary or tertiary levels.

Gender gaps in education access at primary, lower secondary, and upper secondary levels appear to be reversing over time. Girls are slightly more likely than boys to be enrolled in lower and upper secondary school (see figure 2A.3, panel a). The growth in women's enrollment at a tertiary level has been remarkable and substantially higher than men's enrollment growth: women's enrollment has nearly tripled over time, and women's gross enrollment has overtaken that of men (see figure 5.3). The differences in the education profile of men and women at a postsecondary level are substantial, as are the differences in their chosen fields of study (figure 2A.3, panel b). Women are more likely than men to study business and education and are less likely to be studying technical fields such as IT, engineering, science, and craftsmanship. These gender differences in the choice of field of study are also seen among current students—68 percent of urban women engaged in postsecondary education report studying business, compared to approximately 30 percent of men. In comparison, 45 percent of men are engaged in studies in IT, science, or craftsmanship, compared to only 7 percent of women.

Figure 2A.2 Gender Differences in Social and Behavioral Skills and Openness to Experience, after Accounting for Education and Age

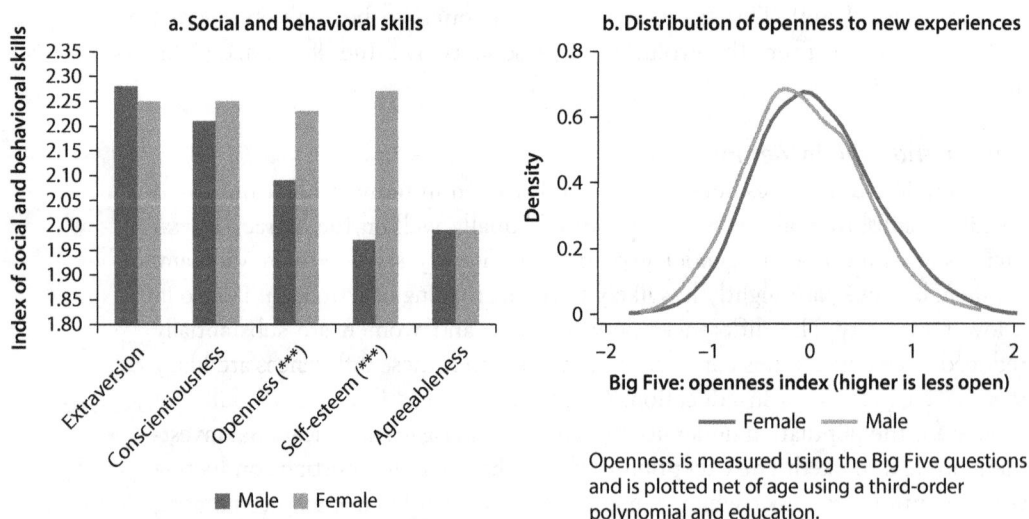

Openness is measured using the Big Five questions and is plotted net of age using a third-order polynomial and education.

Source: World Bank staff estimates using STEP household survey data.
Note: STEP = Skills Toward Employment and Productivity. n = 3,405. *** = statistically significant difference between female and male at a 1 percent level.

Figure 2A.3 Gender Gaps in Enrollment in Secondary Education and Choice of Fields of Study

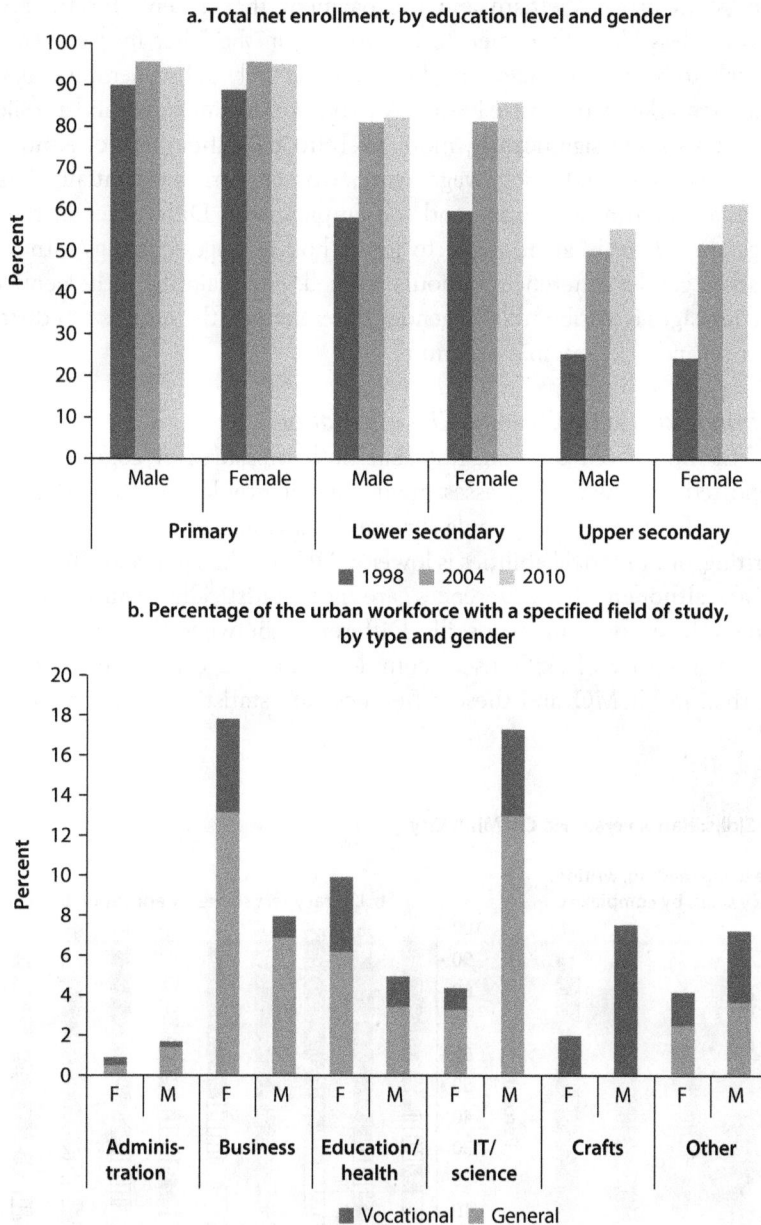

a. Total net enrollment, by education level and gender

b. Percentage of the urban workforce with a specified field of study, by type and gender

Sources: Panel a: World Bank staff estimates using VHLSS data; panel b: World Bank staff estimates using STEP household survey data.
Note: F = female; M = male; STEP = Skills Toward Employment and Productivity; VHLSS = Vietnam Household Living Standards Survey. *N* = 3,405 of which 1,493 have studied in a specified field at upper secondary level or above. Of the 1,493, 683 are male and 810 are female. The higher number of females does not reflect a greater propensity for females to have studied a specific field of study, but is instead reflective of a greater number of female respondents in the STEP survey (60 percent).

Although there is little evidence of gender differences in cognitive skills in the workforce, there are substantial differences in the types of work that men and women do in urban Vietnam and the payment they receive for their work. Women are less likely than men to be working in the labor market—they are more likely to be inactive than men, but no more likely to be unemployed. Once in the labor market, women are less likely to be working for wages and are slightly, but not statistically significantly, more likely to be self-employed. Among the men and women conducting wage work, women earn substantially less per month than men in both wage and self-employment. Differences in monthly earnings are primarily attributable to lower hourly wages/earnings rather than any marked gender differences in hours worked. The majority of the gender difference in wages is attributable to gender differences in the returns to education, experience, and occupational premium.

Comparing Skills in Ho Chi Minh City and Hanoi

The STEP household data suggest that both measures of cognitive skills—self-reported and the literacy assessment—are slightly lower in HCMC than in Hanoi. The fraction of the population conducting any tasks that involve reading, writing, or numerical abilities is lower in HCMC than in Hanoi (figure 2A.4, panel a), although the differences are not statistically significant at the 10 percent level for numeracy skills. Differences between the two cities show up in the intensity of skills used: complex skills usage is more prevalent in Hanoi than in HCMC, and these differences are statistically significant across

Figure 2A.4 Cognitive Skills: Hanoi versus Ho Chi Minh City

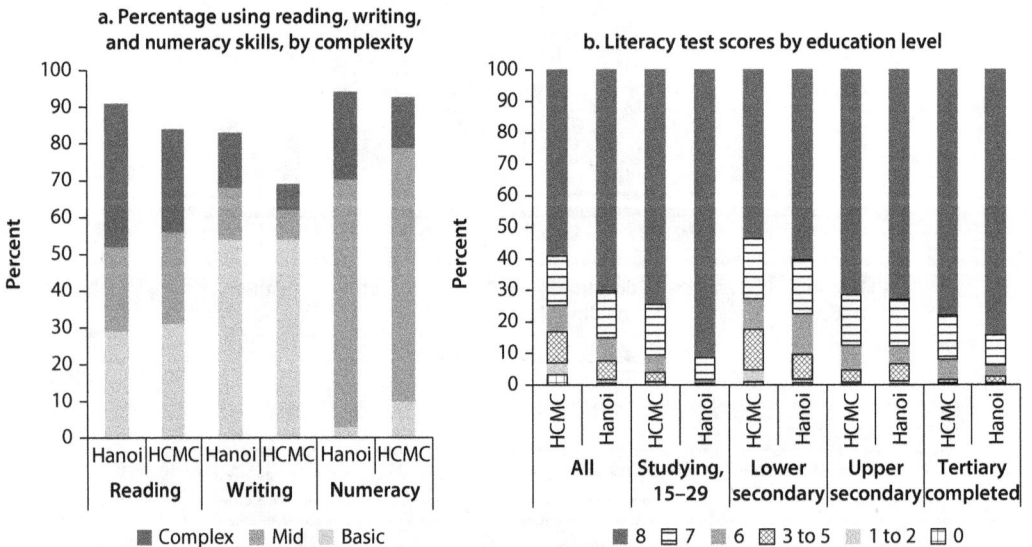

Source: World Bank staff estimates using STEP household survey data.
Note: HCMC = Ho Chi Minh City; STEP = Skills Toward Employment and Productivity. Panel a, $n = 3,405$. Panel b, $n = 3,328$.

all three skill categories. A similar pattern emerges from the scores on the literacy assessment (figure 2A.4, panel b). The fraction of the population attaining full marks is lower in HCMC overall, and in particular among students aged 15–29. To ensure that these differences are not driven just by differences between the two cities' education levels, we examine whether there are differences in test scores among individuals who have completed the same level of education. We find statistically significant differences in the fraction obtaining full marks among those who have completed lower secondary or tertiary education, although no difference is found for those with upper secondary education (figure 2A.4).

Hanoi and HCMC also differ on a number of social and behavioral skill scales. For example, residents of Hanoi tend to score lower on the agreeableness, openness to experience, and extraversion scales (figure 2A.5). Hanoi residents are more risk averse than residents of HCMC, less conscientious, and display lower levels of grit, which captures perseverance for long-term goals. Higher levels of grit have been found to be positively associated with labor market outcomes and educational performance (Duckworth et al. 2007).

Finally, the use of technology is higher in Hanoi than in HCMC. For example, 78 percent of residents in Hanoi reported using technology compared to only 73 percent of residents in HCMC (figure 2A.6). HCMC residents were also less

Figure 2A.5 Social and Behavioral Skills: Hanoi versus Ho Chi Minh City

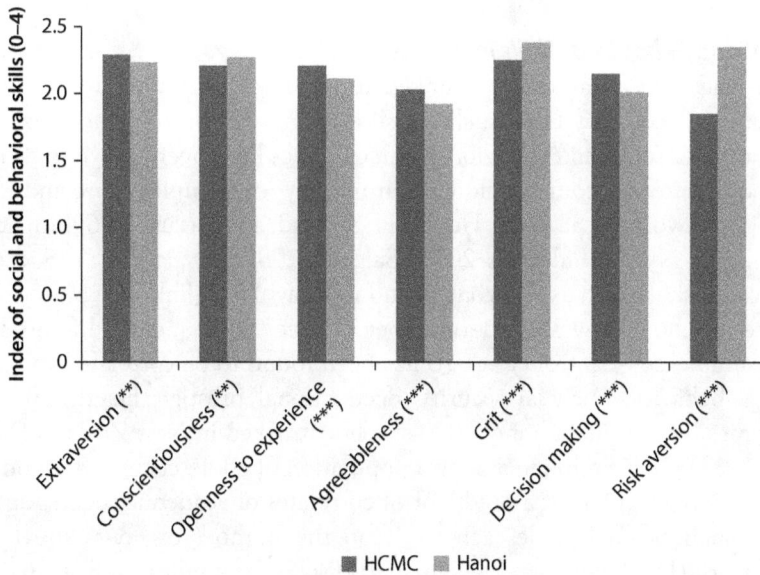

Source: World Bank staff estimates using STEP household survey data.
Note: HCMC = Ho Chi Minh City; STEP = Skills Toward Employment and Productivity. N = 3,405. Index varies between 0 and 4. Higher values imply a lower level of the social and behavioral skill.
Significance level: * = 10 percent, ** = 5 percent, *** = 1 percent.

Figure 2A.6 Technical Skills: Hanoi versus Ho Chi Minh City

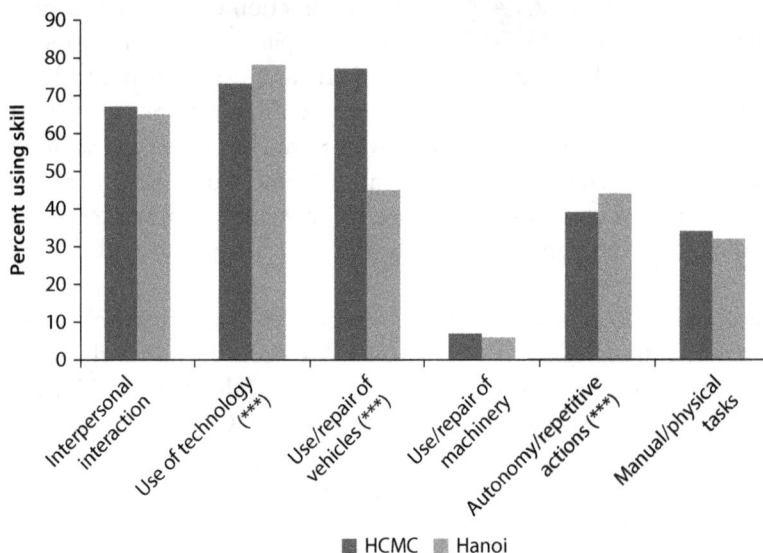

■ HCMC ■ Hanoi

Source: World Bank staff estimates using STEP household survey data.
Note: HCMC = Ho Chi Minh City; STEP = Skills Toward Employment and Productivity. *N* = 3,405.

likely to be in repetitive jobs and more likely to be operating or repairing vehicles. No statistically significant difference in interpersonal interaction, use or repair of machinery, or manual and physical tasks were found.

Social and Behavioral Skills in Vietnam

Social and behavioral skills are linked to good educational and labor market outcomes. Personality traits such as self-esteem, self-control, emotional stability, and other social and behavioral characteristics have been shown to be linked to labor market outcomes including earnings, type of employment, and experience (Duckworth et al. 2007; Heckman, Stixrud, and Urzua 2006; Mueller and Plug 2006; Nyhus and Pons 2005; Salgado 1997; Urzua 2008). Social and behavioral skills such as self-control and grit have been linked to better performance in school as well as to a number of other consequential life outcomes. For example, self-control at age 10 has been found to be correlated to income, savings behavior, financial security, occupational prestige, health, and other outcomes later in life among 1,000 students tracked in New Zealand (Moffitt et al. 2011). Self-discipline among a population of adolescents was found to be as statistically significant a predictor of correlates of academic success and diligence, such as final grades achieved and the number of hours spent doing homework (Duckworth and Seligman 2005). Some studies suggest that social and behavioral skills are actually more important than cognitive skills for determining labor market outcomes (Bowles, Gintis, and Osborne 2001; Goff and Ackerman 1992; Segal 2008, 2012).

Social and behavioral skills, such as conscientiousness and openness, vary with education. Figure 2A.7 shows differences in openness to experience by age and across two different education levels. Panels a and b show openness to experience and conscientiousness for individuals who have completed primary- and university-level education, after taking into account age and sex. Individuals educated at a higher level of education are more open to new experiences and are more conscientious. The lowest levels of both openness and conscientiousness are found among those who have completed only primary school (those who have six years of education). Among those who have completed primary school or less, both conscientiousness and openness to experience decline systematically with education. These patterns resemble those seen in other countries, where higher educated individuals display

Figure 2A.7 Index of Openness to Experience and Conscientiousness, by Education Level and Age

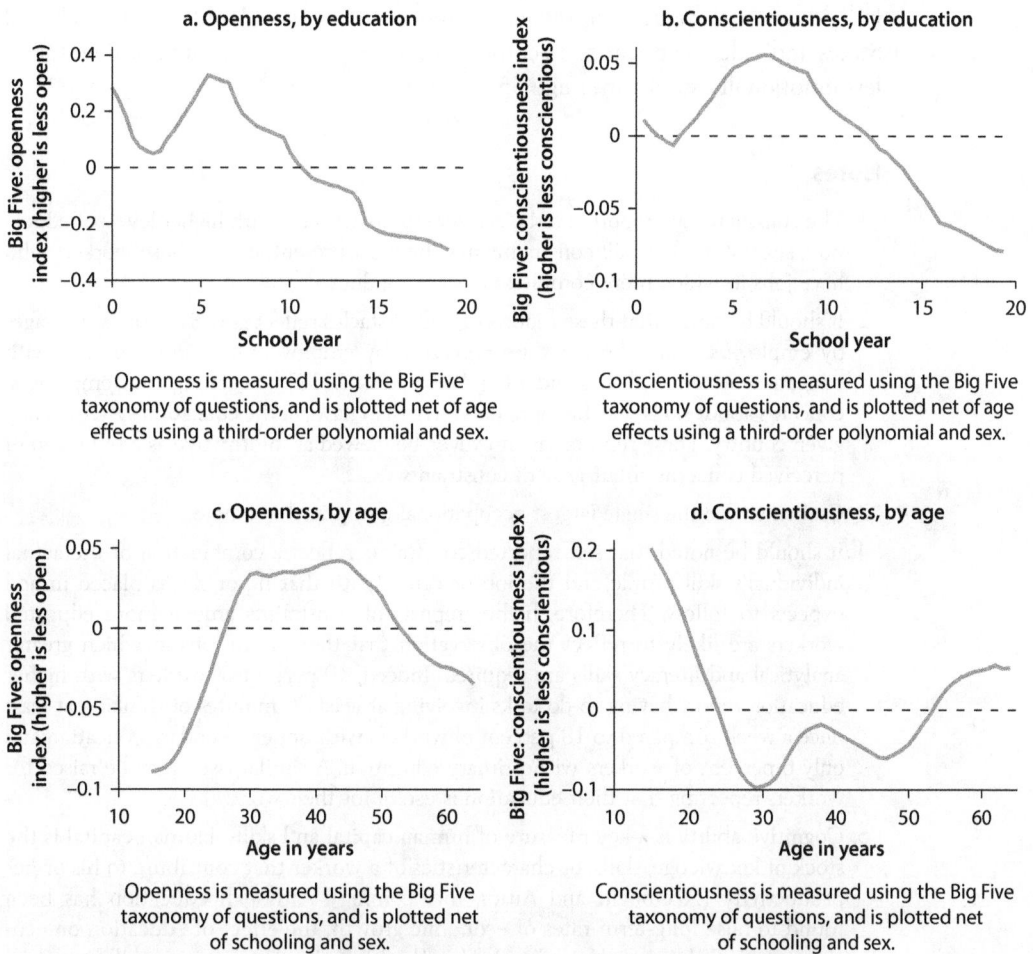

a. Openness, by education

Openness is measured using the Big Five taxonomy of questions, and is plotted net of age effects using a third-order polynomial and sex.

b. Conscientiousness, by education

Conscientiousness is measured using the Big Five taxonomy of questions, and is plotted net of age effects using a third-order polynomial and sex.

c. Openness, by age

Openness is measured using the Big Five taxonomy of questions, and is plotted net of schooling and sex.

d. Conscientiousness, by age

Conscientiousness is measured using the Big Five taxonomy of questions, and is plotted net of schooling and sex.

Source: World Bank staff estimates using the STEP (Skills Toward Employment and Productivity) household survey data.

higher levels of grit, openness, and conscientiousness, but lower levels of extraversion and agreeableness.

Personality traits evolve with age in Vietnam (see figure 2A.7, panels c and d), mirroring patterns found across the world but with notable differences. Personality traits respond to changes in a person's environment but also evolve with age due to biological processes. For example, attitudes toward risk have commonly been found to be highest among adolescents and fall in people in their early twenties (Paulsen et al. 2012; Spear 2000). This observation has been linked to development changes in the prefrontal cortex and limbic regions of the brain among adolescents, which include an apparent shift in the balance between mesocortical and mesolimbic dopamine systems (Spear 2000). Older people in other countries have been found to be more socially dominant, conscientious, and emotionally stable (Roberts, Walton, and Viechtbauer 2006), while openness to experience rises early in life and falls with old age. The Vietnamese data corroborate these patterns for social dominance, conscientiousness, and emotional stability, but suggest that openness to experience is lowest for middle-aged individuals and higher for teenagers and older people. Unlike in the United States, individuals appear to become less risk averse, less socially dominant, and less emotionally stable after age 55.

Notes

1. The constraints are reported to be greater among workers with higher levels of education, suggesting that skill constraints may be most present among those workers who have jobs in which more complex tasks are conducted.
2. It should be noted that these reports of skill obstacles reflect perceived skills shortages by employers. Skills shortages are perceived by employers in many countries with education systems of all standards (World Bank 2012), suggesting that employers' concerns about skills may be more pervasive than flaws in the education system in any given country. These reports can, however, be viewed as informative as a reflection of perceived concerns about growth constraints.
3. Craftsmen are the single largest occupational group in the sample.
4. It should be noted that self-reported constraints reflect a combination of the actual individual's skill profile and the job or career path that he or she is placed in and expects to follow. Therefore, higher reports of constraints among more educated workers are likely to reflect the observation that they are in jobs in which greater analytical and literacy skills are required. Indeed, 40 percent of workers with higher education report having to do tasks involving at least 30 minutes of thinking at least once a week compared to 18 percent of workers with upper secondary education and only 6 percent of workers with primary education. A similar issue may be raised for workers reporting that their education is useful for their work.
5. Cognitive ability is a key measure of human capital and skills. Human capital is the stock of knowledge, skills, or characteristics of a worker that contribute to his or her productivity (Acemoglu and Autor, forthcoming). Although education has been found to raise long-term rates of economic growth, the effect of education on economic growth has been found to be largely driven by the cognitive skills acquired through the education process (Barro 2001; Hanushek and Woessmann 2008, 2012).

The evidence suggests that expanding educational enrollment without ensuring improvements in cognitive skills may not result in economic growth (Hanushek and Woessmann 2008). This evidence does not imply that social and behavioral skills are unimportant for economic growth, as cognitive skills are likely to be closely related to social and behavioral skills. Therefore, the effect of cognitive skills on economic growth may indeed reflect a combination of cognitive and social and behavioral skills.

6. The test covers foundational reading skills, including word meaning, sentence processing, and passage comprehension. More information on the measurement of literacy skills can be found in annex 2A.

7. It should be noted that factors other than differences in education quality could also explain a decline in score with age among individuals with similar levels of education, such as differences in the use of their literacy skills, differences in motivation to learn across age cohorts (regardless of the quality of schooling offered), and a decline in mental faculties.

8. Although the literacy assessment is the preferred measure of cognitive skills, the test captured only basic literacy skills; therefore, we turn to examining self-reported skills to look at more advanced skills.

9. Data on wages paid by international firms versus local businesses in Vietnam are not available. Evidence from the Vietnam Household Living Standards Survey (VHLSS) suggests that there is a substantial wage premium for working in foreign firms compared to domestic businesses for workers with similar characteristics.

10. It should be noted that the return to emotional stability is not statistically significant at a 10 percent level among self-employed individuals.

11. Dominant models of personality assume a hierarchical taxonomy similar to that used to model intelligence, but without the prevalence of a single factor equivalent to g (Almlund et al. 2011).

12. These differences continue to be found after accounting for age and education differences within the sample studied.

References

Acemoglu, D., and D. Autor. Forthcoming. *Lectures in Labor Economics.* http://economics.mit.edu/files/4689.

Almlund, M., A. L. Duckworth, J. Heckman, and T. Kautz. 2011. "Personality Psychology and Economics." In *Handbook of the Economics of Education,* edited by E. A. Hanushek, S. Machin, and L. Woessmann, 1–181. Amsterdam: Elsevier.

Barrick, M. R., and M. K. Mount. 1991. "The Big Five Personality Dimensions and Job Performance: A Meta-Analysis." *Personnel Psychology* 44 (1): 1–26.

Barrick, M. R., M. K. Mount, and T. A. Judge. 2001. "Personality and Performance at the Beginning of the New Millennium: What Do We Know and Where Do We Go Next?" *International Journal of Selection and Assessment* 9: 9–30.

Barro, R. J. 2001. "Human Capital and Growth." *American Economic Review* 91 (2): 12–17.

Borghans, L., A. L. Duckworth, J. Heckman, and B. ter Weel. 2008. "The Economics and Psychology of Personality Traits." *Journal of Human Resources* 43 (4): 972–1059.

Bowles, S., H. Gintis, and M. Osborne. 2001. "Incentive-Enhancing Preferences: Personality, Behavior, and Earnings." *American Economic Review* 91 (2): 155–58.

Carroll, J. B. 1993. *Human Cognitive Abilities: A Survey of Factor-Analytic Studies.* New York: Cambridge University Press.

Cattan, S. 2010. "Heterogeneity and Selection in the Labor Market." PhD thesis, University of Chicago.

Cattell, R. B. 1971. *Abilities: Their Structure, Growth, and Action.* Boston, MA: Houghton Mifflin.

Cornwell, C., D. B. Mustard, and J. Van Parys. 2013. "Non-cognitive Skills and the Gender Disparities in Test Scores and Teacher Assessments: Evidence from Primary School." Unpublished manuscript, University of Georgia.

Costa, P. T. Jr., and R. R. McCrae. 1992. "Four Ways Five Factors Are Basic." *Personality and Individual Differences* 13 (6): 653–65.

Coxhead, I., and D. Phan. 2012. "Long-Run Costs of Piecemeal Reform: Wage Inequality and Returns to Education in Vietnam." Staff Paper Series 566, University of Wisconsin, Agricultural and Applied Economics.

Diaz, J. J., O. Arias, and D. V. Tudela. 2012. "Does Perseverance Pay as Much as Being Smart? The Returns to Cognitive and Non-Cognitive Skills in Urban Peru." Working Paper, World Bank, Washington, DC.

Digman, J. M. 1990. "Personality Structure: Emergence of the Five-Factor Model." *Annual Review of Psychology* 41: 417–40.

Duckworth, A. L., C. Peterson, M. D. Matthews, and D. R. Kelly. 2007. "Grit: Perseverance and Passion for Long-Term Goals." *Journal of Personality and Social Psychology* 92 (6): 1087–101.

Duckworth, A. L., and M. E. P. Seligman. 2005. "Self-Discipline Outdoes IQ in Predicting Academic Performance of Adolescents." *Psychological Science* 16 (12): 939–44.

Goff, M., and P. L. Ackerman. 1992. "Personality Intelligence Relations: Assessment of Typical Intellectual Engagement." *Journal of Educational Psychology* 84: 537–53.

Hanushek, E. A., and L. Woessmann. 2008. "The Role of Cognitive Skills in Economic Development." *Journal of Economic Literature* 46 (3): 607–68.

———. 2012. "Do Better Schools Lead to More Growth? Cognitive Skills, Economic Outcomes, and Causation." *Journal of Economic Growth* 17: 267–321.

Heckman, J. J., J. Stixrud, and S. Urzua. 2006. "The Effects of Cognitive and Non-Cognitive Abilities on Labor Market Outcomes and Social Behavior." *Journal of Labor Economics* 24 (3): 411–82.

Horn, J. L., and R. B. Cattell. 1967. "Age Differences in Fluid and Crystallized Intelligence." *Acta Psychologica* 26: 107–29.

Jacob, B. A. 2002. "Where the Boys Aren't: Non-cognitive Skills, Returns to School and the Gender Gap in Higher Education." *Economics of Education Review* 21 (6): 589–98.

John, O. P., and S. Srivastava. 1999. "The Big Five Trait Taxonomy: History, Measurement and Theoretical Perspectives." In *Handbook of Personality: Theory and Research*, edited by L. A. Pervin and O. P. John, 102–38. New York: Guilford Press.

McClelland, D. C., and R. E. Boyatzis. 1982. "The Leadership Motive Pattern and Long-Term Success in Management." *Journal of Applied Psychology* 67 (6): 737–43.

McCrae, R. R., and P. T. Costa., Jr. 1987. "Validation of the Five-Factor Model of Personality across Instruments and Observers." *Journal of Personality and Social Psychology* 52 (1): 81–90.

Moffitt, T. E., L. Arseneault, D. Belskya, N. Dickson, R. J. Hancox, H. Harrington, R. Houtsa, R. Poulton, B. W. Roberts, S. Ross, M. R. Sears, W. M. Thomson, and A. Caspi. 2011. "A Gradient of Childhood Self-Control Predicts Health, Wealth, and Public Safety." PNAS (Proceedings of the National Academy of Sciences) USA 108: 2693–98.

Mueller, G., and E. J. S. Plug. 2006. "Estimating the Effect of Personality on Male and Female Earnings." *Industrial and Labor Relations Review* 60 (1): 3–22.

Neisser, U., G. Boodoo, T. J. Bouchard, Jr., A. W. Boykin, N. Brody, S. J. Ceci, D. F. Halpern, J. C. Loehlin, R. Perloff, R. J. Sternberg, and S. Urbina. 1996. "Intelligence: Knowns and Unknowns." *American Psychologist* 51 (2): 77–101.

Nyhus, E. K., and E. Pons. 2005. "The Effects of Personality on Earnings." *Journal of Economic Psychology* 26 (3): 363–84.

OECD (Organisation for Economic Co-operation and Development). 2013. *OECD Skills Outlook 2013: First Results from the Survey of Adult Skills.* Paris: OECD Publishing.

Paulsen, D. J., M. L. Platt, S. A. Huettel, and E. M. Brannon. 2012. "From Risk-Seeking to Risk-Averse: The Development of Economic Risk Preference from Childhood to Adulthood." *Frontiers in Psychology* 3. doi: 10.3389/fpsyg.2012.00313.

Pierre, G., M. L. Sanchez Puerta, and A. Valerio. Forthcoming. *STEP Skills Measurement Surveys: Innovative Tools for Assessing Skills.* Washington, DC: World Bank.

Roberts, B. W., K. E. Walton, and W. Viechtbauer. 2006. "Patterns of Mean-Level Change in Personality Traits across the Life Course: A Meta-Analysis of Longitudinal Studies." *Psychological Bulletin* 132: 1–25.

Salgado, J. F. 1997. "The Five Factor Model of Personality and Job Performance in the European Community." *Journal of Applied Psychology* 82 (1): 30–43.

Segal, C. 2008. "Classroom Behavior." *Journal of Human Resources* 43 (4): 783–814.

———. 2012. "Working When No One Is Watching: Motivation, Test Scores, and Economic Success." *Management Science* 58 (8): 1438–57.

Seibert, S. E., and M. L. Kraimer. 2001. "The Five-Factor Model of Personality and Career Success." *Journal of Vocational Behavior* 58: 1–21.

Seibert, S. E., M. L. Kraimer, and J. M. Crant. 2011. "What Do Proactive People Do? A Longitudinal Model Linking Personality and Career Outcomes." *Personnel Psychology* 54 (4): 845–75.

Spear, L. P. 2000. "The Adolescent Brain and Age-Related Behavioral Manifestations." *Neuroscience Biobehavioral Review* 24: 417–63.

UNESCO (United Nations Educational, Scientific, and Cultural Organization). 2013. Tertiary Education Statistics. UNESCO Institute for Statistics, Paris.

Urzua, S. 2008. "Racial Labor Market Gaps: The Role of Abilities and Schooling Choices." *Journal of Human Resources* 43 (4): 919–71.

World Bank. 2012. *World Development Indicators 2012.* Washington, DC: World Bank.

Zhao, H., and S. E. Seibert. 2006. "The Big Five Personality Dimensions and Entrepreneurial Status: A Meta-Analytical Review." *Journal of Applied Psychology* 91 (2): 259–71.

Skills Formation and the Importance of the Early Years

The skills of Vietnam's future workforce are being built now—before birth and after, and in kindergartens, schools, in higher education, and on the job. To make the most of the resources devoted to skills development, Vietnam needs to align its skills policy with the critical junctures at which skills are built. This chapter summarizes key aspects of the emerging literature on skills formation. It shows that the most sensitive moments for skill development differ by type of skills, with cognitive and behavioral skills formed earlier in life and technical skills later. Investing early can have a multiplier effect because new skills build off those already learned. A child who learns how to read fluently by second grade will be better prepared to learn mathematics during third grade than a child who is unable to read fluently. The early years are the most sensitive for laying the foundations of cognitive skills, and they are also when children from disadvantaged backgrounds start to irrevocably fall behind.

Because the early childhood period is critical for the development of strong cognitive skills, creating the right conditions for early childhood development is more effective and less costly than trying to rectify problems at a later age. This important early period marks the first step of skills development, particularly for closing the gaps between children from poorer and better-off households. This chapter discusses early childhood development in Vietnam and argues that Vietnam still has important policy gaps: almost a quarter of children below the age of 5 are stunted mostly as a result from inadequate feeding practices in early age, and stunting severely negatively impacts cognitive development. Vietnam is successfully expanding access to full-day preschool for children aged 5, but more attention should be directed to helping parents make better choices for their youngest children, especially disadvantaged and poor parents.

What Do We Know about the Formation of Cognitive, Social and Behavioral, and Technical Skills?

The skills that a Vietnamese worker brings to the labor market reflect investments made throughout their lifetime—from the stimulation and nutrition he or she received as a baby to on-the-job learning as an adult. For all people, adult human capital, such as workforce skills and cooperative behavior, builds on capacities that are developed early in childhood and continue to be built through training and learning by doing. The skills of young workers entering the labor market are the consequence of decisions made throughout their childhood and adolescent years, including their home and school environments. The skills of older and more experienced workers additionally reflect knowledge and know-how acquired through learning by doing and training in their workplaces.

There are critical and sensitive moments when a skill is the most responsive to investment and when skills can be most effectively and efficiently formed. The foundations of cognitive and behavioral skills are set early on. Because these foundations are the platform upon which later skills are built, a skills strategy must be built up from the early investments made during early childhood. Figure 3.1 summarizes the different points in childhood and early adulthood

Figure 3.1 The Process of Skill Formation

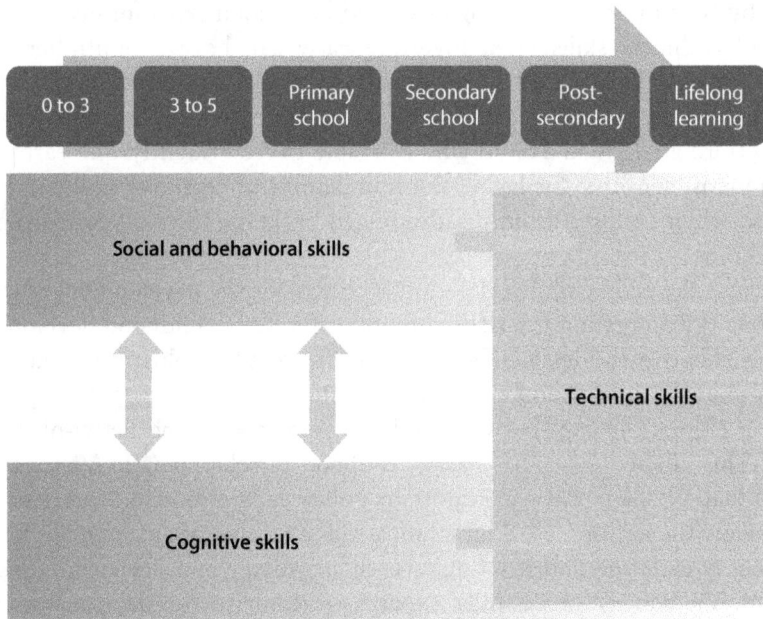

Source: Authors' illustration based on international evidence from a range of disciplines studying the development of abilities, including psychology, economics, and neuroscience.
Note: An overview of this literature can be found in Shonkoff and Phillips (2000), Naudeau et al. (2011), Almlund et al. (2011), Cunha, Heckman, and Schennach (2010), and Cunha and Heckman (2007). It should be noted that the research underlying this figure is fast moving, complex, and includes many questions that remain to be solved. This schematic portrays one model for understanding the formation of skills, but this model may be subject to evolution as the research continues to expand.

during which cognitive, social and behavioral, and technical skills may be formed. The four noteworthy features of skill formation summarized in figure 3.1 are explored in greater depth in this chapter.

First, there are sensitive and critical periods for building skills, and it is more efficient and effective to build skills at these periods than to address skill deficits at a later age. In the figure, the most sensitive moments for skill acquisition are depicted in dark shading. Periods during which the skills are less sensitive to investment are indicated in light shading, and periods during which sensitivity is most limited are indicated in white. Cognitive skills are more intensively formed in the earliest years of a child's life. Behavioral skills begin to be formed in the early years and continue to evolve throughout adult life.

Second, new skills are built off old skills and benefit from previous investments. A child who has learned to read by second grade will be able to absorb more in third grade than a child who cannot yet read fluently. This implies that earlier investments are likely to have a greater and longer-term impact on skills, as it is easier and less costly to build these skills when children are most receptive to learning.

Third, behavioral skills are valuable early in a child's life because they feed into, and benefit from, cognitive skills. A child who has more initiative and greater self-confidence is more likely to be imaginative and creative. Such children are likely to apply themselves more diligently at school. This implies that these skills are valuable both in themselves and because they feed into the development of strong cognitive skills.

Fourth, strong cognitive and behavioral skills beget strong technical skills. Technical skills—often acquired last, through technical and vocational education and training (TVET), higher education, and on-the-job learning—will benefit from the stronger cognitive and behavioral skills acquired earlier in the education system. The skills learned in formal education will help workers to continuously update their technical skills during their working lives.

Sensitive and Critical Periods for Building a Skill

There are sensitive and critical moments in a person's life when cognitive, social and behavioral, and technical skills are most responsive to investments. The "malleable" moments are depicted in dark shading in figure 3.1, and periods when the skills are less sensitive to change are depicted in white.[1] A critical period is one for which there is no substitute, which means that a similar investment at another point in life is unable to change that ability. A period is defined as "sensitive" if an investment during that period can have a greater impact than during others (Cunha and Heckman 2008; Doherty 1997).

The foundations of an individual's intelligence are formed early in life. During the first few years of life, brain development occurs rapidly and in a bottom-up manner whereby the simple circuits and skills formed provide the scaffolding for more advanced circuits and skills over time. During this period of rapid brain development, the foundations are set for later development, resulting in path dependence: adverse circumstances such as malnutrition, stressful home environments, or a lack of stimulation during this period can have long-term consequences on adult capacities. Food supplementation to address nutritional deficits before age 5 have been found to have strong positive impacts on cognitive ability, motor development, and mental development, but are less effective thereafter (Walker et al. 2005).

The foundations of an individual's intelligence are fairly well set early in life. Two seminal and widely discussed factors of an individual's intelligence are fluid intelligence and crystallized intelligence. Fluid intelligence reflects the capacity to perceive and act upon complex problems under novel conditions, independent of acquired knowledge (Cattell 1971). In contrast, crystallized intelligence reflects learned skills and knowledge, and is therefore dependent on education and the formation and learning of knowledge (Horn and Cattell 1967). IQ scores, which capture to a greater degree fluid intelligence, become stable between ages 8 and 10, suggesting a particularly sensitive period for their formation before age 10 (Hopkins and Bracht 1975). There is, however, evidence to suggest that the development of fluid intelligence continues until age 16 (Garlick 2002).

Children continue to acquire knowledge and cognitive skills based on early cognitive foundations. Although a person's analytical and deductive capacity is most responsive to investments early in childhood, knowledge accumulation continues throughout adolescence and into adulthood and continues to grow with further education and on-the-job training (see annex 2A; Almlund et al. 2011).

Social and behavioral skills also begin to form in the early years and continue to evolve throughout adult life. There is evidence that social and behavioral skills are malleable during adulthood and that they may be *more* responsive to interventions during adolescence than in early childhood (Almlund et al. 2011). Interventions to strengthen behavioral skills can, therefore, be successful throughout a person's life. For example, the Jóvenes programs targeting disadvantaged youth in many Latin American countries combine socioemotional learning with the acquisition of technical skills (see chapter 5). Personality traits, like cognitive traits, are responsive to environmental stimulus but are also subject to evolution due to predictable biological processes. Attitudes toward risk have been found to be highest among adolescents and fall in the early twenties (Paulsen et al. 2012; Spear 2000).

The focus on behavioral skills formation early in life is growing worldwide. Because personality traits have been found to causally impact performance at school and in the labor market, interventions targeting social and behavioral skills are likely to be more effective when conducted earlier in life—before path-changing decisions are taken, such as whether to drop out of upper secondary school. Higher levels of perseverance and persistence have been found to be positively related to attendance and grades at school (Duckworth and Seligman 2005; Moffitt et al. 2011). Efforts are under way to anchor socioemotional learning in preschool and school curricula (e.g., the Tools of the Mind program in the United States), to establish standards for socioemotional learning (e.g., in Colombia), to record behavioral skills in student report cards (e.g., in Germany and the United States), and to provide relevant training to teachers.

Evidence from Vietnam indicates that consistent with international patterns, foundational cognitive skills are more malleable in childhood. The Young Lives survey in Vietnam follows a sample of children from early childhood to adolescence. The survey allows assessing changes in test score ranks as children mature, notably using the Peabody Picture Vocabulary Test (PPVT), a widely used test for cognitive ability at age 5 to measure vocabulary, and a Cognitive Development Assessment (CDA) to capture notions of quantity. Panel a of figure 3.2 shows rising correlations in the ranks of children in math and vocabulary tests as children grow older. This indicates that an individual's rank in the population becomes more stable over time—a sign of reduced malleability of cognitive skills with age. Panel b shows the scores achieved by children of different ages on the same test, on average and by wealth tercile. Two noteworthy messages emerge from this data. First, the children who performed relatively poorly at a younger age are less likely to overtake those who performed better, and those performing better are more likely to stay ahead of their lower-scoring peers. Second, older children attain higher scores in the vocabulary test than younger children. Therefore, although an individual's intelligence rank within a population becomes more stable over time, the knowledge they have expands over time and results in better performance on these tests.

Creating the right conditions for skill development in early childhood is more effective than rectifying gaps at later ages. Because the brain develops in a bottom-up manner, as described in box 3.1, it is harder to alter its capacity after it has stabilized with age. The windows of opportunity for skill development and

Figure 3.2 Changes in Cognitive Skills as Children Age

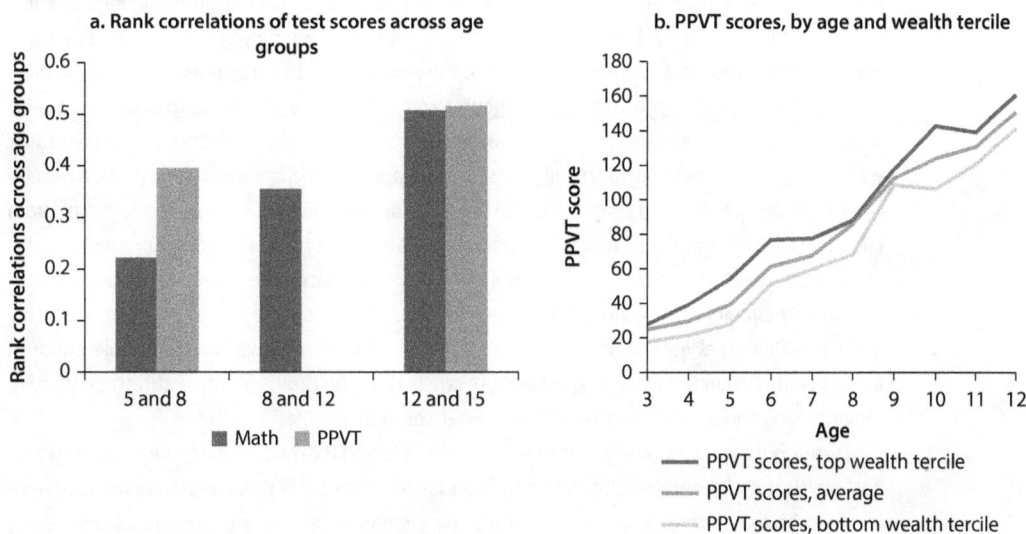

Sources: World Bank staff estimates using data from Young Lives survey, 2002, 2006–07, and 2009.
Note: PPVT = Peabody Picture Vocabulary Test. Panel a uses information from repeated rounds of the Young Lives survey to examine rank order correlations between rounds. Panel b uses information from the 2009 round of the Young Lives survey, in which a single PPVT was adminstered to younger children and their siblings of different ages.

Box 3.1 Why Are the Early Years So Fundamental for Building Skills?

Brains are built over time, in a process that starts before birth and continues into childhood. Building a brain is similar to building a house—the foundations must be laid, rooms framed, and the electrical system wired in a predictable sequence. The architecture of the brain, similar to a house, eventually incorporates distinctive features that reflect increasing individuality over time. The wiring occurs under the influence of both genetics and environment—that is, the environment a child is born into can affect the architecture of the brain through stimulating and secure interaction that promotes healthy development or continuous "toxic" stress that can have a damaging impact on early development. Toxic stress can occur as a result of prolonged exposure to extremely trying circumstances, such as extreme poverty or violence, that are not mitigated by the strength of reciprocal and nurturing relationships that can help a child to cope.

The brain's architecture is built over a succession of sensitive moments, each of which is associated with the formation of particular neural circuits—connections among brain cells— that are associated with specific abilities. The development of increasingly complicated skills and their underlying circuits builds on the circuits and skills that were formed earlier.

Brain circuits that process basic information are wired earlier than those that process more complex information. Higher-level circuits build on lower-level circuits, and adaptation at higher levels is more difficult if lower-level circuits were not wired properly. Parallel to the construction of brain circuits, increasingly complex skills build on the more basic, foundational capabilities that precede them. For example, the ability to recognize and then say the names of objects depends upon earlier development of the capacity to differentiate and reproduce the sounds of one's native language. And the circuits that underlie the ability to put words together to speak in phrases form a foundation for the subsequent mastery of reading a written sentence in a book. Stated in simple terms, circuits build on circuits and skill begets skill.

As the maturing brain becomes more specialized to assume more complex functions, it is less capable of reorganizing and adapting to new or unexpected challenges. Once a circuit is wired, it stabilizes with age, making it difficult to alter. Scientists use the term *plasticity* to refer to the capacity of the brain to change. Plasticity is maximal in early childhood and decreases with age. The windows of opportunity for skill development and behavioral adaptation remain open for many years, but trying to change behavior or build new skills on a foundation of brain circuits that were not wired properly when they were first formed requires more work and is more "expensive." For the brain, this means that greater amounts of energy are needed to compensate for circuits that do not perform in an expected fashion. For society, the expense may be costly. Remedial education and other professional interventions for vulnerable children living in difficult circumstances may be more costly than the provision of nurturing, protective relationships and appropriate learning experiences earlier in life.

Through this process, early experiences create a foundation for lifelong learning, behavior, and physical and mental health. A strong foundation in the early years increases the probability of positive outcomes, and a weak foundation increases the odds of later difficulties.

Source: This box draws heavily upon National Scientific Council on the Developing Child 2007.
Note: Research in this area is fast moving and complex and includes many questions that are far from resolved.

behavioral adaptation remain open for a period of years, but it becomes more difficult and more expensive to change behaviors or to build new skills on the foundation of brain circuits that were not wired properly when first formed. Remedial and second-chance education and training interventions are typically more costly than the provision of an appropriate learning and development environment earlier in life.

The environment that a child is born into has a fundamental influence on his or her development and has the ability to alter their genetic inheritance (see box 3.1). Stimulating interactions and stable responsive relationships with caregivers provide the sensory inputs necessary to build a healthy brain needed for lifelong learning and behaviors. Negative experiences such as malnutrition or exposure to toxins before birth or in early childhood are built into the architecture of the developing brain, putting in place a biological memory that not only can affect physical and mental health but also can impair future learning capacity and behavior.

A child growing up in a particularly stressful environment can have difficulties in learning, memory, and self-regulation because of disruptions in brain development at an early age. Being raised in a stressful environment without an adult who provides a protective barrier to support the child can disrupt the architecture of a developing brain and result in harmful long-term consequences. This type of stress is termed *toxic stress* and includes adverse repeated events that are coupled with limited consistent, supportive relationships to help the child cope with the circumstances. The circumstances that can lead to toxic stress include extreme poverty, chronic neglect, and repeated exposure to violence in the community or family. Excessively stressful conditions early in childhood have been linked to a number of changes in the brain that can compromise healthy development and life trajectories. Extreme poverty can also weaken marital and parenting relationships as families struggle to make ends meet and parents' distress in the economic domain spills over to more detached and less nurturing and stimulating parenting that is not responsive to a child's needs (Duncan, Ziol-Guest, and Kalil 2010).

New Skills Are Built Off Earlier Skills and Benefit from Previous Investments

Skills learned later in life benefit from earlier foundations. In the early years of brain development, the brain is shaped by genetics as well as by the environment in which it is formed, from prenatal nutritional supplements to supportive and responsive adult interactions. These early years and investments lay down the foundation for learning and behavior. Therefore, early investments have a multiplier effect because early abilities provide the foundations upon which later skills are constructed. This process has been referred to as *dynamic complementarity* in skill formation (Carneiro and Heckman 2003).

Unless corrected, early disadvantages compound into poorer performance throughout school. Children with lower initial cognitive and behavioral skills are able to absorb less knowledge (Cunha et al. 2006). When children spend their early years in a less stimulating, or less emotionally and physically supportive environment, brain development is affected and leads to cognitive, social, and behavioral delays. High levels of adversity and stress during early childhood have been found to increase the risk of stress-related disease and learning problems later in life (Grantham-McGregor et al. 2007; National Scientific Council on the Developing Child 2007).

In Vietnam, children who fall behind early on are likely to have difficulty catching up, consistent with earlier disadvantages compounding into poor performance later in life. Children from disadvantaged backgrounds display a lower ability to recognize words and to read fluently, which affects their ability to acquire further knowledge at school. An Early Grade Reading Assessment in primary education conducted in round 3 of the Young Lives survey in 2009 showed that children from poorer households had a lower level of reading fluency than children from richer households, and they also had lower levels of word recognition on average. At age 8, children living in the poorest 25 percent of households recognized approximately 22 fewer words per minute on average than children born to households in the richest quantile, and they displayed lower levels of oral fluency—they read 40 fewer words per minute. Fifty-six percent of children with the bottom 20 percent of scores were found in the poorest wealth quantile. This has an implication for comprehension of written texts: children from poorer backgrounds show poorer comprehension of these texts.

Technical skills learned at higher educational establishments are built off the basis of the foundational cognitive and behavioral abilities developed in childhood. Investment in technical skills later in life will have a greater impact on workforce development, the greater an individual's initial cognitive and behavioral skills (Cunha and Heckman 2007). Technical skills that focus on knowledge specific to occupations, jobs, and vocations are often acquired later in life, undergo continuous change, but benefit from cognitive skills acquired earlier— for example, individuals with better numeracy abilities are likely to make more competent engineers.

Social and Behavioral Skills Feed into Cognitive Skills and Vice Versa

Higher perseverance and an interest in learning have been associated with children staying longer in school. Policies that shape behavioral skills are likely to be pathbreaking when conducted earlier in life before important decisions, such as whether to drop out of upper secondary school, are taken. Behavioral skills such as self-control and determination (or grit) have been linked to better performance in school and a number of other consequential life outcomes. Self-control at age 10 was found to be associated with higher levels of income, savings behavior, financial security, occupational prestige, better health, and other outcomes later in life among 1,000 students tracked in New Zealand (Moffitt et al. 2011). Similarly, self-discipline among a population of adolescents was found to be a strong predictor of academic success and diligence such as the final grades achieved and the number of hours spent doing homework (Duckworth and Seligman 2005).

Evidence from Vietnam supports the importance of social and behavioral skills for the accumulation of cognitive skills. A school survey with an assessment of competencies in mathematics and Vietnamese language at grade 5 conducted as part of the Young Lives project in 2012 included questions to assess a student's academic confidence and academic effort at the beginning and the end of the school year. The evidence from this exercise underscores the importance of children's behavioral skills for their learning outcomes in mathematics and Vietnamese language over the course of the school year in grade 5. Academic confidence and effort are important for learning success even when controlling for initial scores and student background characteristics. At the same time, scores in mathematics and language were associated with increases in academic confidence and effort, highlighting the dynamic interaction between cognitive and social and behavioral skill formation (Yorke and Rolleston, forthcoming). The results also suggest that to be effective, teaching in early childhood and general education should not place emphasis only on the accumulation of knowledge but also on behavioral skills such as academic confidence and self-esteem. Social and behavioral skills are not just demanded by employers, as shown in chapter 2; they also contribute to the accumulation of learning in school.

Step 1: School Readiness through Early Childhood Development

The evidence in skills formation suggests that early childhood development and education interventions for children below the age of 6 to promote their readiness for school should be the first step in a holistic skills development strategy for Vietnam. The concept of school readiness has emerged over the past decade or so and represents the ability of children entering primary school to succeed at school. Offord Centre for Child Studies in Canada (2013) defines readiness to learn as a "child's ability to meet the task demands at school" and as a "child's ability to benefit from the educational activities provided by the school." School readiness is considered to be the product of a young child's cognitive, physical, and socioemotional development from an early age onward (Hair et al. 2006; Naudeau et al. 2011, 36). Figure 3.3 presents interventions to promote school readiness of children entering primary school as the first step in skills development. The right nutrition and stimulation through effective parenting before the age of 3 and quality preschool between 3 and 5 contribute to children's readiness for school.

A recent assessment of school readiness of 5-year-olds confirms that much of the inequality in learning outcomes between different types of young Vietnamese observed in primary education and beyond is already established before the age of formal schooling. In 2012 the Ministry of Education and Training (MOET) assessed school readiness among 5-year-old children in public preschools (MOET 2012). The survey adapted the Early Development Instrument (EDI) (Offord Centre for Child Studies 2013) to measure the development of children across five domains: physical health and well-being, social knowledge and competence, emotional health/maturity, language and cognitive development, and general

Figure 3.3 Step 1 in Skills Development: Promoting School Readiness to Help Children Learn in School

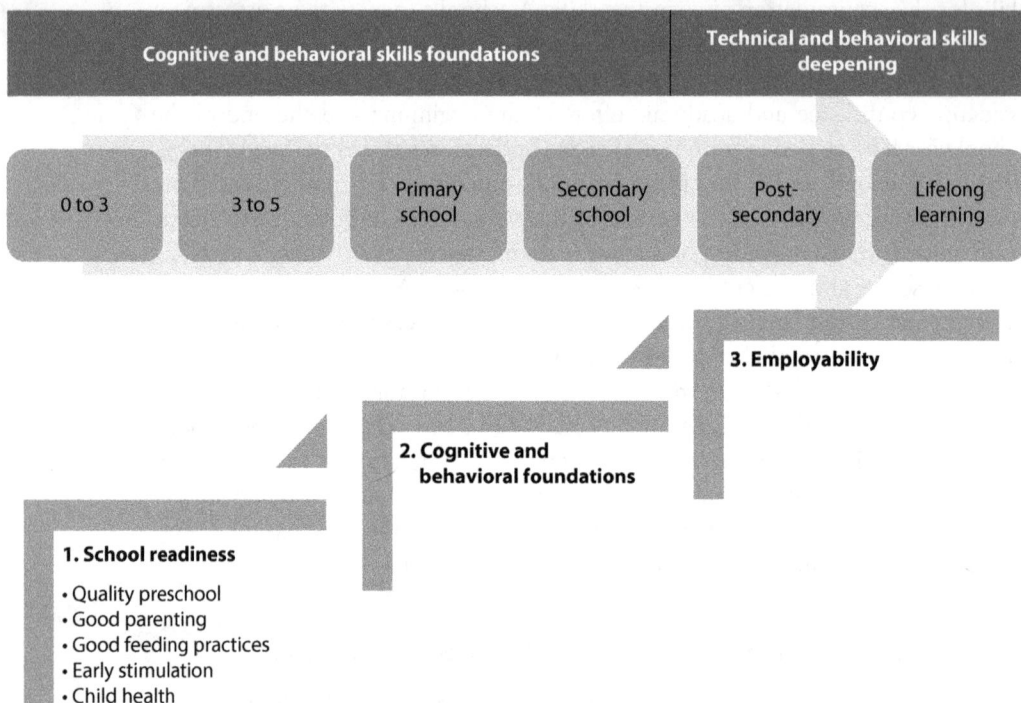

Cognitive and behavioral skills foundations				Technical and behavioral skills deepening	
0 to 3	3 to 5	Primary school	Secondary school	Post-secondary	Lifelong learning

3. Employability

2. Cognitive and behavioral foundations

1. School readiness

• Quality preschool
• Good parenting
• Good feeding practices
• Early stimulation
• Child health

knowledge and communication skills. Shares of children at various levels of school readiness can be determined from scores for each of the five domains. Children who scored in the lowest decile in one or more of the domains are considered vulnerable in terms of school readiness. Although the EDI cannot be used to diagnose whether a particular child is ready or not ready for school, it can be used to identify the shares and types of children who are most vulnerable to not being ready.

The degree of school readiness varies substantially across Vietnam's primary school entrants. Children from poor households in Vietnam run a greater risk of being limited in the various domains of school readiness. Figure 3.4 shows the percentage of Vietnamese 5-year-olds in the bottom 10 percent—the EDI definition of vulnerable—between households officially deemed poor and those deemed not poor. Children living in poor households are more likely to be vulnerable in each of the five developmental domains. More than 40 percent of children from poor households are vulnerable in at least one domain—almost twice the incidence of vulnerability among children in nonpoor households. Children are most vulnerable in the domains of communication and general knowledge, also the domain with the largest difference across poor and nonpoor households, as well as in the domains of physical health and well-being and language and cognitive development.

Figure 3.4 Percentage of 5-Year-Olds in the Lowest Decile of Each School Readiness Domain

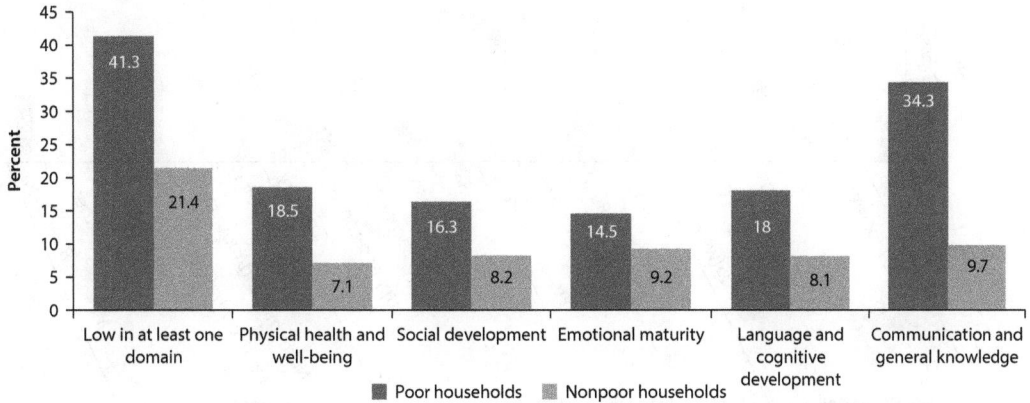

Sources: World Bank staff estimates using Vietnam's Early Development Instrument (EDI) and MOET 2012.

Effective Parenting for Children Aged 0–3

The arguably gravest form of inequality of opportunity manifests itself quickly in life—in the form of chronic child malnutrition, which remains one of Vietnam's biggest human development and skills challenges. Vietnam's youngest population is at a high risk of malnutrition and in particular of stunting. Although Vietnam has made considerable progress on improvement of child nutrition, in 2010 almost a quarter of children below the age of 5 remained stunted; that is, they had low height for age as a result of chronic malnutrition (GSO and UNICEF 2011; see figure 3.5). Rates are considerably higher among ethnic minority children, children from the poorest households, and children whose mothers have not attended school, as well as in certain, predominantly rural, regions across the country. Child malnutrition has substantial negative effects on a child's brain development and therefore on his or her cognitive skill formation. Confirming international evidence, analysis using data from Young Lives suggests that stunting at age 1 has a long-term impact on cognitive development in Vietnam, independent of birth weight, environmental factors, or parental and home background. Le Thuc Duc (2009) finds that an increase on one standard deviation in the height for age Z-score at age 1 leads to an increase by 24 percent in the log score in the PPVT.

Apart from poverty and living conditions such as access to clean water and sanitation, child malnutrition can be explained by inadequate infant and young child feeding (IYCF) practices. The role of parents in cognitive and behavioral skill development through their care for and stimulation of their young children is critical. But not all parents are taking, or are capable of taking, the right decisions for their infants and young children. Table 3.1 presents estimates of key breastfeeding indicators for Vietnam and for the poorest and wealthiest quintiles of the population. The World Health Organization (WHO) recommends that children be breastfed within one hour of birth, be exclusively breastfed for the first six months, and continue to be breastfed in addition to receiving solid food

Figure 3.5 Percentage of Children under 5 with Low Height for Age

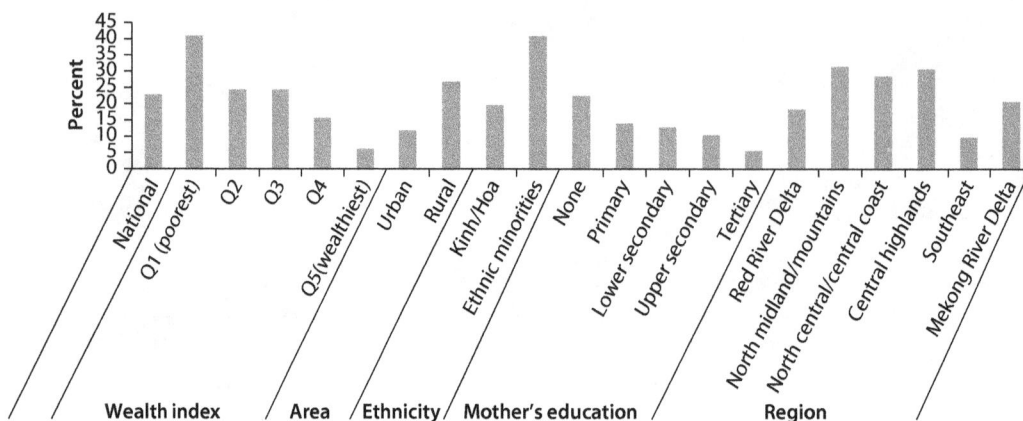

Source: GSO and UNICEF 2011.
Note: Percentage below two standard deviations.

Table 3.1 Feeding Practices for Young Children

	All	Poorest quintile	Wealthiest quintile
Breastfed within one hour of birth (percentage of last-born children in the past two years)	40	52	33
Percentage of children 0–5 months exclusively breastfed	17	28	11
Percentage of 20- to 23-month-old children still being breastfed	19	39	4

Source: GSO and UNICEF 2011.

for two years or longer (WHO 2010). As table 3.1 shows, adherence to these recommendations is very low in Vietnam. Only 40 percent of children born in the two years prior to the survey were breastfed within the first hour of birth. Only 17 percent of children aged 0–5 months were exclusively breastfed, and only 19 percent of children aged 20–23 months were still being breastfed.

Wealthier Vietnamese parents are less likely to breastfeed their infants than are the poor. It is not clear whether parents stray from optimal feeding practices because of a lack of knowledge or value for these practices or because of the opportunity cost of doing so. Parents in the wealthiest quintile are less likely to follow optimal feeding practices than parents in the poorest quintile, possibly because alternatives to breast milk are more accessible among wealthier households. But it also suggests a lack of value or knowledge. These patterns also reflect differences in work habits and the jobs that women do—women in the wealthiest quintile may be engaged in work that is incompatible with breastfeeding.

Beyond sound feeding practices, early stimulation of children is essential for cognitive development. More parents in Vietnam are engaging in educational and school readiness activities for young children. Table 3.2 presents the prevalence of activities in households to promote children's education and school readiness. Educational and school readiness activities include reading or looking at picture

Table 3.2 Activities to Promote Learning and School Readiness in the Past Three Days

	All	Poorest quintile	Wealthiest quintile
Percentage of children aged 35–59 months			
With whom adult household members engaged in four or more activities	77	63	94
With whom the father engaged in at least one or more activities	61	55	79
Mean number of activities			
Any adult household member engaged with the child	4.5	3.8	5.4
The father engaged with the child	1.6	1.2	2.4

Source: GSO and UNICEF 2011.

books with the child, telling stories, singing songs to or with the child, taking the child outside the home, playing with them, and naming, counting, and drawing things with the child. Among 3- to 5-year-old children, 77 percent had an adult member engage in four or more of these types of activities in the three days prior to the survey. The father engaged in at least one of these types of activities for 61 percent of children. On average, adult members engaged in 4.5 of these types of activities, and fathers engaged in 1.6 activities.

Vietnam's better-off parents are more likely to engage in educational activities with their young children. The father in the wealthiest households was engaged in twice as many activities on average as fathers in the poorest households. These differences may be due to wealthier parents being more aware of educational needs of children or valuing education more. They may also reflect parental presence; poorer parents may have to devote more time to income-generating activities to make ends meet. None of these activities except for one (reading and showing books) requires the household to own learning materials; consequently, it is unlikely that the poorest are unable to provide as many activities due to income constraints.

Enhancing parenting capacity for feeding and stimulation among disadvantaged parents is an important element of early childhood development. International evidence shows that parent counseling and curriculum-based parenting classes have been effective at improving parenting practices, particularly related to feeding. Interventions that have been found to be effective range from individual and group counseling for breastfeeding (see Bhutta et al. 2008 and Britton et al. 2007 for reviews) to curriculum-based parenting classes (Naudeau et al. 2011). Community-based learning may also be effective for influencing parenting practices. Evaluation of community meetings to identify and resolve childbirth and childcare issues for mothers in Bolivia, India, and Nepal found positive effects on parenting behavior and subsequent health outcomes. A community-based mechanism for providing information to mothers on nutrition practices in Senegal also yielded improvements in nutrition practices (see Naudeau et al. 2011, 115 for a review). A long-term evaluation of an early childhood development program in Jamaica launched in 1986–87 and targeted to mothers of babies that were stunted due to malnutrition showed that support and guidance on how to stimulate their babies' cognitive, physical, and emotional development proved more effective than the provision of nutritional supplements. A survey 20 years later showed that beneficiaries of this program were earning higher wages than a control group and that they had caught up to their peers who had not suffered from malnutrition in early age (Gertler et al. 2013).

Support for the development of children aged 0–3 remains underdeveloped in Vietnam. Despite high rates of stunting among children under the age of 5 and evidence of low and declining use of breastfeeding, child nutrition and IYCF are not adequately prioritized in government policy. Recent consultations with government leaders at central and local levels on the reasons for high child malnutrition in Vietnam showed that a majority of leaders acknowledge that the overall policy framework for addressing malnutrition was reasonably accurate, but that the main problems lie in implementation (Alive and Thrive 2012).

The weaknesses in early childhood development in Vietnam can be explained through both coordination and policy disconnects. First, key agencies at the central and local levels are not sufficiently aligned to coordinate government policy in the multisectoral arena of early childhood development. The Ministry of Health is in charge of young child health, the MOET is in charge of early childhood education, and the Ministry of Labor, Invalids, and Social Affairs is in charge of child welfare issues, but there is no apparent coordination mechanism to bring these disparate strands of early childhood development into an integrated and focused policy and implementation framework. Second, there is significant scope to be more systematic in promoting breastfeeding and child stimulation through a variation of parallel interventions in hospitals after birth, in local health stations, in communities, and through communication campaigns (Alive and Thrive 2012). The extensive poverty reduction policies in place for poor families with children, including through a myriad of more than a dozen cash transfer programs, are mostly aimed at families with children of school age and not at young children below the age of 5. The availability of parenting programs and support to parents from disadvantaged backgrounds through social workers or community volunteers remain limited and not systematic, even though the Women's Union has piloted and is gradually expanding a program of women-led parenting groups. Institutional childcare for children below the age of 3 through crèches is very limited and largely concentrated in urban areas in the Red River Delta (Jarvie 2010).

International evidence suggests that an integrated approach to early childhood development aimed at improving parental information and capacity constraints can help to overcome malnutrition and to get children off to the right start. Improving nutrition outcomes and early stimulation in the earliest years, in particular for children growing up in disadvantaged circumstances, requires addressing information and capacity constraints for parents. An integrated early childhood development package for children aged 0–3 could involve three connected pillars, all of which require close institutional coordination both at the policy and service delivery levels. First, a targeted cash transfer program for poor families with children from birth could help address income poverty and improve the financial capacity of parents to make good decisions for their children. Second, curriculum-based parenting programs focused on feeding and early stimulation, complemented by regular visits to families by social workers or community volunteers, could help to address information and knowledge capacity gaps. Third, greater outreach by community health stations could help facilitate access to child health services.

High-Quality Preschool for Children Aged 3–6

The promotion of preschool for children aged 3–6 is currently the main policy lever of the government of Vietnam to enhance school readiness. The government recognizes the importance of early childhood education to better prepare children, particularly the most disadvantaged children, for school. This is why it has modernized the preschool curriculum, has launched a program to universalize full-day preschool for 5-year-old children (Program 239), and is making investments to facilitate access to preschool among the most disadvantaged children aged 3–5. While access to some form of preschool for 5-year-old children is high countrywide (see figure 3.6), the enrollment in full-day preschool, the key national goal, is still limited and there are wide variations across the country. Moreover, enrollments among children of less than 5 years of age are often significantly lower.

An enhanced focus on quality can help to further strengthen early childhood education. Vietnam's early childhood education has many strengths, including a sound policy framework, child-focused curriculum, and rapidly expanding provision, particularly for 5-year-olds. But a disconnect still exists between policies

Figure 3.6 Preschool Enrollment Rates across Regions in Vietnam, 2011–12

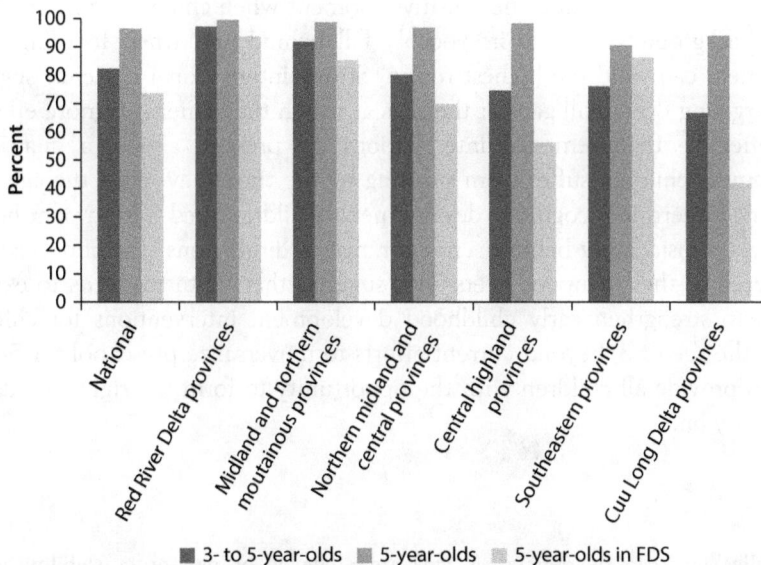

Legend: ■ 3- to 5-year-olds ■ 5-year-olds 5-year-olds in FDS

Source: Education statistics from Ministry of Education and Training, 2011/12.
Note: FDS = full-day preschool, including lunch in line with Program 239.

to promote access and quality at the national level and the actual provision of facilities in the provinces. As a result, there are wide variations in quality and access, with significant weaknesses in provision for disadvantaged children. While promoting access remains a priority, particularly in underserved regions, the government's focus should concentrate on improving the quality of provision. Taking advantage of its modern and child-centered curriculum and translating it into higher-quality provision across all classrooms require investment in the effectiveness of teachers and principals through major teacher training reforms and through upgrading the competence of the current workforce. Also required is a special focus on ethnic minority children, including through increasing the number of ethnic minority teachers and integration of ethnic minority teaching assistants (Jarvie 2010).

Summary and Conclusion

Skills formation happens throughout life, but the early years are particularly important in setting the cognitive and behavioral foundations. The most sensitive moments for skill development vary across different dimensions of skills, with cognitive and behavioral skills formation more sensitive to interventions earlier in life and technical skills later. Behavioral skills and cognitive skills formation are intertwined: evidence from Vietnam shows that academic confidence helps with learning, and learning success fosters academic confidence. And good cognitive and behavioral skills facilitate the formation of technical skills. The stronger their cognitive and behavioral foundation skills, the better Vietnamese workers will be able to acquire technical skills and keep them up to date with accelerating technological progress over longer working lives.

The early years are also the sensitive moment when children from disadvantaged backgrounds start to irrevocably fall behind and when focusing more investment can yield the highest return. Strong international evidence suggests that targeting these skill gaps at the ages at which they emerge is more efficient and effective than remedial interventions. At present, almost a quarter of Vietnamese children suffer from stunting by the time they reach the age of 5. Stunting undermines cognitive development. Children aged 5 from poor households are considerably behind across a range of dimensions of school readiness compared to their nonpoor peers. This suggests that Vietnam needs to expand efforts to strengthen early childhood development interventions for children below the age of 3, beyond current efforts to universalize preschool for 5-year-olds, to provide all children with the opportunity to form the right foundation skills early on.

Note

1. Malleability can be defined as rank-order change or rank-order stability, which establishes the extent to which an individual's ordinal ranking of a trait remains stable over time. Although the rank order of scores remains stable after a pivotal moment,

IQ scores exhibit absolute changes over time. Therefore, individuals continue to see changes in the absolute levels of their scores, although the order of scores within a population exhibits greater stability over time. Malleability can also refer to change over time in absolute levels of a trait. IQ scores have been shown to become relatively *rank* stable at age 10 or so (Hopkins and Bracht 1975; Roberts and Del Vecchio 2000), although *absolute* changes in IQ within a population are observed throughout the life cycle.

References

Alive and Thrive. 2012. *Policy Support for Infant and Young Child Feeding: Leader Perspectives.* Hanoi.

Almlund, M., A. L. Duckworth, J. Heckman, and T. Kautz. 2011. "Personality Psychology and Economics." In *Handbook of the Economics of Education,* edited by E. A. Hanushek, S. Machin, and L. Woessmann, 1–181. Amsterdam: Elsevier.

Bhutta, Z. A., T. Ahmed, R. E. Black, S. Cousens, K. Dewey, E. Giugliani, B. A. Hairder, K. Kirkwood, S. S. Morris, H. P. S. Sachdev, M. Shekar, and the Maternal and Child Under-Nutrition Study Group. 2008. "What Works? Interventions for Maternal and Child Under-Nutrition and Survival." *The Lancet* 371 (9610): 417–40.

Britton, C., F. M. McCormick, M. J. Renfrew, A. Wade, and S. E. King. 2007. "Support for Breastfeeding Mothers." *Cochrane Database of Systematic Reviews* (1): CD001141.

Carneiro, P., and J. J. Heckman. 2003. "Human Capital Policy." In *Inequality in America: What Role for Human Capital Policies?* edited by J. J. Heckman, A. B. Krueger, and B. M. Friedman, 77–239. Cambridge, MA: MIT Press.

Cattell, R. B. 1971. *Abilities: Their Structure, Growth, and Action.* Boston, MA: Houghton Mifflin.

Cunha, F., and J. J. Heckman. 2007. "The Technology of Skill Formation." *American Economic Association Papers and Proceedings* 97 (2): 31–47.

———. 2008. "Formulating, Identifying and Estimating the Technology of Cognitive and Noncognitive Skill Formation." *Journal of Human Resources* 43 (4): 738–82.

Cunha, F., J. J. Heckman, L. Lochner, and D. V. Masterov. 2006. "Interpreting the Evidence on Life Cycle Skill Formation." In *Handbook of the Economics of Education,* vol. 1, edited by E. A. Hanushek and F. Welch. Amsterdam: North Holland.

Cunha, F., J. J. Heckman, and S. M. Schennach. 2010. "Estimating the Technology of Cognitive and Noncognitive Skill Formation." *Econometrica* 78 (3): 883–931.

Doherty, G. 1997. "Zero to Six: The Basis for School Readiness." Research Paper R-97-8E, Applied Research Branch, Strategic Policy, Human Resources Development, Canada. citeseerx.ist.psu.edu.

Duckworth, A. L., and M. E. P. Seligman. 2005. "Self-Discipline Outdoes IQ in Predicting Academic Performance of Adolescents." *Psychological Science* 16 (12): 939–44.

Duncan, G. J., K. M. Ziol-Guest, and A. Kalil. 2010. "Early Childhood Poverty and Adult Attainment, Behavior, and Health." *Child Development* 81 (1): 306–25.

Garlick, D. 2002. "Understanding the Nature of the General Factor of Intelligence: The Role of Individual Differences in Neural Plasticity as an Explanatory Mechanism." *Psychological Review* 109 (1): 116–36.

Gertler, P., J. Heckman, R. Pinto, A. Zanolini, C. Vermeersch, S. Walker, S. Chang, and S. Grantham-McGregor. 2013. "Labor Market Returns to Early Childhood Stimulation: A 20-Year Follow-Up to an Experimental Intervention in Jamaica." NBER Working Paper 19185, National Bureau of Economic Research, Cambridge, MA.

Grantham-McGregor, S., Y. B. Cheung, S. Cueto, P. Glewwe, L. Richter, and B. Strupp. 2007. "Developmental Potential in the First 5 Years for Children in Developing Countries." *The Lancet* 369 (9555): 60–70.

GSO (General Statistics Office—Viet Nam) and UNICEF (United Nations Children's Fund). 2011. *Monitoring the Situation of Children and Women: Vietnam Multiple Indicator Cluster Survey 2011.* Hanoi.

Hair, E. C., T. Halle, E. Terry-Humen, B. Lavelle, and J. Calkins. 2006. "Children's School Readiness in the ECS-K: Predictions to Academic, Health, and Social Outcomes in First Grade." *Early Childhood Research Quarterly* 21 (4): 431–54.

Hopkins, K. D., and G. H. Bracht. 1975. "Ten-Year Stability of Verbal and Nonverbal IQ Scores." *American Educational Research Journal* 12 (4): 469–77.

Horn, J. L., and R. B. Cattell. 1967. "Age Differences in Fluid and Crystallized Intelligence." *Acta Psychologica* 26: 107–29.

Jarvie, W. 2010. "Improving Access to and Quality of Early Childhood Education in Vietnam." Unpublished manuscript.

Le Thuc Duc, L. 2009. *The Effect of Early Age Stunting on Cognitive Achievement among Children in Vietnam.* Young Lives Working Paper 45, Department of International Development, University of Oxford, Oxford, U.K.

MOET (Ministry of Education and Training of Vietnam). 2012. *Early Development Instrument (EDI) in Vietnam.* Hanoi.

Moffitt, T. E., L. Arseneault, D. Belskya, N. Dickson, R. J. Hancox, H. Harrington, R. Houtsa, R. Poulton, B. W. Roberts, S. Ross, M. R. Sears, W. M. Thomson, and A. Caspi. 2011. "A Gradient of Childhood Self-Control Predicts Health, Wealth, and Public Safety." *PNAS (Proceedings of the National Academy of Sciences) USA* 108: 2693–98.

Naudeau, S., N. Kataoka, A. Valerio, M. J. Neuman, and L. K. Elder. 2011. *Investing in Young Children: An Early Childhood Development Guide for Policy Dialogue and Project Preparation.* Directions in Development. Washington, DC: World Bank.

National Scientific Council on the Developing Child. 2007. *The Science of Early Childhood Development.* http://www.developingchild.net.

Offord Centre for Child Studies. 2013. "School Readiness to Learn Project." http://www.offordcentre.com/readiness/.

Paulsen, D. J., M. L. Platt, S. A. Huettel, and E. M. Brannon. 2012. "From Risk-Seeking to Risk-Averse: The Development of Economic Risk Preference from Childhood to Adulthood." *Frontiers in Psychology* 3: doi: 10.3389/fpsyg.2012.00313.

Roberts, B. W., and W. F. Del Vecchio. 2000. "The Rank-Order Consistency of Personality Traits from Childhood to Old Age: A Quantitative Review of Longitudinal Studies." *Psychological Bulletin* 126: 3–25.

Shonkoff, J. P., and D. A. Phillips. 2000. *From Neurons to Neighborhoods: The Science of Early Childhood Development.* Washington, DC: National Academy Press.

Spear, L. P. 2000. "The Adolescent Brain and Age-Related Behavioral Manifestations." *Neuroscience Biobehavioral Review* 24: 417–63.

Walker, S. P., S. M. Chang, C. A. Powell, and S. M. Grantham-McGregor. 2005. "Effects of Early Childhood Psychosocial Stimulation and Nutritional Supplementation on Cognition and Education in Growth-Stunted Jamaican Children: Prospective Cohort Study." *The Lancet* 366: 1804–07.

WHO (World Health Organization). 2010. *Guidelines on HIV and Infant Feeding 2010.* Geneva: WHO.

Yorke, L., and C. Rolleston. Forthcoming. *The Importance of Non-Cognitive Skills for Academic Achievement in Vietnam.* Young Lives Working Paper, Department of International Development, University of Oxford, Oxford, U.K.

CHAPTER 4

Cognitive and Behavioral Foundation Skills in the General Education System

General education has been important in advancing basic cognitive skills among Vietnam's children and workforce over the last two decades. Vietnam's general education system has undergone a remarkable transformation since the đổi mới reforms. Enrollments have expanded dramatically at every level, and Vietnam's population has become increasingly well educated. An initial successful focus on expanding access to and completion of primary education, as called for under the Millennium Development Goals, has opened the way to an increased emphasis on expanding pre-primary and secondary education enrollments. Available evidence suggests that the education system succeeds in equipping graduates with basic literacy and numeracy skills, perhaps more successfully than education systems in richer countries.

Strengthening higher-order cognitive and social and behavioral skills among all school graduates means entering a new phase in Vietnam's education development from expanding access to deepening quality. In other words, with employers highlighting the importance of advanced cognitive and social and behavioral skills, Vietnam needs to strengthen its system further to provide graduates with those needed foundation skills and to overcome inequalities in learning outcomes. It is the second step of a holistic skills development strategy (figure 4.1). This chapter provides a snapshot of the current general education system and discusses how Vietnam can do more to build the right cognitive and behavioral foundations. It calls for *more schooling*, with expanded full-day instruction at primary level and enhanced access to secondary education; *better schooling*, with a curriculum and teaching methods that foster the development of higher-order cognitive and behavioral skills in students; and *schooling that involves parents and local communities* more. Vietnam is in a good position to implement such reforms—the school infrastructure is there, and because of the declining birthrate, the school population is also declining.

Figure 4.1 Step 2 in Skills Development: Developing the Cognitive and Behavioral Skills Foundation

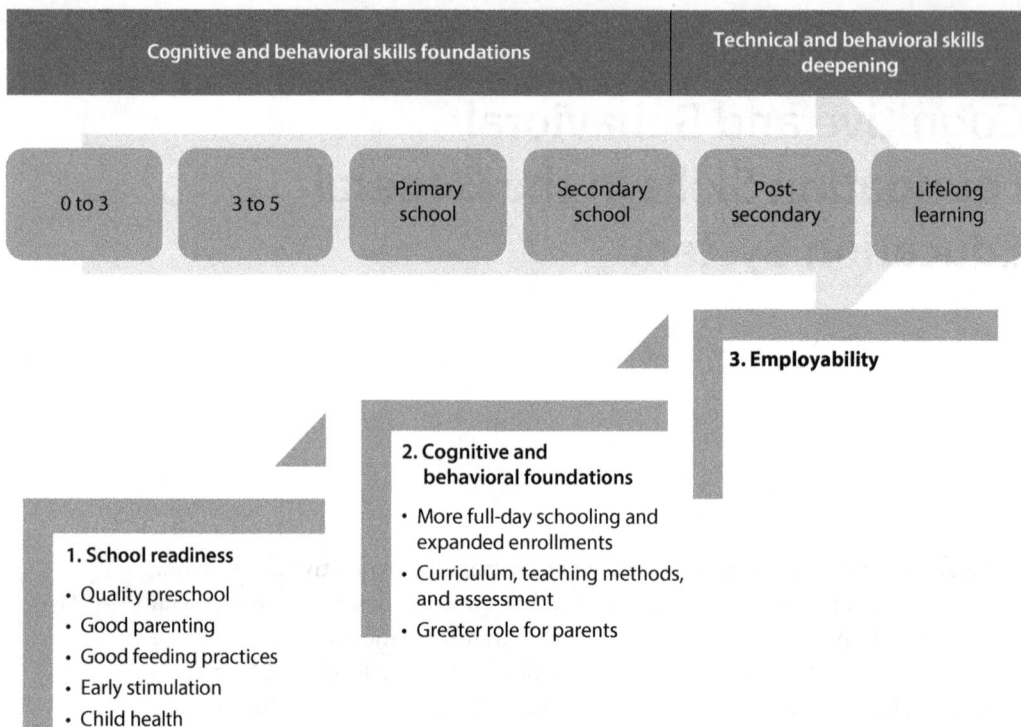

Cognitive and behavioral skills foundations				Technical and behavioral skills deepening	
0 to 3	3 to 5	Primary school	Secondary school	Post-secondary	Lifelong learning

3. Employability

2. Cognitive and behavioral foundations
- More full-day schooling and expanded enrollments
- Curriculum, teaching methods, and assessment
- Greater role for parents

1. School readiness
- Quality preschool
- Good parenting
- Good feeding practices
- Early stimulation
- Child health

General Education in Vietnam at a Glance

Ever greater shares of Vietnamese children and young people attend and complete primary, lower secondary, and upper secondary education, but inequalities exist in enrollment at the postprimary level. Primary enrollment is universal today, and lower and upper secondary enrollments were above 80 percent and close to 60 percent, respectively, in 2010 after considerable increases in enrollments since 1998 (figure 4.2, panel a). The universality of primary enrollment is evident from the breakdown by wealth quintile (panel b): 90 percent of children from the poorest households are enrolled in primary education. Primary education in Vietnam is compulsory and involves formal half-day provision, which is free of charge. Secondary education is not compulsory, and schools levy tuition fees, which are exempt for children from registered poor households. Despite this assistance, net enrollment rates at secondary level vary significantly between rich and poor children, in particular at the upper secondary level. The failure by many children from less well-off households to progress to upper secondary education is also a key predictor of their subsequent underrepresentation in higher education. A nuanced picture emerges: in Vietnam today, primary education is for all, and upper secondary and above is mainly for the wealthy.

Half-day tuition time in primary education is short relative to the needs of children and compared to other countries. Half-day schooling runs between

Figure 4.2 Net Enrollment Rates and Enrollment by Wealth Quintile

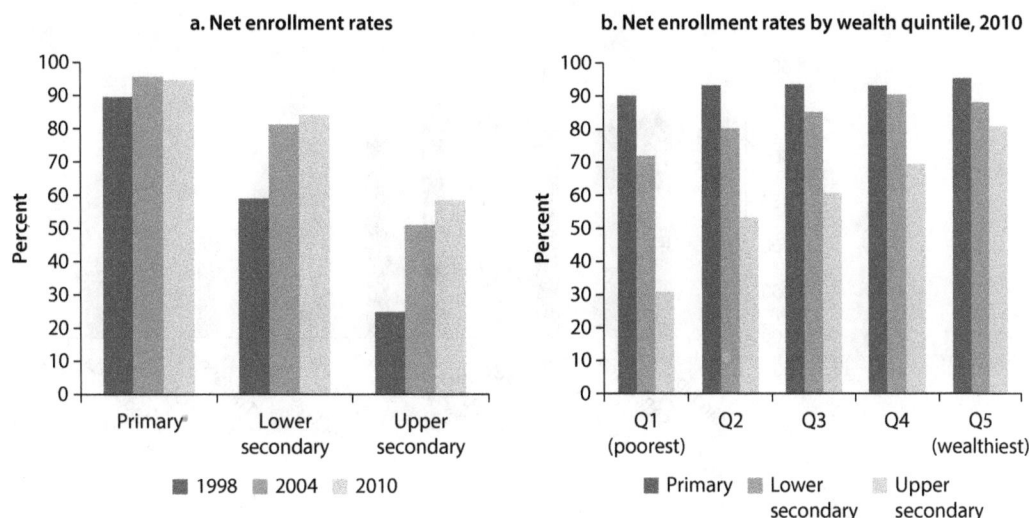

a. Net enrollment rates

b. Net enrollment rates by wealth quintile, 2010

Legend (a): ■ 1998 ■ 2004 ▪ 2010

Legend (b): ■ Primary ■ Lower secondary ▪ Upper secondary

Source: World Bank staff estimates based on VHLSS 1998, 2004, and 2010 data.
Note: VHLSS = Vietnam Household Living Standards Survey.

23 and 25 instruction periods (40 minutes long) per week over a school year of 36 weeks (that is, between 550 and 600 hours per year). The amount of time in school is deemed too short to cover the curriculum adequately. Teachers in Vietnam are paid for 40 hours (the norm of working hours in the civil service), but deliver only about 15.3 hours of tuition a week (23 periods). The amount of tuition time per teacher is low compared to other countries with established full-day schooling. In advanced economies, teachers typically spend between 22 and 25 hours per week teaching, which corresponds exactly to the amount of tuition received by students (on average between 800 and 1,000 hours of tuition each year) (SEQAP 2012).

Even with relatively short formal instruction time, the Vietnamese general education system performs well in imparting basic cognitive skills such as literacy and numeracy. Vietnam's participation in the 2012 Programme for International Student Assessment (PISA) allows, for the first time, for the benchmarking of its educational outcomes internationally (figure 4.3). Like their peers in many other East Asian countries, Vietnam's 15-year-old students showed stronger achievements in mathematics, science, and reading than the average of much wealthier countries in the Organisation for Economic Co-operation and Development (OECD). PISA assesses competencies of 15-year-olds in school, which means that it captures only those Vietnamese students who remain in upper secondary education—typically the better-off, and likely better-performing, students—and excludes those who have already dropped out.

Vietnam's overall impressive performance in mathematics hides significant variation in students' competencies across different dimensions of mathematics use. PISA allows differentiating between the formulating domain (translating a

Figure 4.3 Mean 2012 PISA Mathematics Scores, Selected Cities and Countries

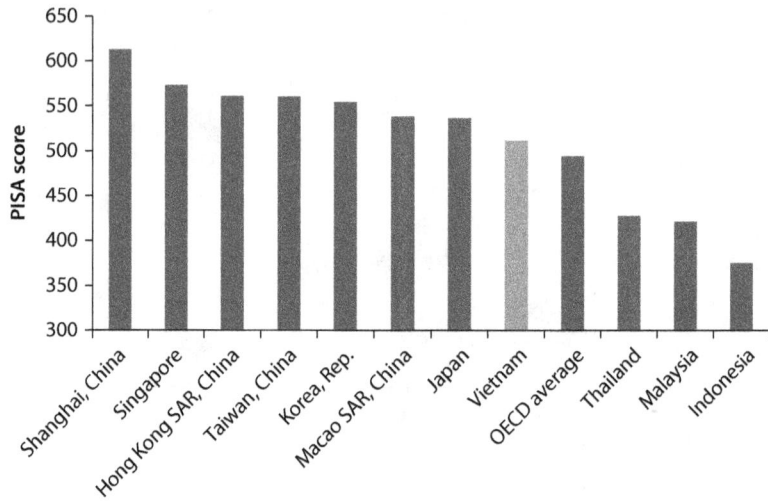

Source: OECD 2013.
Note: OECD = Organisation for Economic Co-operation and Development; PISA = Programme for International Student Assessment.

real-world problem into a mathematics problem), the interpretation domain (linking the mathematical outcome to the situation of the problem), and the employing domain (choosing the right mathematical tools to solve a math problem). Vietnam's performance on the formulating and interpretation domains is significantly lower than its average score, while its performance on the employing domain is relatively higher (figure 4.4). The scores suggest that Vietnamese students are not equally familiar with different dimensions of mathematics and relatively less so in formulating and interpreting mathematical problems.

Gaps in student performance are large between disadvantaged and other children, but primary schooling shows some success at helping children from disadvantaged backgrounds catch up. The Young Lives School Survey in 2012 involved a curriculum-based test at the beginning and the end of grade 5 (figure 4.5, panels a and b). It shows, first, that there are large gaps in curriculum mastery between ethnic Kinh and ethnic minority children both at the beginning and end of the school year. It also demonstrates, however, that ethnic minority children in grade 5 reduced the performance gap with their ethnic Kinh peers in curriculum mastery in Vietnamese language and mathematics over the course of the school year. Catch-up in Vietnamese language was particularly pronounced. In mathematics, the learning progress was fast for all the children, with less bridging in the learning outcome gap. In mathematics, the gap at the end of grade 5 remains the equivalent of one year of instruction (the average increase in scores between the first and second rounds was 41 points—less than the difference in performance between ethnic Kinh and minority children).

Primary education overall is not able to help disadvantaged children fully make up for unequal starting positions. Figure 4.5 (panels c and d) shows data from multiple rounds of Young Lives surveys presenting the evolution of learning outcomes of children over time by the wealth index of the children's households (panel c). Differences in learning outcomes between children from different socioeconomic groups are already well established at age 5, consistent with the evidence from the Early Development Instrument (EDI) shown in chapter 3. Although there is some narrowing of the gap in learning outcomes between

Figure 4.4 PISA Mean Mathematics Scores, by Subscale, 2012

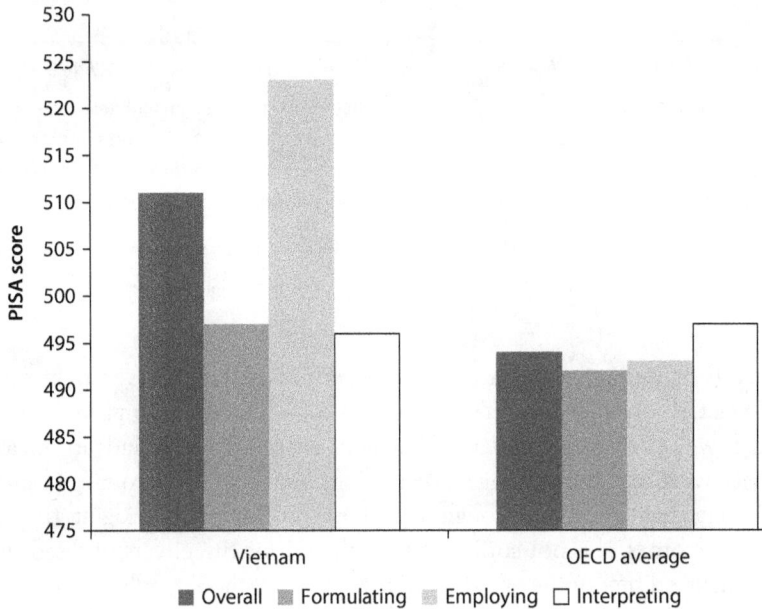

Legend: ■ Overall ■ Formulating ▨ Employing □ Interpreting

Source: OECD 2013.
Note: OECD = Organisation for Economic Co-operation and Development; PISA = Programme for International Student Assessment.

Figure 4.5 Math and Language Test Scores of Children of Different Backgrounds

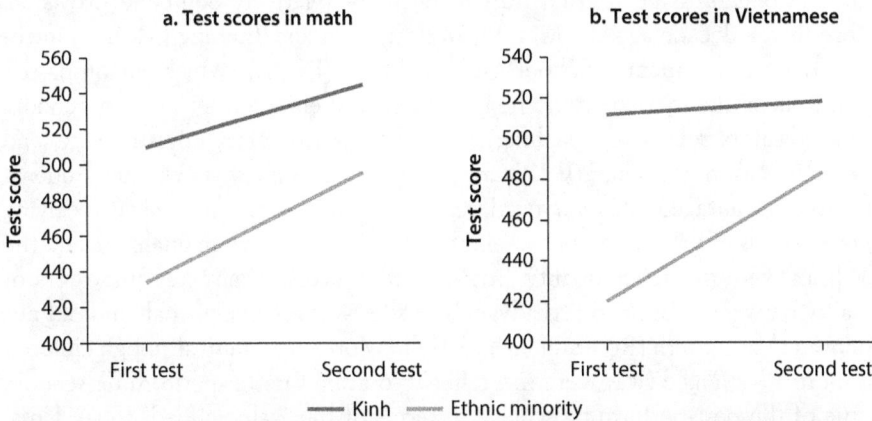

a. Test scores in math

b. Test scores in Vietnamese

Legend: —— Kinh ----- Ethnic minority

figure continues next page

Figure 4.5 Math and Language Test Scores of Children of Different Backgrounds *(continued)*

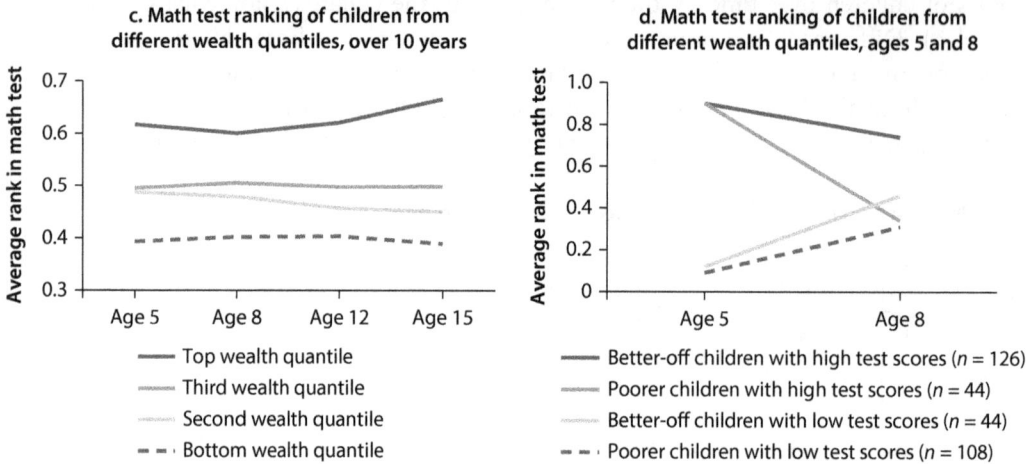

c. Math test ranking of children from
different wealth quantiles, over 10 years

d. Math test ranking of children from
different wealth quantiles, ages 5 and 8

——— Top wealth quantile
——— Third wealth quantile
········· Second wealth quantile
– – · Bottom wealth quantile

——— Better-off children with high test scores ($n = 126$)
——— Poorer children with high test scores ($n = 44$)
········· Better-off children with low test scores ($n = 44$)
– – · Poorer children with low test scores ($n = 108$)

Sources: Rolleston et al. 2013, using Young Lives survey data (panels a and b); World Bank staff estimates using Young Lives survey data (panels c and d).

children in richest and poorest households within grade 5, gaps remain through time. In fact, the average rank in mathematics and Vietnamese language test scores of initially well-performing students from disadvantaged backgrounds are not able to keep pace with well-performing students from better-off backgrounds (panel d).[1] This finding suggests that although schooling contributes to bridging the gap in learning outcomes, it is not sufficient to make up for the effects of disadvantage already incurred before the age of 6, that is, gaps in school readiness. To improve learning outcomes among disadvantaged children, it is necessary to look not only at the classroom—the quality of the teacher—but also at how the situation at home can be improved, including through engagement with the parents and targeted additional support for children from disadvantaged backgrounds.

Vietnam's focus on ensuring minimum quality standards across all primary schools appears to be bearing fruit in terms of relatively equitable provision. More than a decade ago the Ministry of Education and Training (MOET) introduced the Fundamental School Quality Level (FSQL), which encompassed indicators of quality that would be monitored and enforced for primary schools. The indicators related to teaching staff, teaching materials, infrastructure, and school management. The 2012 Young Lives School Survey shows that students in more advantaged sites surveyed across Vietnam were on average receiving more periods of instruction per week, their teachers were more qualified, and the facilities were of higher quality. But the difference in many key indicators of quality between more and less advantaged sites was relatively small and did not follow a clear pattern (Rolleston et al. 2013).[2] More important, although children in more advantaged sites were more likely to attend better-performing schools, some of the best-performing schools in terms of the "value added" to students' learning achievement are in disadvantaged sites.

Step 2: Building Cognitive and Behavioral Foundation Skills in General Education

Vietnam's general education system is successful in providing graduates with good basic cognitive skills, and any reforms should carefully build on the system's strengths. Shifting the emphasis in general education toward making sure that more children learn and acquire the higher-order cognitive and behavioral skills demanded in Vietnam's labor market does not mean that the system needs wholesale reform. Instead, it needs careful adjustments, building on its strong features. Building stronger cognitive and behavioral skills will require (a) *more schooling*, with full-day instruction and expansion of access to secondary education; (b) *better schooling*, with a curriculum, teaching methods, and assessments that foster the development of higher-order cognitive and behavioral skills in students; and (c) *greater involvement of parents and communities in schooling*. All three requirements are particularly important to help students from disadvantaged backgrounds catch up. The move to full-day schooling presents many opportunities to broaden the curriculum and find time to build on strong foundations through exposure to a wider range of learning experiences.

More Schooling

Improving cognitive foundation skills among Vietnam's next generation will require that children spend more time in school. First, education careers need to be extended through increasing the progression rates from primary to lower secondary and from lower secondary to upper secondary. Second, the tuition time in primary education needs to be extended through introducing full-day schooling. More schooling carries additional costs, which need to be covered by the government or parents or both. A decline in the number of students offers an opportunity to rebalance public spending toward the new priorities of expanded secondary education and full-day schooling.

More students need to enroll and complete general secondary education. As figure 4.6, panel a, demonstrates, gross enrollment rates for lower secondary education are broadly on par with Malaysia, the Philippines, and Thailand but are below those in China and significantly below those in the Republic of Korea, where lower secondary education is universal. Even though Vietnam is trailing Korea on upper secondary gross enrollment rates today, Vietnam is aiming to do as well as Korea in the future. To provide some orientation: Vietnam's combined upper and lower secondary net enrollment rate in 2010 stood at 72 percent—the equivalent of Korea's in the early 1980s (see figure 4.6, panel b). At that time Korea's share of employment in professional and technical occupations, which require at least secondary education, was roughly similar to Vietnam's today. Its considerable expansion of employment in these occupations was associated with expansions in secondary enrollment.

Expanding secondary enrollments requires an expansion in the supply of secondary schooling and a strengthening of demand by easing the financial constraints of less well-off households. Progressing to lower and upper secondary

Figure 4.6 Gross and Net Secondary Enrollment Rates in Vietnam and Neighboring Countries

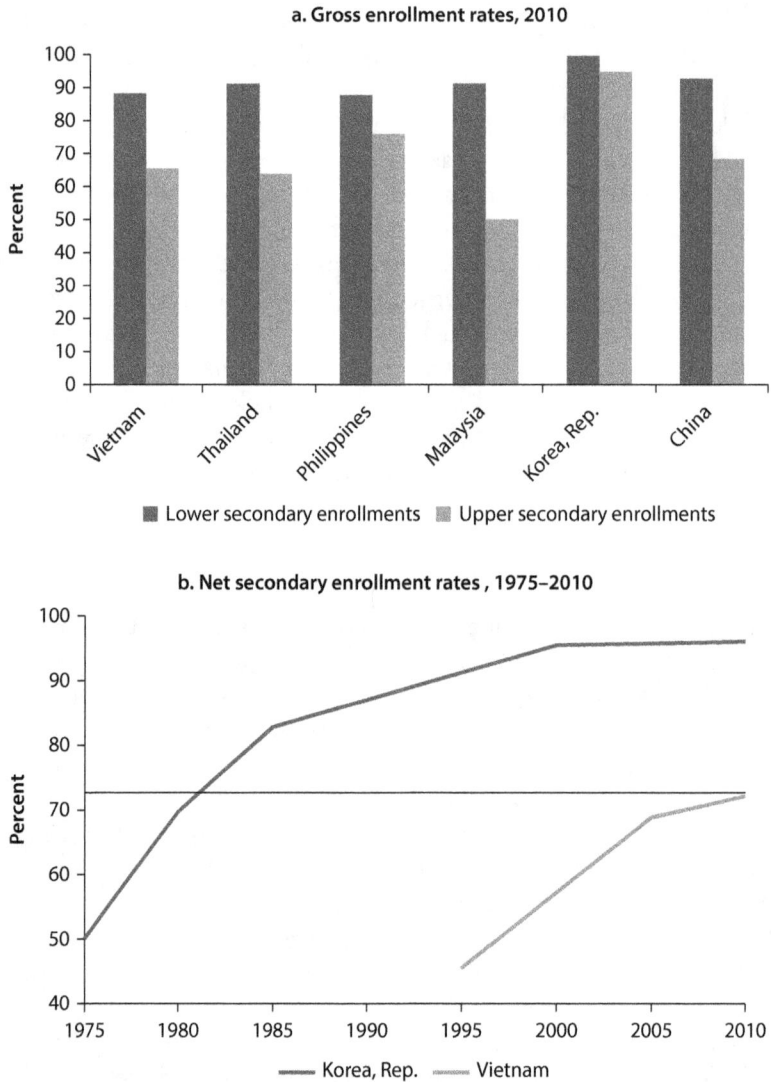

a. Gross enrollment rates, 2010

■ Lower secondary enrollments ■ Upper secondary enrollments

b. Net secondary enrollment rates , 1975–2010

——— Korea, Rep. ——— Vietnam

Source: World Bank EdStats (http://datatopics.worldbank.org/education/).
Note: In panel a, Philippines data are from 2009. In panel b, 1995 data for Vietnam are from 1998, and 2005 data are from 2004.

education involves considerable costs to households. This involves both a direct cost and the indirect cost of not earning income on the labor market. Figure 4.7 presents the private cost of education by level of education and by type of expenditure in 2010. At around 4.2 percent of overall household expenditure, the private cost of upper secondary is large and significantly larger than for primary education (around 1.7 percent) and lower secondary (around 2.5 percent). The shares of private expenditures are broadly similar across

Figure 4.7 Private Spending on Secondary Education, 2010

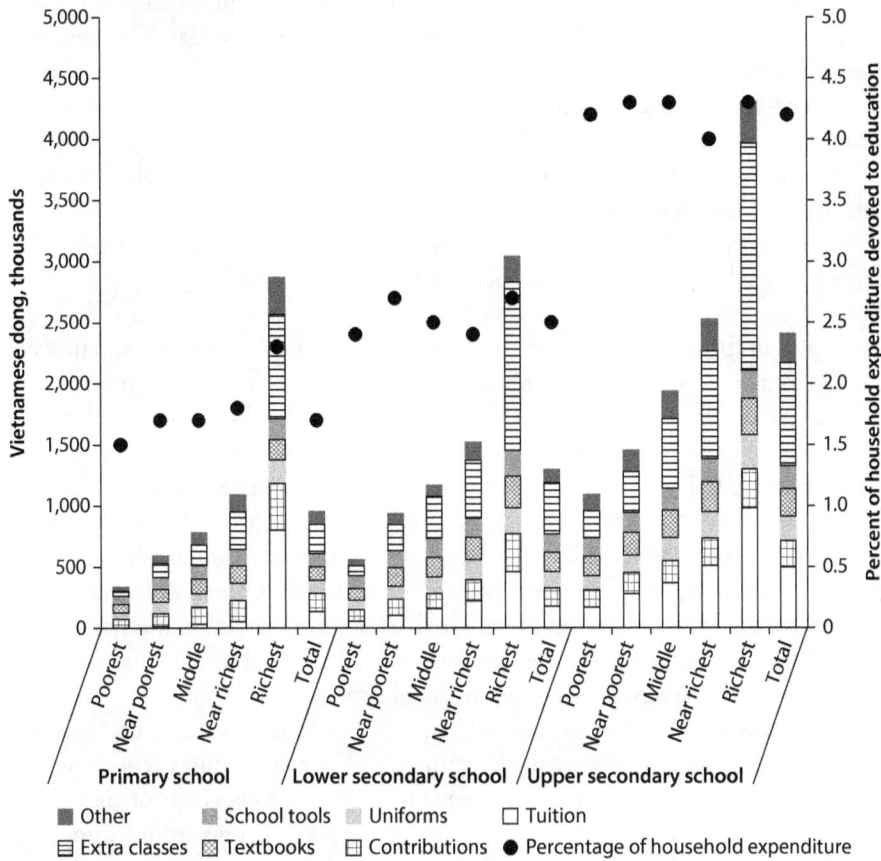

Source: World Bank staff estimates based on VHLSS 2010 data.
Note: VHLSS = Vietnam Household Living Standards Survey.

household wealth quintiles, but the poorest households spend significantly less than richer households in absolute terms, with expenses on tuition, contributions, and extra classes making the biggest difference. Larger expenses for formal tuition and contributions at the upper secondary level likely reflect that upper secondary schools are fewer in number than lower secondary schools and are located on average farther away, which imposes transport and boarding costs that may be unaffordable to less well-off households.

Formal tuition is not the main driver of private spending, and tuition exemptions alone do not offset all private costs. In addition to tuition, households must pay for books, equipment, and uniforms, which suggests that only waiving the tuition for children from poorer households may not be sufficient to encourage their higher enrollment at secondary levels. International experience shows that well-targeted and adequate cash transfers for poor households, conditional on a child's school enrollment or attendance, can help to offset direct and opportunity costs associated with schooling and thereby expand the demand for secondary education (Grosh et al. 2009). And targeting resources to the poor, particularly to the hardest-working children, can help to expand enrollments and raise learning outcomes. Recent evidence from a scholarship program in Cambodia showed that scholarships that were allocated based on a combination of income-based and merit-based targeting mechanisms had the highest impact on test scores (Barrera-Osorio and Filmer 2013).

Wealthier parents already demand more schooling than is formally provided, which is evident in the prevalence of extra classes. Parents pay for their children to attend regular core academic lessons typically by their own teachers after school hours. Vietnam's policy of socialization builds on parents' financial contributions toward education, including complementing publicly funded half-day provision in primary education. Traditionally, many children in urban areas in Vietnam have participated in informal extra classes that are taught in the afternoons. Extra classes are not only a Vietnamese phenomenon; they are encountered across several countries in East Asia. But they are prominent in Vietnam: in 2010 parents of 33 percent of primary students and 49 percent of lower secondary students reported some expenditure on coaching sessions for academic subjects (VHLSS 2010). The actual number of children whose parents pay for extra classes may be much higher. For example, in the 2009 Young Lives survey, 70 percent of 14- and 15-year-old students attended extra classes, and extra classes amounted to an average additional 10 hours of instruction per week, representing 27 percent of total instructional time.

Extra classes are problematic in several ways. First, if they focus on the same academic material that is part of the formal half-day curriculum (coaching sessions for compulsory subjects), as opposed to activities such as arts or sports that can help build behavioral skills, they risk consuming precious tuition time that could be allocated for alternative activities. Second, extra classes are often informal and not regulated. They place teachers in an undue position of power in relation to parents. There is evidence that many parents are asked to make unofficial payments to schools and teachers (World Bank 2012a; CECODES, VFF-CRT, and UNDP 2013). Third, richer households are able to spend much larger amounts on extra classes (see figure 4.7), and extra classes are mainly an urban phenomenon. The risk, therefore, is that extra classes may deepen inequalities in learning, as opposed to bridging them. Fourth, extra classes serve exams, which reward heavy preparation in terms of memorization and model answers, but which are not demanding in terms of creativity and critical thinking. Changing the nature of exams, especially those that act as gatekeepers, may help change some of the practices around extra classes.

Expanding formal full-day schooling may well be the best strategy to limit extra classes. MOET has attempted to regulate the provision of informal extra classes, but with little apparent effect. An alternative to regulating extra classes is to expand formal full-day schooling to reduce the time available for teachers to offer private tuition and to help make up for the revenue loss related to forgone extra classes. An expansion of full-day schooling can be financed by a mix of budgetary and private resources. Well-off parents who currently finance extra classes for their children could be asked to provide formal cofinancing to schools for full-day schooling as opposed to informal payments to teachers who provide extra classes.

The shift toward ensuring full-day primary schooling has already begun, but does not yet cover the whole country. The incidence of formal extra classes in rural settings is lower than in urban settings, and a significant share of children at primary level remains in half-day provision. This is why MOET is promoting the expansion of formal full-day schooling and has launched a program to expand full-day schooling in primary schools in the 35 poorest provinces with support from the School Education Quality Assurance Program (SEQAP) cofinanced by Belgium, the United Kingdom, and the World Bank. A foreseen increase of tuition time under full-day schooling to at least 30 instructional periods by 2015 and 35 by 2020 would allow Vietnam to catch up with international standards (Cerbelle 2013).[3]

A decline in student numbers in general education may open fiscal space to further expand full-day schooling and enrollments at the secondary level. Vietnam is beginning to undergo a dramatic demographic transition with declining cohort sizes among the young and expanding among the old. According to Vietnamese census data, the size of the population cohort below the age of 15 declined by 17 percent between 1999 and 2009. Data from the annual census of primary schools from the District Fundamental School Quality Level Audit (DFA) presented in figure 4.8 show that the number of students in primary schools declined by 11 percent between 2005 and 2010. Fewer students need fewer teachers, so the number of teachers has also declined, although by a smaller percentage. While managing a decline in student numbers is challenging, it may open fiscal space. Excess teachers can

Figure 4.8 Changes in the Number of Teachers and Students in Primary Schools, 2005–10

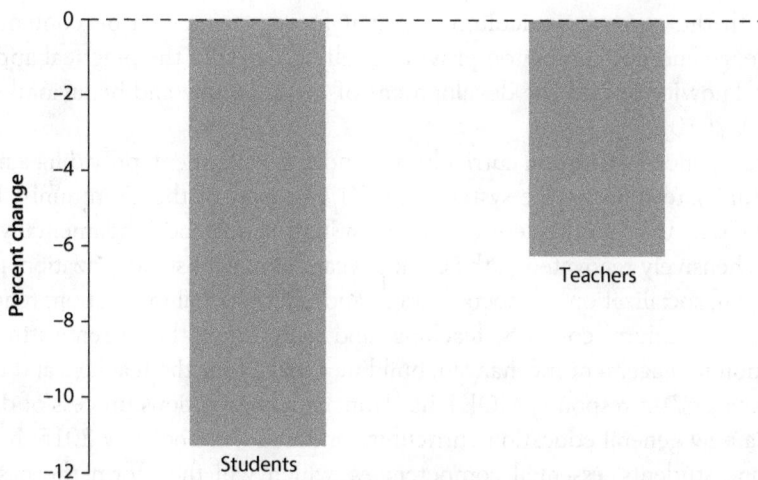

Source: World Bank staff estimates using District Fundamental School Quality Level Audit (DFA) 2005 and 2010 data.

be reallocated to help deliver full-day schooling, or savings from a smaller teaching workforce can be reallocated to pay remaining teachers for longer instruction times. Beyond reallocating resources within primary education, the demographic decline may free up resources for expanding schooling at the secondary level, including progressively abolishing tuition fees at the secondary level and enhancing financial support to students from poor families.

Better Schooling

What matters is not just more schooling but more quality schooling with a curriculum and teaching methods that foster the formation of higher-order cognitive and behavioral skills. Vietnam already has a successful education system that performs well in imparting core basic cognitive skills. This is also true for children from disadvantaged backgrounds who do not appear to be falling further behind in primary education. How to make schooling in Vietnam better, therefore, is not an obvious proposition, but the Vietnamese authorities are already embarking on a reform aimed at making schooling better—through a modernized, competency-based curriculum, more student-centered teaching methods, and enhanced competency of the teaching workforce. Children from disadvantaged backgrounds are likely to benefit disproportionately from such reforms.

Curriculum

Vietnam's current general education curriculum is more focused on teaching content and knowledge rather than on developing higher-order cognitive and behavioral skills in students. Vietnam's general education curriculum, which was adopted in 2000, sets out, among other goals, to strengthen students' ability to cooperate and self-study and to apply knowledge in practice as objectives of education activity. MOET, however, acknowledges that these goals do not go far enough to meet today's needs. According to the ministry, the problem with the current curriculum is that it focuses too much on content and knowledge and not enough on providing self-study skills, the practical application of knowledge, and the development of the cognitive and behavioral skills (MOET 2010).

A new general education curriculum is under development, providing a major opportunity to reorient the system. The XI Congress of the Communist Party in 2011 said the "Vietnamese education system should be fundamentally and comprehensively renovated in the coming years, aiming at standardization, modernization, socialization, democratization, and international integration; renovating the curriculum, contents, teaching, and learning methods; renovating the education management mechanism, building capacity for the teachers and training managers." In response, MOET has launched an ambitious process of developing a new general education curriculum and new textbooks by 2015. It aims to define students' essential competencies, which will then form the basis of educational objectives, standards, learning content, teaching methods, and assessment. The vision is to ensure the curriculum's coherence from grade 1 through grade 12, but with more broad-based content focus in basic education (primary and lower secondary) and more electives in upper secondary education. It should be nationally consistent but enable provinces to adjust a certain flexible share of the curriculum. It will define half-day provision but provide schools with guidance on how to arrange full-day provision. A strong emphasis is placed on modernizing teaching methods and student assessment.

Vietnam's chosen direction for curriculum reform follows that chosen by other countries in East Asia and worldwide. In 1997 Singapore adopted the "Thinking Schools, Learning Nation" initiative, which aims to promote active learning and creative and critical thinking in schools. The initiative involved the explicit teaching of critical thinking and problem-solving skills, for example, through a new secondary school subject called knowledge and inquiry and a reduction of subject content (Tan and Gopinathan 2000). Korea's new national curriculum places more emphasis on critical thinking skills and creativity than in the past. In both cases changes to assessment methods and approaches were critical elements of the reforms. In Korea, university entrance exams use essays that test writing and logical thinking, and in Singapore university admission criteria were widened beyond secondary graduate certificate and an entrance examination to results in project work in schools and extracurricular activities.

Pedagogy and Teaching Methods

Curriculum change and textbook reform are important steps, but the resulting changes in the teaching methods and instruction in the classroom are even more important. In other words, implementation matters most and requires enhancing the skills of teachers and school principals and parental involvement. Translating a new general education curriculum into concrete change in the classroom will, therefore, require modernization of teacher professional development, both in-service and pre-service, and sustained investment in its rollout across Vietnam's teacher workforce. Change will also involve the need to continue strengthening student assessment. Vietnam is already testing new teaching methods that are more geared toward developing cognitive and behavioral skills. MOET has begun introducing the model of *Escuela Nueva* from Colombia into primary schools in Vietnam on a pilot basis (see box 4.1) with the aim of informing the renovation of the general education curriculum, the teaching methods used, and how to manage its possible rollout.

Teachers matter most for better schooling. Enhancing the competencies of the teaching workforce is the single most important investment to create the preconditions for the formation of higher-order cognitive and behavioral skills. The skills and abilities of the teaching workforce significantly affect the quality of learning in the classroom. Teacher education and qualifications have been found to be a positive and significant predictor of student achievement worldwide—and in grade 5 examinations in Vietnam (World Bank 2011; Rolleston et al. 2013). A well-qualified teacher workforce is likely better equipped to translate a changing curriculum into the reality of changed teaching methods in the classroom. Because the aggregate teacher wage bill exceeds 80 percent of total education

Box 4.1 Vietnam Escuela Nueva

Escuela Nueva is a model of organizing schools and classrooms in a way that enhances the development of core cognitive and behavioral skills, such as problem solving and teamwork. It was launched in Colombia in 1975 by the Fundación Escuela Nueva, a Colombian nongovernmental organization (NGO), to help improve schooling outcomes among children in disadvantaged circumstances, and is now serving more than 5 million children across 16 countries worldwide. The Ministry of Education and Training (MOET) has adapted the model to the Vietnamese circumstances and is piloting the Vietnam Escuela Nueva (VNEN) in close to 1,500 primary schools across the country with financial support from the Global Partnership for Education (GPE). VNEN puts forward five key elements of innovative teaching:

- Students at the center of the learning process, with encouragement and support to develop their own learning goals and with the necessary tools and resources to realize those goals
- Cooperation and collaboration between small groups of learners that not only lead to higher academic achievement, but also promote independence, self-esteem, and interpersonal skills and relationships
- Active and reflective learning methods that take place in a supporting classroom environment, encourage student inquiry and discovery, provide problem-solving opportunities, and generate maximal cognitive engagement to students interspersed with adequate resting periods
- Linkages in students' knowledge building as the basis of the pedagogical content—new information is integrated with existing knowledge structures, including the use of innate human inductive skills, to derive patterns and apply them to solve problems
- Empowerment of the local community to ensure that school life is integrated with the child's social and family life and that local cultural practices are valued in the school just as they are at home.

These innovations mean that teaching and learning in VNEN are quite different from the traditional model currently in use in schools in Vietnam. The main visible difference is the seating arrangement—children are seated in clusters of four or five students as compared to the row and bench seating in traditional classrooms. VNEN classrooms also contain more material to provide intellectual stimuli to the children—math and reading corners, a "tree of words" to depict different groups of words, and community maps. VNEN encourages parents and the community to take part in the life of the school—especially in ethnic minority areas, where parents and others come to school to pass on their traditions.

VNEN follows the same general education curriculum as the traditional classrooms, but presents the curriculum in a way that will better engage the students. For example, teaching under VNEN includes a 3-in-1 learning guide (textbook, workbook, and guide together in one book) with more interactive exercises to complement the stories that make learning more fun and engaging for children. Teachers engage in less reading and writing on the board, and students spend more time on tasks. VNEN provides tools, such as materials, protocols,

box continues next page

Box 4.1 Vietnam *Escuela Nueva* (continued)

and methods, that enable even teachers of an ordinary level of ability to provide an enriching learning experience.

VNEN is planned to undergo a rigorous impact evaluation that will provide policy makers with in-depth information on success factors that could be expanded systemwide as part of the planned general education curriculum reform.

Sources: Epstein and Yuthas 2012; World Bank 2012b.

---

expenditures in Vietnam, improving what teachers do in the classroom is also the main investment into quality that the government can make.

The quality of Vietnam's teaching workforce is already an asset. The primary education teacher workforce has become significantly better qualified in recent years. Nearly 60 percent of all primary school teachers now hold a college or university degree—almost double the share of 2006. The share of teachers with only 9 or 12 years of academic schooling followed by 3 or 2 years of teacher training has also declined significantly (figure 4.9, panel a). Increased teacher qualification matters: evidence from the 2012 Young Lives School Survey suggests that high-performing schools have higher shares of teachers with a college or university degree. High teacher capacity is also evident in their capability to correctly assess their students' abilities, which is critical to help them provide the support their students need. Data from Young Lives show a strong correlation between teacher ratings and mean test scores in mathematics for the same students (figure 4.9, panel b). Moreover, teacher attendance in Vietnam is very high—another strong feature of the Vietnamese education system. The already high capacity and rising qualifications of the teaching workforce can be expected to provide a sound foundation for further professional development related to the new curriculum and teaching methods.

Investing in in-service professional development to equip teachers with the skills to teach a renovated curriculum is one of the most important tasks for Vietnam's education system in the coming years. Vietnam can build on an increasingly well-qualified teaching workforce at the primary level through the use of in-service professional development, but there is much to improve. First, the evidence from the DFA suggests that in-service professional development among primary teachers is limited and its use has been declining. Second, the content and methods of in-service professional development require modernization. The content will need to be reformulated in line with the changes that the new general education curriculum will bring. In reforming the method of delivery, teacher training needs to shift away from the traditional cascading model (MOET trains trainers who train other trainers to deliver training in the summer months) to a method of delivery in which capacities in provincial teacher training colleges are enhanced to provide more tailored programs all year round and with new teaching methods. A special emphasis will be required to equip teachers with the right skills and tools, especially those in the most

Figure 4.9 Primary Teachers' Professional Training, and Correlation of Student Test Scores and Their Teachers' Ratings

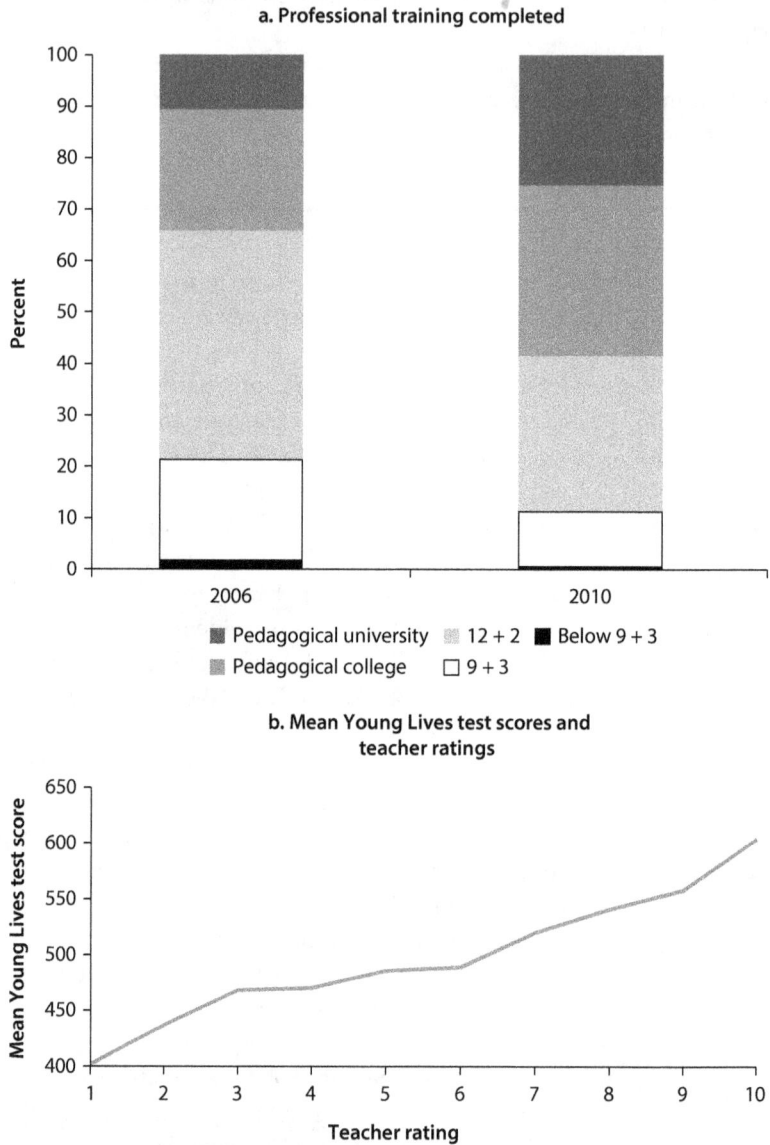

a. Professional training completed

Pedagogical university   12 + 2   Below 9 + 3
Pedagogical college   9 + 3

b. Mean Young Lives test scores and teacher ratings

Sources: Panel a, World Bank staff estimates based on District Fundamental School Quality Level Audit (DFA) data, 2006 and 2010; panel b, Rolleston et al. 2013.
Note: 9 + 3 = 9 years of academic training followed by 3 years of teacher training; 12 + 2 = 12 years of academic training followed by 2 years of teacher training.

challenging circumstances, such as those teaching in remote regions and those teaching students from ethnic minority backgrounds.

Teacher training needs to focus not only on how to teach curriculum content but also on how to impart behavioral skills. Chapter 3 describes how behavioral skills are associated with learning success and the acquisition of cognitive skills.

Pupils with greater academic confidence make more progress, holding other factors constant (Yorke and Rolleston, forthcoming). An effective teacher in Vietnam, therefore, needs to be good at teaching mathematics, Vietnamese, and other subjects and to excel at helping students to build confidence and show good effort. Teacher effectiveness begins with attitude and motivation. Evidence from the 2012 Young Lives School Survey shows that teachers in high-performing schools had more confidence that their students would succeed (and not be hampered by their family backgrounds) compared to teachers in less well performing schools with respect to the learning prospects of children from disadvantaged backgrounds. Effective teachers were more likely to disagree with the statement that the amount a student can learn is primarily driven by family backgrounds and more likely to agree that a student's home experience can be overcome by good teaching (Rolleston et al. 2013). A teacher with a more fatalistic or discriminatory attitude is unlikely to be able to effectively foster behavioral skills such as academic confidence and effort by students. Explicitly influencing teacher attitudes in teacher training and professional development, therefore, is likely to raise teacher effectiveness.

Assessment

Beyond curriculum and teaching methods, student assessment needs to be aligned with the objective of fostering higher-order cognitive and behavioral skills. Once the curriculum and standards in general education are adjusted to better reflect higher-order cognitive and behavioral skills, the student assessment system needs to be equipped with the tools to help evaluate these skills in students, see how schools perform in imparting these skills, and to hold schools and local education authorities accountable for results. Efforts to promote the formation of critical and creative thinking and behavioral skills in Singapore and Korea have involved changes to student assessment and university admission criteria.

Educational assessment is firmly anchored in Vietnam's general education system and consists of the three main categories of assessment. First, *classroom assessments* involve written and oral tests, and marked assignments and homework are used in classrooms across the country with the objective of providing real-time feedback on students' performance to inform teaching. Second, *national examinations* for making high-stakes decisions about students' progression to the next level in the education system are firmly established and widely accepted as a mechanism for selecting students for further education, both at grade 9 (in some provinces) and the school-leaving examination at grade 12 (the results of which are used mainly for entry to vocational and professional colleges), and the university entrance examination. Further tests are being conducted according to provinces' preferences and capacities. Third, Vietnam has conducted *large-scale surveys* of grade 5 (2001, 2007, and 2011) and grade 6 and grade 9 (2009), and in 2012 participated for the first time in PISA, which is organized by the OECD.

The potential for using classroom assessments for improving student learning is not yet fully exploited. MOET has issued curriculum standards to guide the design and structure of classroom assessments, but so far the evidence of the utilization of these standards in test development in practice is limited. Teacher capacity in using assessment techniques is one obstacle. Teachers often cite the difficulty in translating the standards into specific test items given that the standards are presented in a very general way. Instead, they often use textbooks and teachers' guides as the basis for devising tests. In upper secondary schools, teachers acknowledge that the tests they develop are heavily influenced by the structure and content of the high-stakes examinations (grade 12 graduation and university entrance). Moreover, the results from classroom assessments and examinations are not routinely utilized in schools to guide quality improvements in teaching, including by effectively communicating results to parents. Further efforts to raise teachers' capacity in using classroom assessment and improved monitoring and feedback to teachers on the quality of classroom assessments are necessary to make effective use of this important tool to promote quality of teaching (World Bank 2009).

The system of national examination is well established, but its potential could be leveraged more. The General Department of Testing and Accreditation (GDETA) manages national examinations and is accountable to MOET. The examination questions are based on an examination framework for each subject that tends to follow the relevant textbook in use in schools rather than the official curriculum. The grade 12 examination consists of multiple-choice questions only, while the university entrance examination also includes open-ended questions. The university entrance examination is perceived as more rigorous and valid than the grade 12 test. There are no mechanisms in place, such as pilot testing or pretesting, to ensure the quality of the examinations. The quality of national examinations and public confidence could be enhanced by making publicly available high-quality, independent technical reports, and by introducing systematic and transparent mechanisms to ensure quality at key stages of the examination process, including training the GDETA staff on contemporary assessment practices. Quality could also be enhanced by independent research on the impact of national examinations, creating a permanent oversight committee, or conducting regular quality reviews (World Bank 2009).

Large-scale national assessments are perhaps the weakest link in the system. Large-scale surveys at grades 5, 6, and 9 are not a formal element of the system. They have been conducted on an irregular basis with the financial and technical support from the World Bank and the Asian Development Bank (ADB). Although significant capacity has been built for the management of national assessments, the quality of the grade 5 assessment in 2011 was regarded as weak, underscoring the need to further enhance capacity. The principal constraint is that the national assessments have been ad hoc and not part of a system. They have typically been managed out of project management units and do not have an organizational "home" or a standard system built around them.

Student assessment needs to become more varied and involve test items designed to assess higher-order cognitive skills such as creative thinking and problem solving. Students' behavioral skills can be assessed by teachers and, as in some German states, be communicated regularly to parents in student report cards. More generally, student assessment should be reflective of the full curriculum, not just those things that can be easily tested, including through multiple-choice tests, such as mathematics. Multiple-choice tests have much to recommend them in a situation in which over a million students are being assessed, but the testing approach needs to be broadened if the quality of learning is to be improved. Students need to know that other abilities are also valued, such as being able to write, speak, and listen in language studies and being able to design and carry out experiments in science or projects in geography. The introduction of more open-ended questions would allow for greater emphasis on higher-order thinking and problem solving.

More Involvement of Parents and Communities in Schooling

A prominent role for parents in schooling is important for several reasons. First, parents have a strong interest in ensuring that their children receive a quality education. Providing parents with information and a forum to voice views and advise the school can make the school more explicitly accountable to them for their children's learning progress. Second, much learning takes place at home, and the home environment is an important contributor to learning success. For example, the availability of a child's own place to study at home has been found to be associated with higher learning achievement at grade 5 in Vietnam (World Bank 2011). Parents need to be aware of the learning process and content in the school and how they can complement them by providing effective support to their children's learning at home—after school and during the long summer vacations. Third, a greater involvement of parents and communities will help make instruction more reflective of local needs, traditions, and contexts. It will also help build bridges where there are cultural and other gaps between school and home, for example, in the case of ethnic minority children who are taught by Kinh teachers. Finally, involvement in school can help raise parenting skills benefiting also any siblings not yet in school.

The opportunities for formal parental involvement in schools beyond making financial contributions are limited in Vietnam. According to government regulations, schools can establish a parents' council for a class or the school as a whole, but where such councils exist they have little formal influence. Councils can channel parents' feedback to teachers on educational issues and allow parents to express their views to the principal on educational activities or school management. Legally, however, the parents' council has very limited weight on influencing the operation and monitoring the performance of a public school. Moreover, school councils do not even have to include parents as members. In practice, the role of the parents' council is often reduced to collecting parents' voluntary contributions to the school. In cases of dissatisfaction, the only way for parents to be heard is via going to the provincial or district education authorities, according to the Law on Complaints.

A greater role of parents in the school usually goes hand-in-hand with the transfer of more decision-making power from education authorities to the school. But it is possible even within the current system of central standards and predominant decision making at the province level. Provinces and districts could cede certain decisions to schools that could be made with the involvement of parents. Schools could be entrusted with deciding the arrangements for full-day schooling, and parents could contribute to this decision making. Parents could advise on how to incorporate extra classes into the formal program and how to arrange afternoon activities under formal full-day schooling. Despite the different models of what roles to assign to parents and community members, it is agreed that parents also need sufficient information and capacity to be effective participants in school governance.

Parental advice on some aspects of budgetary decisions, such as the use of school grants, is usually a first step in the direction of greater involvement. Vietnam has already taken some steps toward greater school-based management and enhancing the role of parents in primary and secondary schools. More could follow. The SEQAP project involves the use of school improvement grants that the school, rather than provincial or district authorities, can decide how to use. Parents could take part in the decision process. Schools participating in VNEN have the freedom to involve parents in the learning process and to contribute to learning content, for example, through introducing local ethnic minority traditions in the program. Augmenting these first steps would be a logical next step.

A greater involvement of parents and communities in schooling is possible even in disadvantaged communities. Vietnam's experiences with SEQAP, VNEN, and earlier pilot projects employing ethnic minority teaching assistants show that greater involvement of disadvantaged parents and communities in schooling is possible and important for the educational process. Experience from rural communities in Pakistan shows how school report cards for parents in very low capacity contexts were successful in helping to raise achievement scores for initially poor-performing schools (Andrabi, Das, and Khwaja 2009).[4]

Summary and Conclusion

Vietnam's general education system is well placed to transition to a new phase in education development from expanding access to deepening quality. After two decades of successful expansion in access to general education, greater emphasis now needs to be placed on ensuring that more children learn and acquire the higher-order cognitive and behavioral skills demanded in Vietnam's labor market. Progress in this direction will require further expanding access to secondary education and expanding instruction time through full-day schooling, thereby also reducing the prevalence of informal extra classes. The reduction in student numbers due to declining age cohorts provides an opportunity. Budget resources can be freed up to cover additional costs associated with expanding enrollments in secondary education and full-day schooling, including progressively abolishing tuition fees at a secondary level. Second, more schooling should mean better schooling through a competency-based, as opposed to content-based, general education curriculum, coupled with the right teaching methods to stimulate creative and critical thinking in primary and secondary school students. Enhanced in-service teacher training capacity will be critical to equip Vietnam's teaching workforce with the capabilities to make a new curriculum a reality in all classrooms in the country. Third, a greater involvement and outreach to parents will help them to hold the school more explicitly accountable for children's learning success and to make sure that children get the best possible learning support at home.

Annex 4A: In Depth

Results from the 2012 Programme for International Student Assessment

Vietnam participated in the PISA for the first time in 2012. Vietnam's 15-year-old students performed significantly above their peers in many much wealthier OECD countries. It also showed a significantly smaller share of low achievers (defined as performance below level 2 of the PISA mathematics scale) than the OECD average, and its results appear to be less driven by socioeconomic and cultural background than in many other participating countries (OECD 2013). Because PISA assesses the competencies of 15-year-olds in school, it excludes the relatively large share of Vietnam's early school-leavers, who are disproportionally from poor and disadvantaged backgrounds and who often perform less well than the average. Table 4A.1 presents the results of PISA 2012 in mathematics, reading, and science.

Table 4A.1 PISA Assessments of Vietnamese 15-Year-Olds and Their Peers in OECD and Other Economies, 2012

	Mathematics			Reading	Science
	Mean score in PISA 2012	Percentage of low achievers (<level 2)	Percentage of top performers (level 5 or 6)	Mean score in PISA 2012	Mean score in PISA 2012
OECD average	494	23.1	12.6	496	501
Shanghai, China	613	3.8	55.4	570	580
Singapore	573	8.3	40.0	542	551
Hong Kong SAR, China	561	8.5	33.7	545	555
Taiwan, China	560	12.8	37.2	523	523
Korea, Rep.	554	9.1	30.9	536	538
Macao SAR, China	538	10.8	24.3	509	521
Japan	536	11.1	23.7	538	547
Liechtenstein	535	14.1	24.8	516	525
Switzerland	531	12.4	21.4	509	515
Netherlands	523	14.8	19.3	511	522
Estonia	521	10.5	14.6	516	541
Finland	519	12.3	15.3	524	545
Canada	518	13.8	16.4	523	525
Poland	518	14.4	16.7	518	526
Belgium	515	18.9	19.4	509	505
Germany	514	17.7	17.5	508	524

table continues next page

Table 4A.1 PISA Assessments of Vietnamese 15-Year-Olds and Their Peers in OECD and Other Economies, 2012
(continued)

	Mathematics			Reading	Science
	Mean score in PISA 2012	Percentage of low achievers (<level 2)	Percentage of top performers (level 5 or 6)	Mean score in PISA 2012	Mean score in PISA 2012
VIETNAM	**511**	**14.2**	**13.3**	**508**	**528**
Austria	506	18.7	14.3	490	506
Australia	504	19.7	14.8	512	521
Ireland	501	16.9	10.7	523	522
Slovenia	501	20.1	13.7	481	514
Denmark	500	16.8	10.0	496	498
New Zealand	500	22.6	15.0	512	516
Czech Republic	499	21.0	12.9	493	508
France	495	22.4	12.9	505	499
United Kingdom	494	21.8	11.8	499	514
Iceland	493	21.5	11.2	483	478
Latvia	491	19.9	8.0	489	502
Luxembourg	490	24.3	11.2	488	491
Norway	489	22.3	9.4	504	495
Portugal	487	24.9	10.6	488	489
Italy	485	24.7	9.9	490	494
Spain	484	23.6	8.0	488	496
Russian Federation	482	24.0	7.8	475	486
Slovak Republic	482	27.5	11.0	463	471
United States	481	25.8	8.8	498	497
Lithuania	479	26.0	8.1	477	496
Sweden	478	27.1	8.0	483	485
Hungary	477	28.1	9.3	488	494
Croatia	471	29.9	7.0	485	491
Israel	466	33.5	9.4	486	470
Greece	453	35.7	3.9	477	467
Serbia	449	38.9	4.6	446	445
Turkey	448	42.0	5.9	475	463
Romania	445	40.8	3.2	438	439
Cyprus	440	42.0	3.7	449	438
Bulgaria	439	43.8	4.1	436	446
United Arab Emirates	434	46.3	3.5	442	448
Kazakhstan	432	45.2	0.9	393	425
Thailand	427	49.7	2.6	441	444
Chile	423	51.5	1.6	441	445
Malaysia	421	51.8	1.3	398	420
Mexico	413	54.7	0.6	424	415
Montenegro	410	56.6	1.0	422	410
Uruguay	409	55.8	1.4	411	416
Costa Rica	407	59.9	0.6	441	429
Albania	394	60.7	0.8	394	397

table continues next page

Table 4A.1 PISA Assessments of Vietnamese 15-Year-Olds and Their Peers in OECD and Other Economies, 2012
(continued)

	Mathematics			Reading	Science
	Mean score in PISA 2012	Percentage of low achievers (<level 2)	Percentage of top performers (level 5 or 6)	Mean score in PISA 2012	Mean score in PISA 2012
Brazil	391	67.1	0.8	410	405
Argentina	388	66.5	0.3	396	406
Tunisia	388	67.7	0.8	404	398
Jordan	386	68.6	0.6	399	409
Colombia	376	73.8	0.3	403	399
Qatar	376	69.6	2.0	388	384
Indonesia	375	75.7	0.3	396	382
Peru	368	74.6	0.6	384	373

Source: OECD 2013.
Note: Economies are ranked by the mean scores in mathematics.

Education and Skills Development in the Republic of Korea

The Republic of Korea is a useful case study for Vietnam. Both countries' education systems are rooted in and are strongly influenced by Confucianism. Korean and Vietnamese citizens view the pursuit of education as an important social value, and industrialization and economic development strategies emphasize human resource development. Vietnam is interested in Korea's experience in skills development and draws lessons from Korea's distinguished achievements, such as high PISA scores and high enrollment rates at all levels of education. The history of Korea's modern education and skills development reforms are summarized in table 4A.2.

Education development at the initial stage of Korea's postwar period focused on promoting literacy through enforcing the universalization of primary education (1948–60). The main focus for educational development during that phase was on reconstruction of educational infrastructure. Educational programs initially launched during 1945–48 and the formal establishment of primary education after the proclamation of Korea in 1948 aimed at reducing the high illiteracy rate (more than half of the population aged 13 and above was illiterate at the time). At this time Korea also established the 6-3-3-4 linear school system: six years of elementary education, three years of middle school education, three years of high school education, and four years of higher education. This system prevents dead ends in education careers and introduces multiple pathways to tertiary education (TE). Last, primary school teachers' qualification requirements were upgraded from upper secondary school diploma holders to four-year teachers' college graduates.

In the period of 1961–80 the emphasis shifted toward an expansion of vocational high school and strengthening of science and technology disciplines. Korea was experiencing strong economic growth and a shift of employment from agriculture to capital-intensive heavy and chemical industries during this phase.

Table 4A.2 Korean Education Development Focus, Policy Goals, Major Concerns, and Resources, 1948 to Present

Periods	1948–60	1961–80	1981–2000	2001–present
Education development focus	Reconstruction of educational infrastructure	Education for economic growth	Decentralization of education Facilitation of local autonomy	Restructuring education system
Policy goal	Universal primary education (compulsory)	Universal secondary education Supply technical manpower Enhance technical and vocational training	Universal tertiary education Quality improvement Vocational training reform	Lifelong learning Human resource development Quality improvement of public schools Research support (TE) Regional development (TE) Human resources development (TE)
Major concerns	Access to education	Growth of quantity—efficiency and control	Quality Autonomy Accountability	Competitiveness in globalization Knowledge society
Resources, tools	Using foreign assistance	Long-term (5-year) planning Law of Local Education Financing Fund Foreign loans to support TVET	Presidential Commission for Education Reform 1995 Education Reform	Education and financial support for TE

Source: KEDI 2007.
Note: TE = tertiary education; TVET = technical and vocational education and training.

Simultaneous population growth and urbanization generated increasing social demand for education. To strengthen education, the government further expanded primary school enrollment and promoted vocational high schools and science and technology education. Expanding primary education enrollment resulted in overcrowded classrooms and raised competition among students for seats in secondary schools. To relieve the burden, Korea moved toward automatic grade promotion and abolished the entrance exams for lower and upper secondary schools in 1969 and 1974, respectively.

Between 1981 and 2000 Korea decentralized its educational administration and shifted from bureaucratic control to increased local education accountability to stimulate improvements in education quality. The growing numbers of secondary school graduates in turn increased the demand for TE. Private tutoring began to flourish. In addition, a widening income gap during this period resulted in unequal access to education. Education reforms aimed to eradicate private tutoring and relieved students from competitive exams. Reforms further lifted government's control over university enrollment, and in 1995 universities were granted more autonomy in recruiting students. The Presidential Commission for Education Reform summarized Korea's new direction for educational development, including more emphasis on learner-centered education, diversification of educational programs, autonomy and accountability of school operations, a new information system, and a new mechanism to allow open access to results of school education evaluation (KEDI 2007).

Since 2001 the East Asian financial crisis and globalization have forced Korea to refocus on strengthening the nation's competitiveness through education. Reforms to Korea's education system have aimed at responding to two challenges: (a) supporting the nation's competitiveness in the global market; and (b) meeting the human resource development needs. The first priority of the government has been to reform higher education in a way that enhances its relevance and the international competitiveness of Korean universities and to strengthen technical and vocational education and training (TVET) to reduce an overreliance on TE. In improving the nation's competitiveness and in preparation for the advent of becoming a knowledge-based society, lifelong learning is considered to be an integral part of the educational system.

Korea has had the advantage of being able to sequentially improve its education system and to shift gears slowly toward rigor and responsiveness to the economic development over the decades. The journey for education development sets an interesting example of how a growing economy could achieve national education success in quantitative expansion and qualitative improvement simultaneously without a trade-off. It also shows how an education system develops from an elite to a mass system and finally to universal access and how doing so can enhance a country's economic development (Jones 2013). Today, a number of features of the Korean education system stand out.

First, teacher salaries in Korea are high in relation to the OECD standard and in relation to GDP per capita. Well-trained and well-remunerated teachers tend to be one of the driving forces for improved quality of education. Figure 4A.1 presents the ratio of the average salary of a teacher in lower secondary education relative to GDP per capita in comparison to that of the United States and the OECD country average in 2008. Korean teachers are significantly better paid than their peers elsewhere in the OECD.

Second, Korea's no-dead-end tracking ensured that 84 percent of secondary school graduates transitioned to college in 2008. The 6-3-3-4 linear track also ensures that all secondary school graduates, whether from an academic or vocational school, are equally qualified to apply to universities. Students are not being streamed into vocational programs that might restrict them from entering academic tertiary programs.

Third, there was shift from rote memorization to knowledge-based education and an emphasis on critical thinking and problem-solving skills. As Korea entered the 21st century, the focus of its education system was no longer only on rote memorization of academic content, but was broadened to impart broader cognitive skills such as problem solving and critical thinking, which have helped Korean students to score high in PISA.

Fourth, Korea's education system is well funded. Total spending on education in Korea is the second highest in the OECD as a share of GDP spending on education (8 percent in 2009). This includes a significant share of private sector contributions, accounting for 40 percent of total education spending (above

Cognitive and Behavioral Foundation Skills in the General Education System

Figure 4A.1 Ratio of Lower Secondary Teachers' Salary to GDP per Capita, 2008

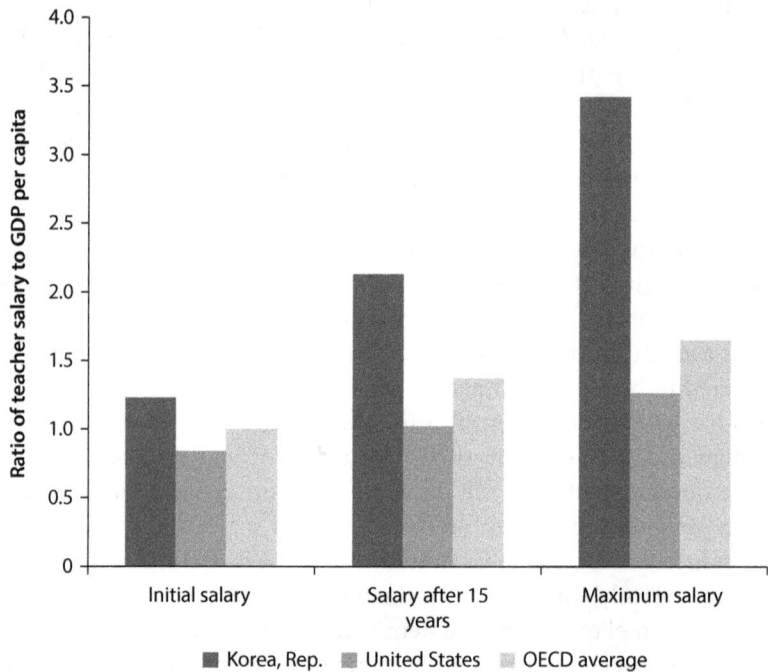

Source: Jones 2013.
Note: GDP = gross domestic product; OECD = Organisation for Economic Co-operation and Development.

50 percent for pre-primary, 25 percent for nontertiary, and more than 70 percent for TE). Spending is not just high but also efficient: relatively high teacher salaries are possible also due to slightly larger average class sizes than elsewhere.

Despite the successes of Korea's education system, some weaknesses remain. Prominent among them is private tutoring, which needs to be further regularized and restricted in the school system. Reliance on private tutoring has been one of the biggest issues in the Korean education system. Private tutoring is expensive, and the reliance on it creates inequalities among students due to differences by socioeconomic status (Jones 2013).

With around 70 percent of high school graduates moving on to TE, Korea has recently focused attention to further improving the TVET system to address the overemphasis on TE. Korea's employer federation estimates 30 months and US$100,000 to train new tertiary graduates in the skill requirements in their jobs, which reflects the reality that students are lacking vocational skills despite strong academic achievements. Vocational education and training has had a long history in Korea, dating since the 1960s. In the 1990s Korea launched a special TVET high school program involving two years in school followed by one year of workplace training, inspired by the German dual system apprenticeship model. The number of schools and students choosing this path started to drop a few years after its introduction (Lee 2007), and the program was abolished.

More recently, to address demand from industry, the government decided to promote innovation in TVET through "meister high schools" to offer customized employment-linked vocational training programs and to reinforce demand-orientation (Park 2011). As part of the reform, 21 meister high schools were founded to train students to become skilled workers in industries such as new media, energy, machinery, mechatronics, and telecommunication. The plan is to expand the number of such schools to 50 by 2015. Moreover, curricula and teaching methodology started to incorporate a competency-based approach. A National Competency Standard (NCS) was developed in 1996 to set standards that define the knowledge and skills required of workers in specific occupational fields and to set systematic criteria based on which individuals may be educated and trained.

The reform also entailed a further strengthening of private sector engagement and collaboration among different ministries to help eliminate the mismatch of skills affecting TVET graduates. The Ministry of Education and the Ministry of Labor collaborate to pursue joint and consistent policies. Similarly, collaboration extended to the private sector and large corporations, small and medium-size companies, sectoral councils, and trade associations.

Notes

1. There may be concern that the decline in relative performance of those with the highest test scores captures mean conversion, for both better- and worse-off students. While mean conversion may well be occurring, it is interesting to note that the decline for worse-off students is substantially greater than for better-off students. The opposite can be said for those students whose rank is rising over time. To check the robustness of the results to these concerns, we examine whether the same results are found when a student performs poorly (or well) on two tests, mathematics and Vietnamese. If a student falls within the bottom 25 percent on both tests, something other than measurement error may be at work. We find similar results both for ranks and normalized scores when we examine the change in their test scores over time, suggesting that these trends are not a statistical artifact but are likely to reflect underlying processes.

2. A notable exception is access to computer and Internet technology in schools, which is far more common in more advantaged urban areas and raises a concern regarding a digital divide. With prospective students in urban areas turning predominantly to online information resources when making educational and career choices, less access to computers and the Internet in rural and remote areas in school risks becoming a key constraint to decision making. See chapter 5.

3. Although in practice wide variation and often not a clear distinction can be found between formal full-day schooling and informal extra classes, full-day schooling is expanding fast. According to MOET data, the share of primary schoolchildren who received 30 or more instructional periods increased from around 60 percent to 73 percent nationwide between 2007–08 and 2011–12 and from 39 percent to 70 percent in the 35 poorest provinces supported under SEQAP.

4. School report cards were distributed that compared learning achievement results across different schools in the same village. Many parents in the villages included in the program were illiterate; as a result, the distribution of report cards had to be done through facilitated village meetings to ensure everyone understood the results and to discuss the factors that influenced learning. This program shows that capacity building is possible for parents to understand learning outcomes and to play a role in their children's schooling even in the lowest capacity contexts.

References

Andrabi, T., J. Das, and A. I. Khwaja. 2009. "Report Cards: The Impact of Providing School and Child Test Scores on Education Markets." Unpublished manuscript, World Bank, Washington, DC.

Barrera-Osorio, F., and D. Filmer. 2013. "Incentivizing Schooling for Learning: Evidence on the Impact of Alternative Targeting Approaches." Policy Research Working Paper 6541, World Bank, Washington, DC.

CECODES (Centre for Community Support and Development Studies), VFF-CRT (Centre for Research and Training of the Viet Nam Fatherland Front), and UNDP (United Nations Development Programme). 2013. "The Viet Nam Governance and Public Administration Performance Index (PAPI) 2012: Measuring Citizens' Experiences." Joint Policy Research Paper, Hanoi.

Cerbelle, S. 2013. "Primary Education Teachers in Vietnam." Unpublished manuscript, World Bank, Washington, DC.

Epstein, M. J., and K. Yuthas. 2012. "Scaling Effective Education for the Poor in Developing Countries: A Report from the Field." *Journal of Public Policy and Marketing* 31 (1): 102–14.

Grosh, M., C. del Ninno, E. Tesliuc, and A. Ouerghi. 2009. *For Protection and Promotion: The Design and Implementation of Effective Safety Nets.* Washington, DC: World Bank.

Jones, R. S. 2013. "Education Reform in Korea." OECD Economics Department Working Paper 1067, OECD (Organisation for Economic Co-operation and Development) Publishing, Paris.

KEDI (Korean Educational Development Institute). 2007. *Understanding Korean Education.* Vol. 5 of *Education and Korea's Development.* Seoul: KEDI. http://eng.kedi .re.kr/khome/eng/education/educationSeries.do.

Lee, Y.-H. 2007. *Workforce Development in the Republic of Korea: Policies and Practices.* Tokyo: Asian Development Bank Institute.

MOET (Ministry of Education and Training of Vietnam). 2010. *Project on Curriculum and Textbook Renovation from 2015 Onwards.* Drafting committee. Hanoi.

OECD (Organisation for Economic Co-operation and Development). 2013. *OECD Skills Outlook 2013: First Results from the Survey of Adult Skills.* Paris: OECD Publishing.

Park, D. 2011. *Korean Policies on Secondary Vocational Education: Efforts to Overcome Skills Mismatch and Labor Force Shortage.* Berufsbildung in Wissenschaft und Praxis (BWP). Bonn: Bundesinstitut für Berufsbildung. http://www.bibb.eu/veroeffentlichungen/en /publication/show/id/6663.

Rolleston, C., Z. James, L. Pasquier-Doumer, and Tran Ngo Thi Minh Tam. 2013. *Making Progress: Report of the Young Lives School Survey in Vietnam.* Young Lives Working

Paper 100, Department of International Development, University of Oxford, Oxford, U.K.

SEQAP (School Education Quality Assurance Program). 2012. "Circular 35/2006—Options for Action: A Discussion Paper." Unpublished.

Tan, J., and S. Gopinathan. 2000. "Education Reform in Singapore: Towards Greater Creativity and Innovation?" *NIRA (National Institute for Research Development) Review* 7 (3): 5–10.

VHLSS (Vietnam Household Living Standards Survey). Multiple years. National Statistics Organization, Hanoi.

World Bank. 2009. *Student Assessment: Vietnam*. SABER (Systems Approach for Better Education Results) Country Report. Washington, DC: World Bank.

———. 2011. *Vietnam: High-Quality Education for All*. Washington, DC: World Bank.

———. 2012a. *Corruption from the Perspective of Citizens, Firms, and Public Officials: Results of Sociological Surveys*. 2nd ed. Hanoi: National Political Publishing House.

———. 2012b. *Vietnam—Global Partnership for Education: Vietnam Escuela Nueva Project*. Washington, DC: World Bank.

Yorke, L., and C. Rolleston. Forthcoming. *The Importance of Non-Cognitive Skills for Academic Achievement in Vietnam*. Young Lives Working Paper, Department of International Development, University of Oxford, Oxford, U.K.

CHAPTER 5

Technical Skills to Promote Employability

Higher education, vocational training, and on-the-job training are the key avenues for acquiring technical skills that help workers succeed in their chosen profession. Higher education prepares graduates for white-collar jobs, and vocational training provides students with applied skills required for vocational tasks. On-the-job training deepens the skills acquired in formal education and training and adapts them to the individual workplace (figure 5.1).

Higher education is booming in Vietnam, but vocational education and on-the-job training are not. Higher education is viewed as the principal driver for raising the quality of human resources by the population, business, and the government. Enrollments have expanded dramatically since 2000, although they remain low in regional comparisons. Moreover, there are concerns about quality, particularly given the fast pace of expansion. Even though vocational training is less popular than higher education, it still absorbs large numbers of young people. Employers are also concerned about the relevance of what students learn in higher and vocational education. Many businesses report that they provide on-the-job training, most of which appears to be internal training, while external training is limited.

Technical skills development in Vietnam suffers from disconnects between universities and vocational schools, businesses, workers, and students. These disconnects are driven by gaps in information, low capacity, and poor incentives. Producing the technical skills that employers are looking for requires: (a) an entirely different model of coordination between businesses and education and training providers; (b) better information for prospective students, better-trained lecturers, teachers, and managers of universities and vocational schools; and (c) more accountability for results to complement increasing autonomy. This chapter provides a snapshot of the state of higher and vocational education and on-the-job training and lays out options for improving technical skills development through *improved information*, the *right incentives*, and *enhanced capacity*.

Figure 5.1 Step 3 in Skills Development: Building Technical Skills for Employment

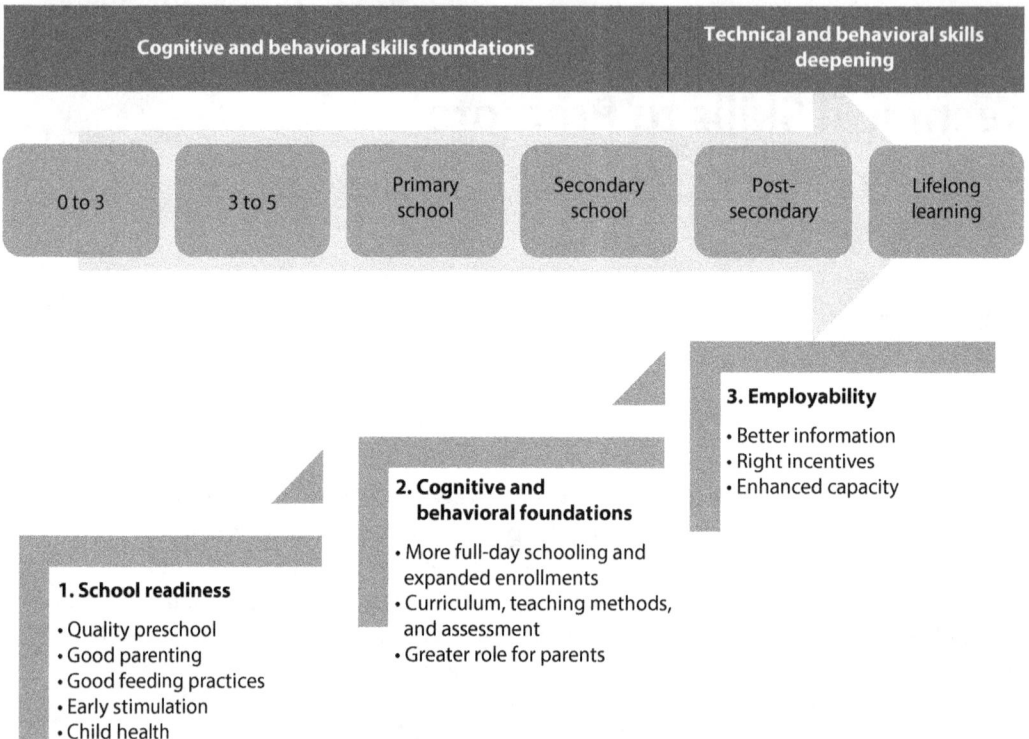

Cognitive and behavioral skills foundations				Technical and behavioral skills deepening	
0 to 3	3 to 5	Primary school	Secondary school	Post-secondary	Lifelong learning

3. Employability
- Better information
- Right incentives
- Enhanced capacity

2. Cognitive and behavioral foundations
- More full-day schooling and expanded enrollments
- Curriculum, teaching methods, and assessment
- Greater role for parents

1. School readiness
- Quality preschool
- Good parenting
- Good feeding practices
- Early stimulation
- Child health

Technical Skills Development in Vietnam at a Glance

Building on long traditions, higher education has grown dramatically since the early 2000s. A thousand years ago, the first university, Temple of Literature, was established for the son of the king. Today, one in four aged 18–24 is enrolled in some form of higher education, and half of the high school graduates find their way to higher education. The number of higher education institutions has doubled to more than 400, including new establishments and upgraded former colleges. All but one of Vietnam's 63 provinces and cities have at least one higher education institution. Around 80 institutions are private, representing 25 percent of college enrollment and 15 percent of university enrollment. Overall, Vietnam's universities and colleges serve more than 2.5 million students, a 31 percent increase in about a decade.

Academic higher education has proved more popular than postsecondary vocational education and training. Academic tertiary education in colleges and universities has seen dramatic expansion, but enrollment in vocational education and training is both lower and more stagnant. Figure 5.2 presents the shares of young Vietnamese aged 19–21 who were enrolled in postsecondary education between 1998 and 2010. The data document the expansion in academic higher education. Vocational enrollments dramatically expanded between 1998 and

Figure 5.2　Percentage of 19- to 21-Year-Olds in Postsecondary Education, 1998–2010

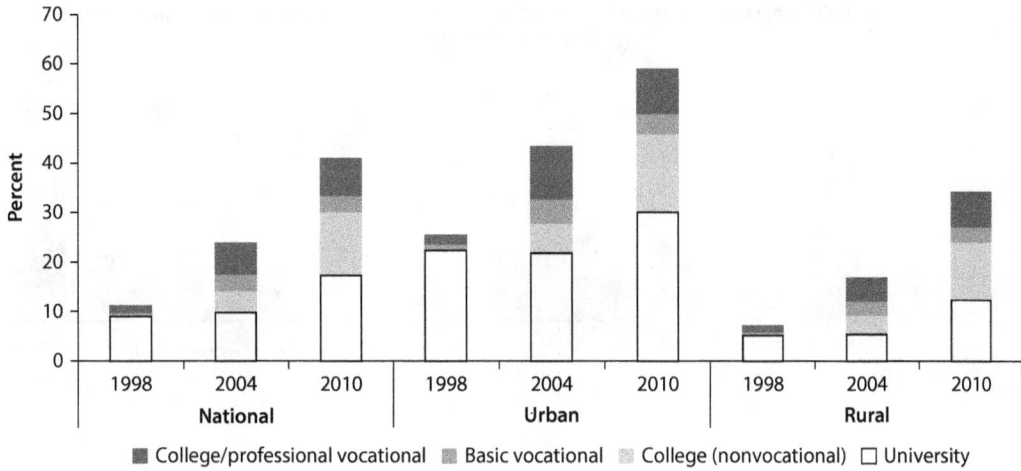

Sources: World Bank staff calculations using the 1998, 2004, and 2010 VHLSS surveys.
Note: VHLSS = Vietnam Household Living Standards Survey. The figure shows the percentage of 19- to 21-year-olds enrolled in vocational training, college, or university.

2004, but stopped expanding and remained at lower levels than academic higher education after 2004. Clearly, the dynamism in the tertiary sector is confined to universities and colleges, not to vocational education and training institutions.

Higher education enrollments are also unequal across socioeconomic groups. Figure 5.3 (panel a) presents higher education gross enrollment rates among people aged 18–24 by geographic area, gender, ethnic group, and wealth quintile. It documents a considerable variation in access to higher education across the country and socioeconomic groups. Gross enrollment rates at 40 percent in urban areas are double those in rural areas. Women, who were behind men in terms of enrollment in 1998, have surged ahead. The gap between majority Kinh and ethnic minorities has deepened. Lastly, access remains unequal. Although enrollments of individuals in the second, third, and fourth expenditure quintile households have surged, they remain considerably behind those of individuals in the richest quintile. Inequalities in access to higher education are predominantly driven by inequalities earlier in the education system, which leads to a premature drop out. But capacity to pay tuition also remains a barrier.

Despite the surge in gross enrollment rates, enrollment is still low compared to neighboring countries, suggesting that Vietnam can expect further expansion. Figure 5.3 (panel b) shows that Vietnam's gross enrollment rates compare favorably to the lower-middle-income country (LMC) average, but they trail those in competitor economies such as China, Malaysia, the Philippines, and Thailand.

As shown in chapters 1 and 2, returns to higher education are high, which foresees continued excess demand over supply. Overall, pursuing higher education remains a rewarding choice, particularly for graduates from prestigious

Figure 5.3 Higher Education Gross Enrollment Rates

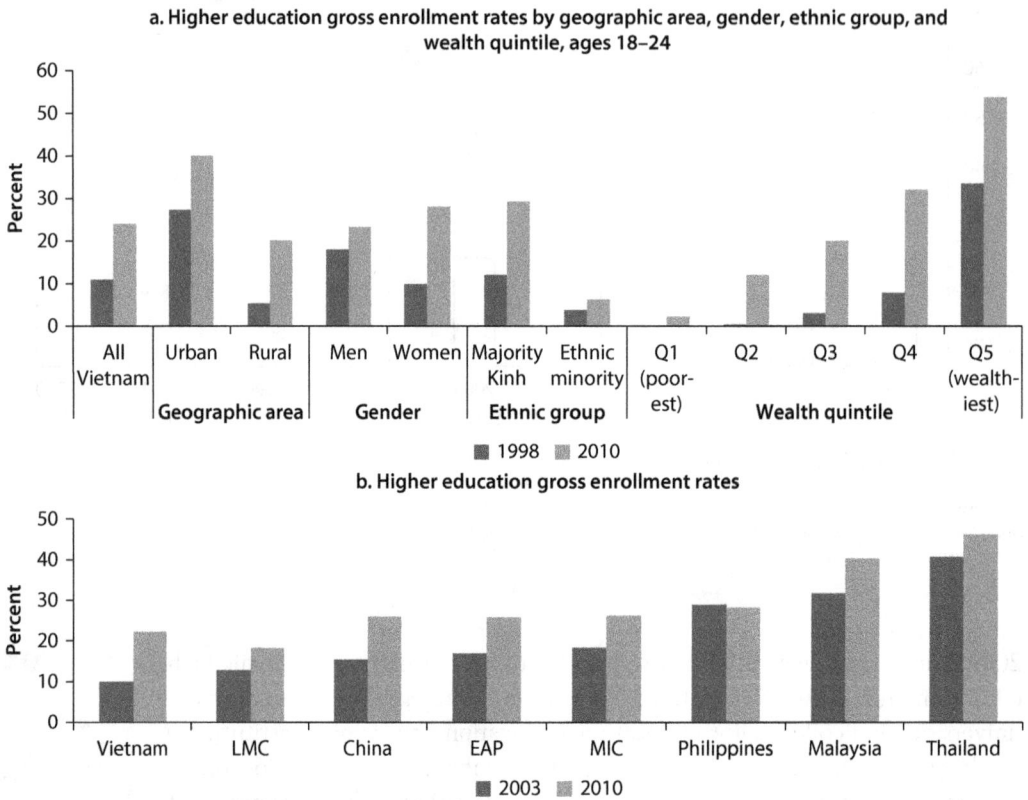

a. Higher education gross enrollment rates by geographic area, gender, ethnic group, and wealth quintile, ages 18–24

b. Higher education gross enrollment rates

Sources: Panel a, World Bank staff estimates using VHLSS data, various years; panel b, World Bank EdStats (http://datatopics.worldbank.org /education/).
Note: EAP = East Asia and Pacific; LMC = lower-middle-income countries; MIC = middle-income countries; VHLSS = Vietnam Household Living Standards Survey.

urban universities. Graduates from rural, remote, and disadvantaged regions may be less fortunate. Evidence from tracer studies conducted in close to two dozen universities involved in the Higher Education 2 Project shows that graduates from 17 well-established universities (group 1) had a close to 75 percent chance of being employed within six months of graduation in 2012, up from below 70 percent in 2007 (figure 5.4). In contrast, graduates from 5 universities in disadvantaged areas, remote mountainous regions, and the Mekong Delta (group 2) saw a significant decline in employment prospects over the same period. This finding is consistent with the data presented in chapter 1 of considerable employment of young higher education graduates in agriculture in rural areas.

Many businesses provide on-the-job training to their workers, but not equally to all workers. As discussed in chapter 2, Vietnam is encountering skill gaps and shortages in the context of expanding enrollments in universities and in vocational schools. Not surprisingly, therefore, some employers seek to equip some but not all of their workers with job- and company-specific skills through on-the-job

Figure 5.4 Percentage of University Graduates Employed within Six Months of Graduation

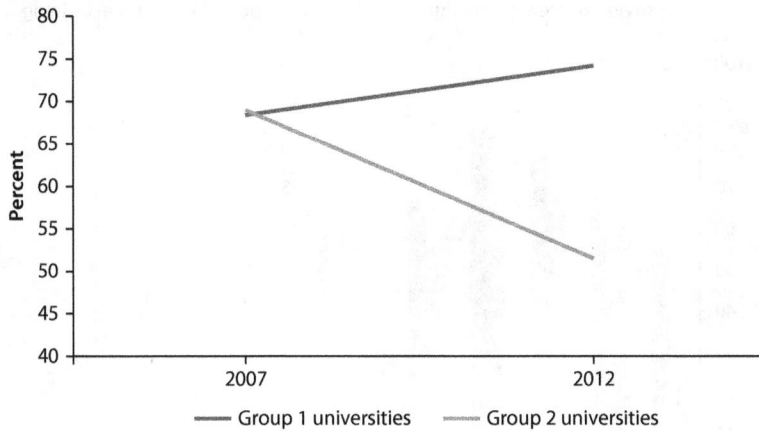

Source: World Bank 2013.
Note: Group 1 universities consist of 17 of the most established, mainly urban universities; Group 2 consists of 5 universities in disadvantaged areas, remote mountainous regions, and the Mekong Delta.

training at the workplace. As figure 5.5, panel a, indicates, more than half of all businesses in the Skills Toward Employment and Productivity (STEP) employer survey reported that they had provided internal training in the 12 months prior to the survey. In line with the picture from across the world, larger businesses conduct training more than smaller businesses. More businesses are providing internal on-the-job training to blue-collar workers than to white-collar workers. The picture changes when looking at external training (figure 5.5, panel b). The difference between large and small business firms becomes even more stark, and significantly more firms provide external training to white-collar than to blue-collar workers.

High shares of businesses that provide on-the-job training do not mean that large shares of workers benefit from training. Training incidence appears considerably more limited when workers are asked about the training they received. Less than 10 percent of wage employees reported to have been in any training lasting for at least 5 days in the last 12 months (figure 5.6, panel a). The data are not fully comparable because the questions are different (the question in the employer survey was not limited to a minimum of 5 days in the last 12 months). Nevertheless, the finding is in line with the picture in many countries: businesses may report training, but not all workers in those businesses participate in training. Even among wageworkers who received training, the initially better educated and those in more advanced occupations were more likely to have been trained (figure 5.6, panels b and c), confirming the training bias found in the employer survey data and evidence worldwide. Curiously, wage employees in state administration, domestic private businesses, and even state-owned enterprises (SOE) were more likely to receive training than workers in foreign-owned businesses (figure 5.6, panel d).

As a fast-growing economy, Vietnam should not be concerned about the existence of skills gaps and occupational skill shortages, but about the ability of the

Figure 5.5 Percentage of Internal and External Training, by Size of Business

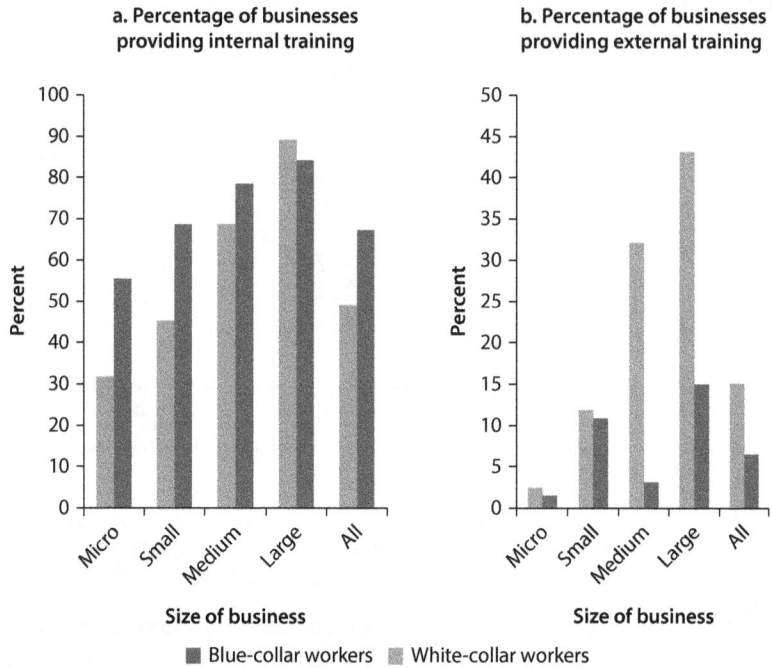

a. Percentage of businesses
providing internal training

b. Percentage of businesses
providing external training

■ Blue-collar workers   ■ White-collar workers

Source: World Bank staff estimates using 2011 STEP employer survey data.
Note: STEP = Skills Toward Employment and Productivity.

skills development system to overcome them. Skills shortages and gaps are indicators of a dynamic economy that creates new, more skill-intensive jobs. The real concern is whether the education and training system is equally dynamic in adjusting quickly to supply graduates with the technical skills to keep up with the constant and accelerating evolution in the demand for such skills. One indicator of responsiveness to expanding demand is the strong expansion in enrollments and in the supply of universities, colleges, and vocational training institutes. But gross enrollments in tertiary education remain lower in Vietnam than those in neighboring countries, suggesting that supply can and will need to expand further. Another indicator is whether the rising numbers of graduates and job applicants bring the skills that employers demand. The evidence provided in this report suggests that they often do not.

Step 3: Building Technical Skills through a Better-Connected System

Vietnam's skill development system today is not as responsive as it needs to be and is suffering from disconnects among employers, students, and universities and vocational schools. An unresponsive, underperforming skills development system is a disconnected system in which actors make choices and act in isolation, and do not sufficiently interact with each other (figure 5.7). Schools and universities may offer programs and produce graduates with skills that do not fully reflect

Figure 5.6 Percentage of Employees Receiving Training, by Education and Employment Type

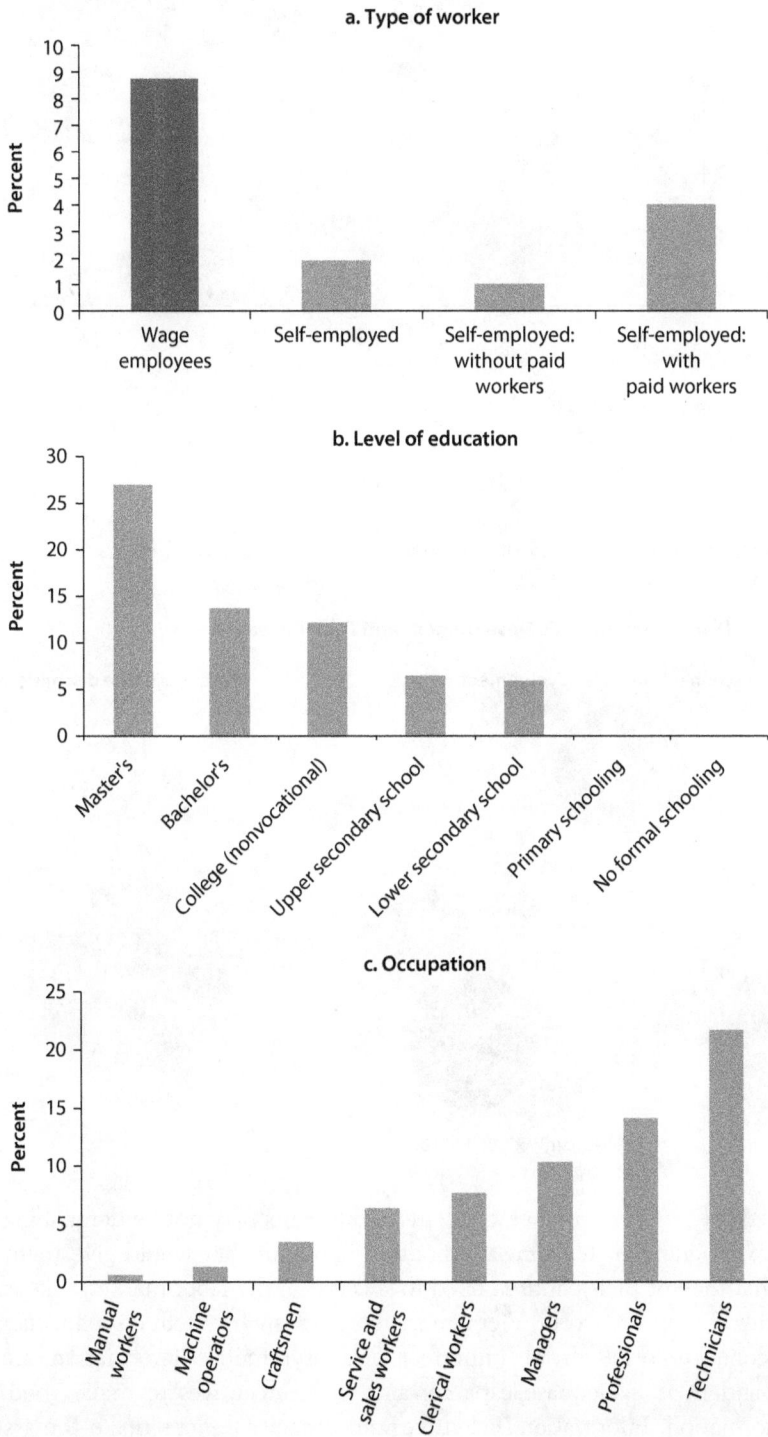

a. Type of worker

b. Level of education

c. Occupation

figure continues next page

Figure 5.6 Percentage of Employees Receiving Training, by Education and Employment Type *(continued)*

d. Type of employer

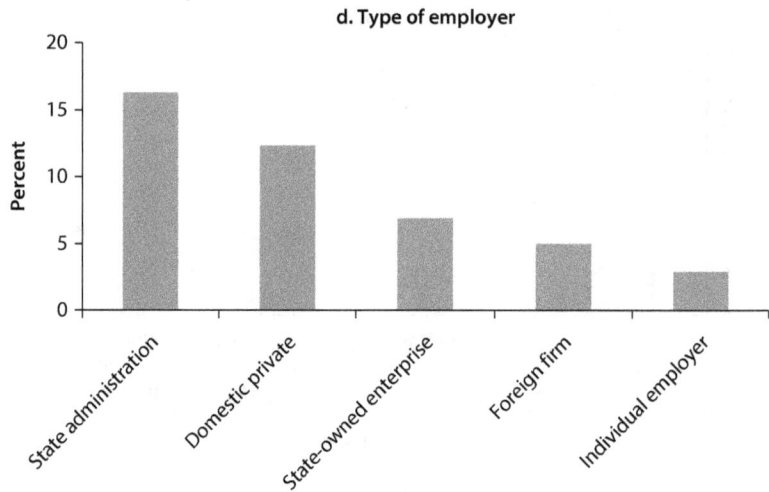

Source: World Bank staff estimates using 2011 STEP household survey data.
Note: STEP = Skills Toward Employment and Productivity.

Figure 5.7 Disconnects in Skills Development and Their Causes

a. Disconnects in skills development   b. Causes of the disconnects

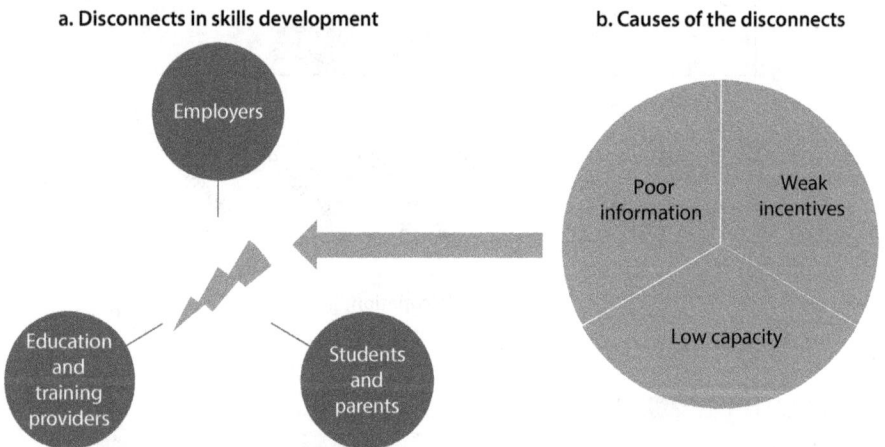

Source: Authors' illustration, adapted from World Bank 2012b.

the needs of the labor market. Students and parents may not be demanding the types of programs or teaching methods and content that would give them the skills that they or their children need to succeed in the labor market. Like many countries around the world, Vietnam suffers from such system disconnects.

Disconnects result from imperfect and asymmetric information among actors and their inadequate capacity and weak incentives to make good use of information. Information, incentive, and capacity deficits make the system less dynamic in responding to the evolving technical skill needs in the economy.

They reflect what economists call market failures.[1] The government is trying to find ways to overcome these market failures. But rather than planning and managing the education and training system centrally and top-down as in the past, the government should help to overcome the disconnects through empowering students, universities, and schools and businesses to make good decisions by facilitating the flow of information, providing the right incentives to schools and universities to be responsive to information, and through carefully investing in raising their capacity. Interventions on these three drivers of system responsiveness are mutually reinforcing and should be conducted in parallel.

Better Information

Information is the oxygen of responsive skills development systems. Education and training providers cannot make good choices on the programs to develop and offer without good information about employers' skill needs, conditions in the labor market, and returns to certain fields of study. Students and parents need the same information to make good decisions about which school or university and which study program to choose. Furthermore, prospective students also need information on the quality of education programs and employment success of graduates. It appears, however, that in Vietnam today information gaps are limiting not only many students' ability to make good choices, but also education and training providers' ability to offer attractive programs and training content.

In urban areas prospective students appear to have good information on the most attractive and rewarding fields of study. Figure 5.8 presents the share of graduates by field of study (panel a) and wage returns by field of study (panel b) for both general and vocational tertiary education. Most university graduates in urban Vietnam have degrees in business, information technology (IT) or science, education, and health. General tertiary degrees in education, business, and

Figure 5.8 Percentage of University Graduates, by Field of Study and Returns to Field of Study

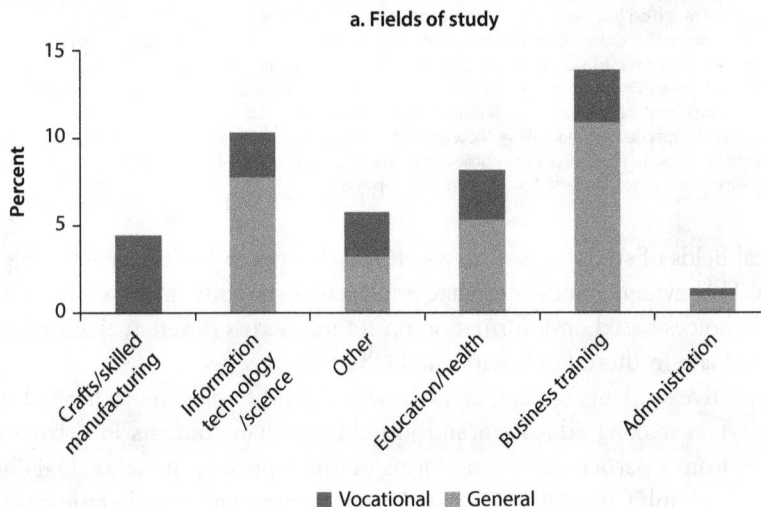

a. Fields of study

■ Vocational ■ General

Figure 5.8 Percentage of University Graduates by Field of Study and Returns to Field of Study *(continued)*

b. Wage returns by field of study

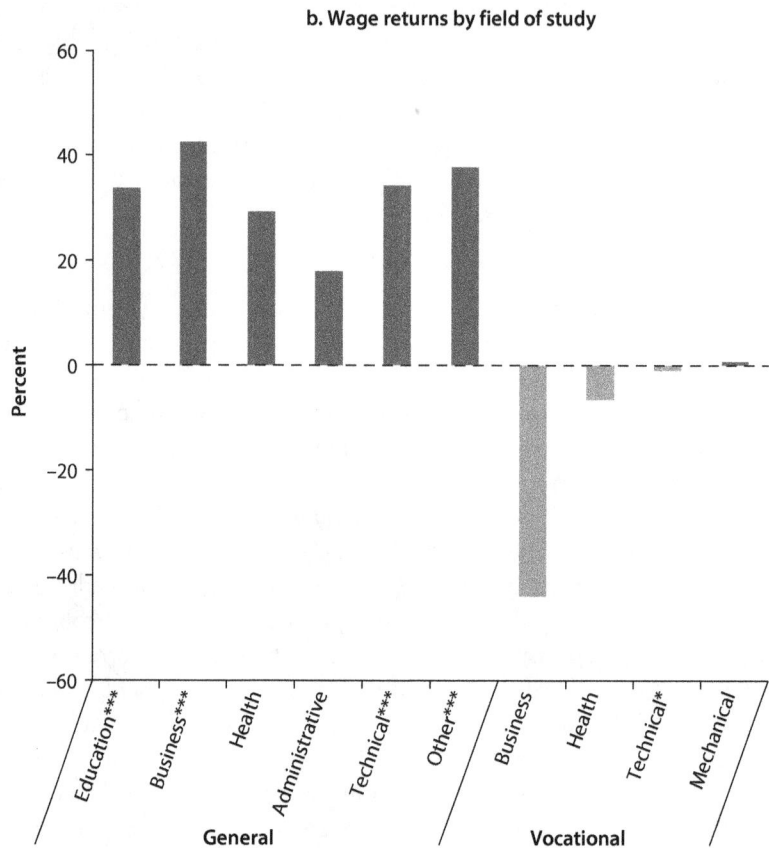

Source: World Bank staff estimates using STEP household survey data.
Note: STEP = Skills Toward Employment and Productivity. The returns to education are estimated using a Mincerian wage regression framework and include controls for demographic characteristics and experience. The sample is restricted to wageworkers who have completed upper secondary education or above, and the returns estimated capture the return to continuing to higher education only having completed a general upper secondary education, by the field of study chosen. The subjects studied are separated into general and vocational training, to allow for a comparison between vocational and general higher education. "Technical" includes information technology and engineering. "Mechanical" training includes manufacturing, auto or home appliance repair, and the building and construction trade. "Other" includes those who have a general or no specified field, agriculture, social and behavioral studies including media, tourism, arts, and humanities, personal care services, and public order and safety. N = 882.
Significance level: * = 10 percent, ** = 5 percent, *** = 1 percent.

technical fields of study as well as vocational degrees in health carry the highest returns. This evidence indicates that prospective students in urban areas make rational choices based on information on returns across different fields of study. They graduate in those fields with the highest returns.

Prospective students in rural areas, however, tend to have more limited information when making education and job choices than students in urban areas. Evidence from a participatory monitoring of urban poverty in Hanoi, Hai Phong, and Ho Chi Minh City (HCMC) in 2012, covering recent school graduates from rural and urban areas, shows variations in the information sources and influences used to make education and career choices (Oxfam and Action Aid Vietnam 2012; see table 5.1 and box 5.1). Urban students reported relying on a greater number and different information sources when making choices, including their own research using newspapers and the Internet, guidance from schools, and a guide to higher education from the Ministry of Education and Training (MOET). In contrast, rural students reported fewer information sources and suggested that they had limited objective information on the employment prospects of studying certain majors or at particular schools. Rural students relied most heavily on the higher education manual provided by MOET, and they did not report having had any education or career guidance from their schools. A highly educated labor market participant from a rural area suggested that the lack of information put students from rural areas in a disadvantaged position: "In this place [HCMC], parents reviewed different colleges several years before their children take the entrance exam. However, in rural areas, our parents are busy all the time and often tell us to choose any college that we like. They cannot give us any career advice even if they want to do so. Our personal experiences show us that we have more disadvantages than our urban peers."

The urban-rural information gap suggests the need to enhance connectivity of prospective students in rural areas. In addition to facing more limited access to good information, prospective students in rural areas are also more vulnerable to misinformation by tertiary education and training institutions, and these students struggle to make a call on the quality of programs and institutions on offer (see box 5.1). Enhancing information and improving choice will require interventions along the following lines: first, prospective students in rural areas need an expanded information base, most prominently through better Internet connectivity and from better labor market information. Evidence from the 2012 Young Lives School Survey shows that schools in rural and remote areas are

Table 5.1 Ranking of Information Sources Used to Make Study Decisions among Students in Urban and Rural Areas

Rank	Urban students	Rural students
1	Newspapers, Internet	MOET's book *What a Student Should Know*
2	Guidance from the youth unions, schools	Relatives with strong academic background who are working in urban areas
3	MOET's book *What a Student Should Know*	Internet
4	Parents	Flyers of some universities and junior colleges
5	Relatives with strong academic background who are working in urban areas	
6	Direct consultation from universities	
7	Flyers of some universities and junior colleges	
8	Student career fairs	
9	Programs such as "being our student for one day" of some universities	

Source: Oxfam and Action Aid Vietnam 2012.
Note: Discussion with four youth groups in two blocks in Ho Chi Minh City's Ward 6. MOET= Ministry of Education and Training.

Skilling Up Vietnam • http://dx.doi.org/10.1596/978-1-4648-0231-7

Box 5.1 Prospective Students in Rural Areas: Limited Objective Career Guidance Information

Youth groups in Hanoi, Hai Phong, and Ho Chi Minh City (HCMC) who participated in a qualitative study indicated that colleges used two main approaches to provide information to students at school:

- *Direct consultation:* In collaboration with Ho Chi Minh youth unions/board of rectors, universities and colleges visited upper secondary schools to deliver presentations about their schools and provide advice to students. This approach was more prevalent in urban areas, although it also occurred in some schools in rural areas.
- *Flyer distribution:* Universities and colleges collaborated with school staff to send flyers to classrooms or to send the relevant information through commune people's committees. This approach was applied in both urban and rural areas.

Among the students that graduated from university or college, some suggested that if they had had more information about the labor market when making their choices, they would have chosen other schools.

They sent flyers to us every year. All of us had their flyers. We did not know anything about their training quality, but they presented all nice things, such as good training quality, employment opportunities guaranteed. After a few years I learned that it would be stupid to trust their consultation.

—Skilled youth group, Kim Chung, Hanoi

The information gaps among rural and poorer students appeared to be even greater. Rural students report that the limited information base on which they were making their choices resulted in some students not continuing to higher education and others choosing the wrong path.

Our secondary school teachers gave no career advice for us. We did not know what to do after graduating from this school.

—Migrant worker, Kim Chung, Hanoi

In recent years, if you ask secondary school students [from rural areas] which field they chose to study, the common answer will be "business management" and "accounting." They follow social trends without considering the professional outlook of disciplines when there are too many people entering the same field of study. Things are different here in the cities: some study economics, foreign trade; some students, who have average performance, choose mechanical engineering, electricity, etc. There are highly marketable jobs in urban areas, meaning that their employment opportunities are more guaranteed.

—Skilled youth group, block 25, HCMC

Source: Oxfam and Action Aid Vietnam 2012.

significantly less well connected to the Internet and are less likely to make use of computers than urban schools (Rolleston et al. 2013). It should be the other way around: improved Internet connectivity can help overcome the information gap resulting from remoteness. Second, prospective students in rural areas need support in making good use of expanded information, including through more tailored and individualized career advice in schools and schools' outreach to businesses to help students obtain a "real life" perspective.

The labor market information system is weak overall, leaving both prospective students and education and training providers short of information to base their choices on. Vietnam now has a quarterly, nationally representative labor force survey that provides up-to-date information on national employment trends. As important as this is, actors are short of disaggregated and localized information on employment developments by sectors and type of work. Big cities have more developed labor market information systems with real-time vacancy data. Private employment agencies that often use online tools provide a more detailed picture of employment patterns. But such information is often lacking in rural areas. Likewise, evidence from STEP surveys shows that most graduates look for, and find, jobs through informal contacts, rather than formal channels such as employment agencies or the Internet (figure 5.9).

Figure 5.9 How Workers Find Jobs

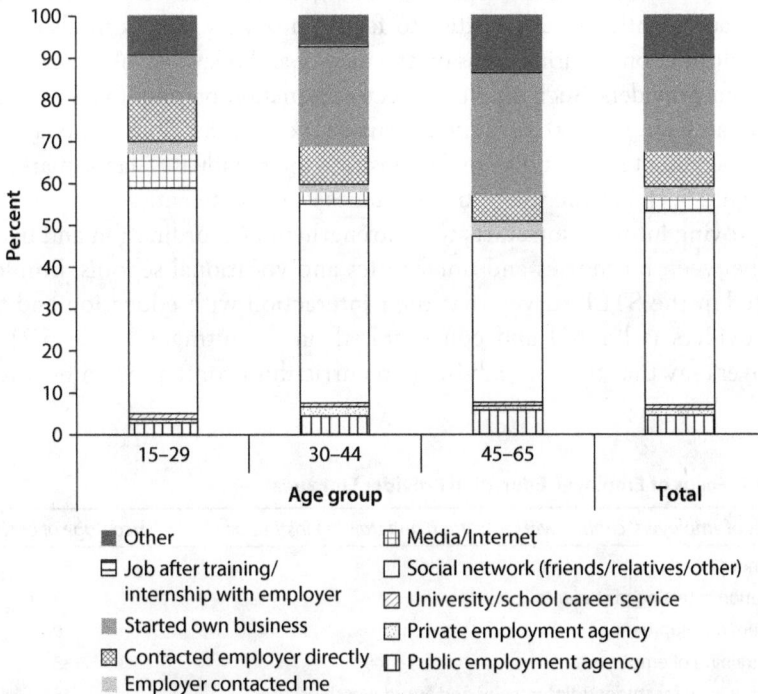

Legend:
- Other
- Job after training/ internship with employer
- Started own business
- Contacted employer directly
- Employer contacted me
- Media/Internet
- Social network (friends/relatives/other)
- University/school career service
- Private employment agency
- Public employment agency

Source: World Bank staff estimates using STEP household survey data.
Note: STEP = Skills Toward Employment and Productivity; *n* = 2,385.

This informal system does not work for graduates with more limited social networks, for example, those in rural areas. Expanding job vacancy information for job search through public and private labor agencies can help improve the matching of skills and inform career choice.

External accreditation of institutions can help to ensure quality in a rapidly expanding system and improve the information base for prospective students and employers. Vietnam's higher education and vocational training system, however, still lacks a functioning mechanism to assess and effectively communicate information on the quality of institutions. Since 2009 higher education institutions are required to disclose information relating to the quality of education facilities, teaching, and management staff, income, and expenditures. More than 150 universities and colleges have introduced internal quality assurance systems, but an agreed quality standard is lacking. The government established the National Accreditation Body in 2008 and charged it with reinforcing the quality assurance system at the central level by specifying and ensuring minimum quality standards. This action has not yet led to the creation of a functioning system of external quality assurance and accreditation. For example, decisions have yet to be made as to whether there will be one or several accreditation agencies and how to secure their independence and funding. The current discussion centers on whether to accredit institutions or programs, which would be extremely costly given the current lack of qualified evaluators.

Better information on graduates' job placements through tracer studies can help future students to choose the best colleges, universities, and programs and provide an incentive to universities to focus on quality. They can also provide useful information to hiring firms on the quality and relevance of education programs and providers. Such studies collect information on employment patterns of graduates after a certain period, usually six months. Some universities in Vietnam conduct such studies to demonstrate their graduates' labor market success (figure 5.4), but the use of tracer studies is not systematic.

Improving information starts with strengthening coordination and partnerships between businesses and universities and vocational schools. Employers reported in the STEP survey that their interaction with education and training providers is limited and concentrated on recruitment (table 5.2). Few employers say that they are advising on curriculum content or on how to test

Table 5.2 Focus of Employer-Education Provider Linkages

Purposes of employers' contact with education and training institutions	Percentage of businesses
Recruitment	83
Participation in testing of students	3
Curriculum development	9
Further training of employees	38
Work experience for students (internships and apprenticeships)	45

Source: World Bank staff estimates using STEP employer survey data.
Note: STEP = Skills Toward Employment and Productivity.

students. Government at central and local levels can improve the flow and availability of information by using its convening power and using incentives to help initiate the establishment of formal and informal partnerships and coordination mechanisms between employers and training providers. Institutional models and set-ups vary across countries, but all successful skills development systems around the world have created such coordination mechanisms. They range from the highly formal and institutionalized "dual system" in Germany, which was established more than 100 years ago, to less formal and localized systems elsewhere. In Vietnam, partnerships already exist between leading businesses and universities, and the challenge is to learn from their experience and spread them further. Today, however, central or local governments rarely act as facilitators of such initiatives. International experience suggests they could and should.

There is also scope to promote partnerships between training providers and firms for promoting demand-driven training and job placement of disadvantaged youth. Several Latin American countries have introduced skills programs for disadvantaged youth who have already left the formal education system. These demand-driven programs, known as *Jóvenes* programs, are regulated by the government but managed by public or nonformal training bodies or nongovernmental organizations (NGOs) in partnership with business. They involve a focus on cognitive and behavioral skills such as problem solving and teamwork, alongside technical and vocational training content and internships. Evaluations have shown that these programs help improve the chances of job placement as well as the quality of jobs young people obtain (Cunningham et al. 2008).

Removing the scope for rent seeking and corruption in education also helps with improving information. Anticorruption surveys show that making unofficial payments in education is widespread (CECODES, VFF-CRT, and UNDP 2013; World Bank 2012a). Corruption and unofficial payments deepen the disconnects by undermining the quality of information. Paying for grades, for example, compromises the information value of grades. With such payments, grades do not fully reflect a student's real performance and thus make diplomas less useful for students in their job search and for businesses in recruitment.

Adequate Incentives

Even in a world of perfect and symmetrical information, students and parents as well as education and training providers may still not be able to make the right choices if they face weak incentives. Universities that are not sufficiently autonomous in their decision making and who have to seek permission from central government on whether to develop a new program, change any curriculum content, or establish a partnership with a university abroad or with local businesses will find it hard to respond to good information. A rigid curriculum that does not give space for vocational schools and universities to adjust their teaching methods and content to the changing and local needs expressed by employers may undermine their responsiveness. Students' choices may be affected by conditions in the labor market. For example, if employment in the public sector is more attractive than in the private sector, prospective students will make education choices to enhance their chances of finding a public sector job.

Greater autonomy of decision making in education and training institutions, coupled with clear accountability for quality, are critical preconditions for enhanced linkages and partnership with industry. The international trend in higher education and vocational training has been toward ensuring greater autonomy and accountability of institutions at the expense of central government control. In line with this trend, Vietnam launched a comprehensive reform of the tertiary education sector that includes steps toward greater autonomy and accountability of higher education institutions. The recently adopted Higher Education Law creates legal conditions for greater institutional autonomy for universities and colleges on many important aspects such as planning, opening and closing units, new programs, financial management, and staffing, and newly instituted university councils provide a tool to enhance accountability. Vocational education and training institutions can choose up to 35 percent of curriculum content locally and can also introduce new study programs at their own initiative, but subject to approval by the Ministry of Labor, Invalids, and Social Affairs (MOLISA). Vocational schools also have autonomy to decide on matters such as staffing and financing.

Despite their expanded de jure autonomy of decision making on curriculum content and study programs, many vocational institutions decide to follow directions from the government. According to national legislation, vocational education and training institutions can choose up to 35 percent of curriculum content locally and can also introduce new study programs at their own initiative, with MOLISA's approval. This degree of autonomy does not translate into different choices in reality. Figure 5.10 presents evidence from a survey of 49 public and private vocational training institutions in Hanoi and HCMC and surrounding provinces on the reasons for introducing new study programs. A majority reported that they introduced new programs at the direction of the government rather than at their own initiative or in response to requests from enterprises. Moreover, their main source of revenue remains government transfers instead of proceeds from tuition fees and partnerships with enterprises. Only 37 percent of institutes reported formal partnerships with enterprises. It should be noted that this evidence is not nationally representative, but it does provide a picture of the realities in vocational education and training institutions in the main areas of economic agglomeration in Vietnam, which can be expected to be at the forefront of connectedness to industry (CIEM and World Bank 2013).

Vietnam's principal challenge in higher education and vocational training now is to translate a legal framework for greater institutional autonomy into de facto autonomy and clear accountability. As in vocational education and training, de facto autonomy of many higher education institutions for decision making in response to labor market needs is still limited, and university councils are not fully empowered to hold universities accountable. Although the

Figure 5.10 New Vocational Training Programs and Their Funding, 2012

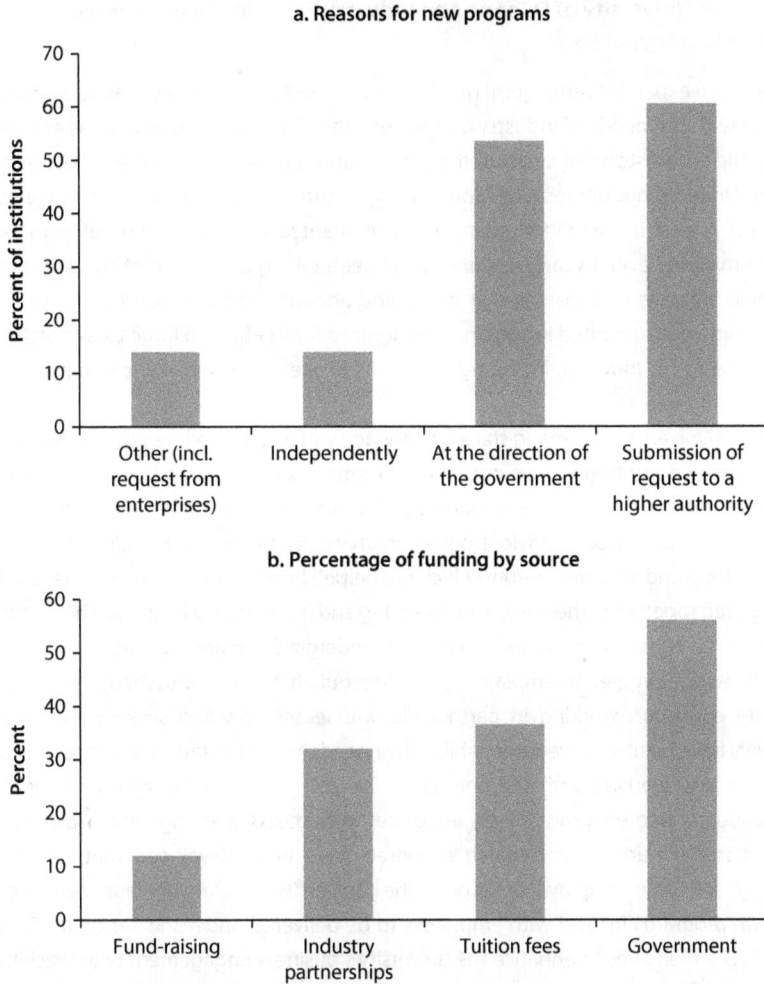

a. Reasons for new programs

b. Percentage of funding by source

Source: CIEM and World Bank 2013.
Note: The charts present evidence from a survey of 49 public and private vocational education and training institutions in Hanoi and Ho Chi Minh City and surrounding provinces.

two national universities in Hanoi and HCMC as well as regional universities are largely autonomous in decision making, public and private universities and colleges have to follow operational and academic policies set by MOET. But there are pockets of excellence. The steps toward greater autonomy of national and regional institutions have demonstrated the benefits of a system in which MOET cedes greater decision making to institutions, for example, in the establishment of partnerships with universities abroad and with local businesses (box 5.2).

Greater institutional autonomy for universities also means that the role of government needs to change from direct management to stewardship of

Box 5.2 The University of Danang and Industry Partnership to Improve Graduate Employability

In an effort to expand its engagement with industry and to align its education and research activities with the needs of industry and society, the University of Danang has entered in a partnership with Aston University in the United Kingdom, as part of the establishment of a Vietnam-United Kingdom research and training institute, and Rolls Royce. The University of Danang is one of the few in Vietnam that was granted a higher degree of autonomy in decision making several years ago, and it has been taking advantage of this autonomy to build new linkages with partners at home and abroad. Aston University, one of the top 30 universities in the United Kingdom, is recognized for its effort to forge close partnerships with business and industry, including with Rolls Royce. The three-way partnership entails two concrete projects.

First, the University of Danang started to engage with local employers to convince them of the benefits of contributing to program development, providing work experience for both undergraduate and postgraduate students and, most important, offering relevant industrial projects to work on. Based on advice from Aston University, the project introduced an industrial advisory group and an alumni forum, which has helped bring alumni, employers, research and teaching staff together in the areas of engineering and international business. The partnership reflects on the current models and practices in undergraduate and postgraduate education. Outreach events targeted to employers are held regularly to share with them a new vision for university education working in partnership with employers and seeking their support. Employers have been surveyed to establish their needs and expectations in terms of graduate employees and working with the university. The end product is an agreed model for an undergraduate degree program to integrate work-based learning alongside academic qualifications. A number of research proposals have been developed that benefit both university staff and employers. Second, the University of Danang launched executive education programs for and with employers to be delivered under the Centre for Executive Leadership, which aims to enhance the university's business engagement with teaching and research and to diversify sources of income for the university.

The role of Aston University has been that of an adviser to the University of Danang, bringing an established model of long-term partnership with groups of companies as well as capacity building on resource mobilization and alumni relations. Apart from content development, industrial placement, and apprenticeships, Rolls Royce committed financial support to both projects and helped leverage its relationships with the British Business Group Vietnam to increase employer participation in these education initiatives.

the system. Despite the recent moves toward promoting greater institutional autonomy, the Vietnamese government still retains a strong say in managing the vocational and higher education systems, for example, by centrally setting enrollment quotas in higher education and regulating and approving curriculum content. In contrast, a more connected, responsive skills development system suggests a different role for government, with a shifting focus from controlling inputs (such as enrollment quotas, curriculum content, and teaching methods), to ensuring minimum quality levels (through accreditation and mandating university councils to hold the autonomous university accountable) and offering incentives for better outputs (such as qualifications and competencies of graduates).

Government can use regulative and financing tools to steer the system. For example, rather than approving the content of a training program to become an electrician, the government could invite employers and training providers to agree on the occupational competency standards an electrician should possess. Government could then focus on certifying electricians based on their competencies, whether they acquired them on the job, from a private or public training provider, or elsewhere. The Republic of Korea provides an interesting example in which government, industry, and technical and vocational education and training providers agreed on a National Competency Standard (NCS) to define the knowledge, skills, and quality required of work in specific occupational fields and to set systematic criteria based on which individuals may be educated and trained (table 5.3). Similar examples of partnership among the government, employers, and providers are becoming more common in Vietnam to determine occupational competencies. (For an example see annex 5A). The government can use financing tools to incentivize excellence in universities, such as by allocating part of its financing based on results or encourage businesses to partner with training providers and expand on-the-job training, for example, through tax breaks (box 5.3).

Table 5.3 The Republic of Korea: Example of National Competency Standards for One Occupation

Traditional construction is the work of building and/or repairing architecture using methods that have been passed down from generations of Korean architects.	
Level	*Performance standards*
5	Is capable of planning and implementing construction projects based on extensive knowledge in his or her own and related areas of expertise; performs the overall supervision and management of the construction project.
4	Is capable of fully comprehending the drawings pertaining to his or her area of expertise; performs the task of managing the construction project.
3	Creates simple drawings pertaining to his or her area of expertise; identifies and estimates the quantity of needed materials; plans and executes the project.
2	Understands the physical properties of materials used in his or her area of expertise, such as woodwork (architectural, furniture), stonemasonry, tiling, plastering, and decorative painting; performs tasks requiring medium-level skills.
1	Performs basic tasks in his or her own area of expertise such as woodwork (architectural, furniture), stonemasonry, tiling, plastering, and decorative painting; assists traditional construction workers who have a higher degree of skills.

Source: Park 2011.

Skilling Up Vietnam • http://dx.doi.org/10.1596/978-1-4648-0231-7

Box 5.3 Promoting Adult Continuous Education and Training

As already mentioned in this chapter, not all businesses train their workers, and even those who do train, do not include all workers. In Vietnam and the world over, larger firms are more likely to train than smaller firms. Likewise, company training often concentrates on younger and better-educated workers rather than on workers who might need it most to stay productive, such as the less well skilled and older workers whose skills may have depleted. Uneven provision of training has created an opening for government intervention to stimulate the demand for training of firms and workers alike. Apart from incentivizing vocational schools and higher education institutions to develop training programs and partner with businesses, governments also use financing tools to stimulate the demand for training by firms and workers.

Countries belonging to the Organisation for Economic Co-operation and Development (OECD) have been using financial tools to incentivize firms to expand training of their workers. Allowing firms to deduct the costs of training from their taxes is one of the most common incentives. Tax deductions for training costs are relatively simple for governments to administer and for firms to use, as they rely on existing tax systems. Critics of tax deductions point out that the deductions may be attractive also to those businesses that would have provided training even without such incentives. Tax incentives could, however, be targeted to certain types of companies and types of workers who are underrepresented in training. Tax deduction schemes can be useful tools to give an initial boost to adult education and training, particularly in environments where few businesses and individuals currently participate in training.

In the Republic of Korea the government partners with large multinational companies and small and medium enterprises (SMEs) to form "training consortia" in which training institutes associated with large businesses organize training for workers in SMEs, subsidized by the government. This program addresses the traditionally lower training participation in SMEs and promotes partnerships between enterprises, including suppliers and subcontractors, and technological spillovers.

Alternatively, incentives can be provided to the individual worker. These usually include tax deductions for training costs (for those who pay income tax) or grants and vouchers that individuals can use to obtain training in accredited providers. For these incentives to be effective in promoting access to job-relevant training programs, individuals need to have good information on which programs are of high quality and what the training will equip them to do.

Sources: Bodewig and Hirshleifer 2011; OECD 2005.

Enhanced Capacity

Even in a world of perfect and symmetrical information and appropriate incentives, students, parents, and providers may still not be able to make the right choices if they face capacity constraints. On the students' side, these constraints may be principally related to the direct and indirect costs associated with education and training. Among schools and universities, capacity constraints may come in the form of insufficiently trained teaching staff or managers, inadequate curricula, or a simple lack of knowledge and experience on how to act on information. Financing capacity constraints can also prevent businesses from investing in their workers' training.

Education and training providers in Vietnam suffer from human and physical capacity constraints. Staff capacity in higher education has not caught up with the expansion in the number of students and institutions. Only around 10 percent of lecturers in universities have a doctorate and although the share increased considerably over time, only another 40 percent hold master's degrees (figure 5.11). The student-faculty ratio of 1:30 in Vietnam is high by international standards. Scholarships and programs to retain students in universities and give them incentives to choose academic careers can help raise the overall qualification profile. But capacity is not limited to teaching and research: private vocational training institutions in Hanoi and HCMC and surrounding provinces report that a lack of strong managerial staff is a major constraint to their ability to deliver effective training services (CIEM and World Bank 2013). This finding suggests that investments in managerial capacity will enable university and vocational school leaders to take advantage of greater autonomy.

Concerns over the quality of local vocational training institutions have resulted in vocational training being held in low esteem. Few participants in the qualitative research study considered vocational training when making their education choices (Oxfam and Action Aid Vietnam 2012). Respondents stated that the perceived quality of vocational training was limited and that they also perceived the employment opportunities emerging from such study as limited.

Figure 5.11 Staff Qualifications in Higher Education Institutions

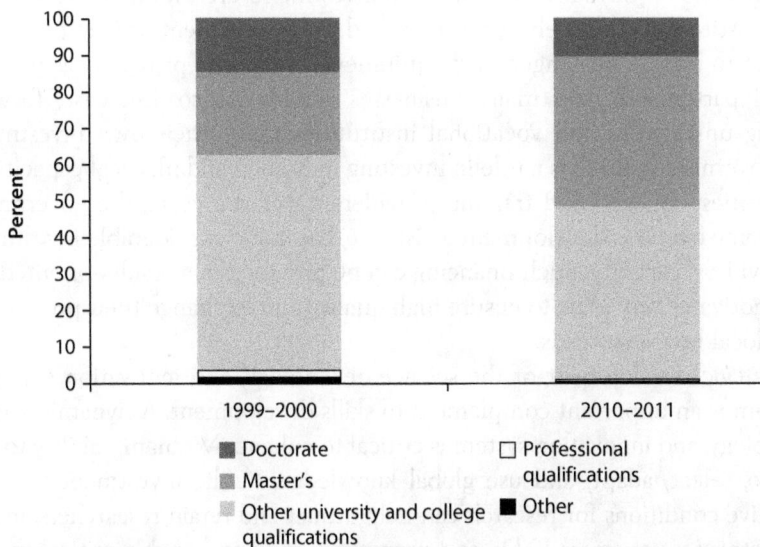

Source: MOET 2012.

Vocational training among these participants was considered only as a last resort if they were unable to enter any tertiary education institutions.

Students with vocational training reported difficulty adapting the technical skills learned at school to real work environments. Among study participants with vocational training, students raised concerns about the content of the courses and their applicability to their work environments. Students expressed an interest in having greater opportunities to gain technical expertise through hands-on learning rather than through classroom sessions focused on theoretical issues. For example, a student of mechanics in Hanoi said, "Classroom sessions dominate the entire training program. It would be lucky if I could use 20–30 percent of what I was taught there in real life." Many graduates reported that they were unable to obtain employment relevant to their field of study. They said the quality of the training they received was limited, with schools placing greater focus on generalized courses and less emphasis on the specialized skills students needed in the labor market (Oxfam and Action Aid Vietnam 2012).

In Vietnam's fast-changing labor market, outdated machinery for training implies that skills learned in vocational school may no longer be applicable to work environments. Recruitment agents in HCMC and former students both suggested that vocational training schools needed to update the machinery used and techniques taught. A graduate from a vocational training school in Hai Phong reported that he is unable to use the knowledge he gained during school because "outdated machines are still being used for training." Recruitment agents in HCMC reported that graduates typically need to be retrained upon entering their positions because some of the machinery used for teaching is outdated (Oxfam and Action Aid Vietnam 2012).

Enhancing the capacity of higher education institutions and vocational training providers requires investment. Such investments are the shared responsibility of institutions themselves, business, and the government. It is in businesses' interest to donate no-longer-used equipment to training providers as part of a formal partnership, and many businesses already do so. Likewise, forward-looking universities and vocational institutions make their own investments. The government also has a role in investing in human and physical capacities in universities, colleges, and training providers. Over the years, the government, with some overseas development assistance, has made considerable investments in providers' capacity. Such financing can be provided in a results-oriented way that motivates providers to ensure high quality and to change their programs to meet local business needs.

Strategic development of the science, technology, and innovation system in Vietnam is an important complement to skills development. A dynamic science, technology, and innovation system is critical to enhance Vietnam's ability to connect to, select, adapt, and use global knowledge. Public investment to create attractive conditions for research can help attract and retain researchers, including Vietnamese overseas PhDs, and promote a growing, capable critical mass of international-level professors at higher education institutions. Strengthening the

Figure 5.12 Private Spending on College Education, by Income Group, 2010

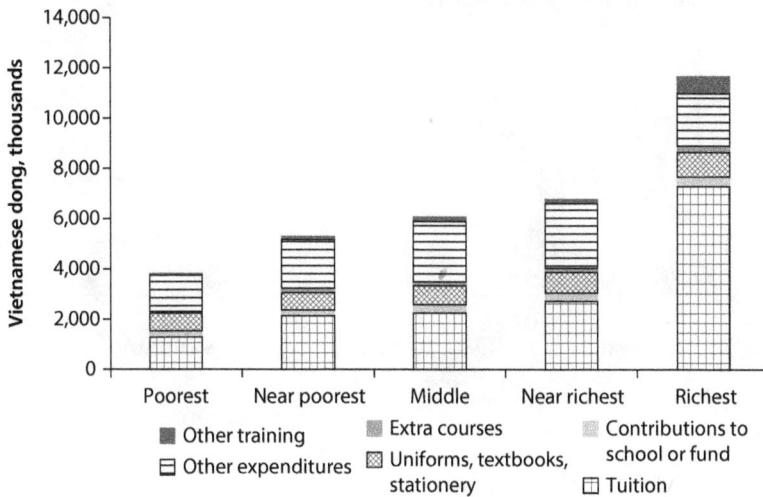

Source: World Bank staff estimates using 2010 VHLSS data.
Note: VHLSS = Vietnam Household Living Standards Survey.

graduate education and advanced training system as well as scholarships and programs to retain students in universities and incentivize them to choose academic careers can help raise the overall qualification profile of teaching and research staff. Improving human capacity is not limited to teaching and research: investments in managerial capacity will enable university and vocational school leaders to take advantage of greater autonomy.

Access to higher education remains inequitable between the haves and have-nots in Vietnam. Even though enrollments in higher education have been rising across all income groups, a higher education degree in effect remains a privilege for the rich (see figure 5.3). Children from poorer backgrounds tend to drop out earlier and not to proceed to higher education. For those who do enroll in university or in college, the ability to pay remains a critical determinant of choice. As expected, private spending on college education varies significantly by income group (figure 5.12).

Measures to safeguard the access to higher education by the poor are in place but can be further strengthened. To promote access to higher education for students who are not able to afford tuition, the government has set up a loan scheme, with a total amount above US$ 1.85 billion to cover 870,000 students in universities and more than US$ 1.3 billion for 760,000 students in colleges in 2012. More than 60 percent of beneficiaries come from registered poor and near poor households. Moreover, Vietnam also has a policy of fee exemptions which is pro-poor (figure 5.13). As Vietnam seeks to expand access to tertiary education, adequate scholarship and fee waiver mechanisms need to be developed and maintained to overcome limits to financing capacity among the poor.

**Figure 5.13 Percentage of Higher Education Students Receiving Fee
Exemptions, by Income Quintiles, 2006–10**

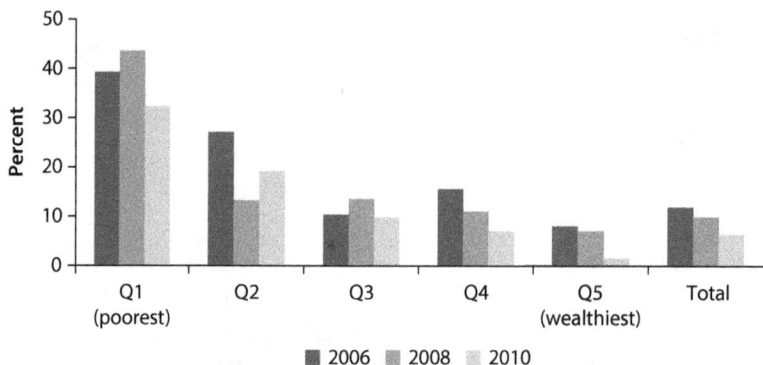

Source: World Bank staff estimates using VHLSS data, multiple years.
Note: VHLSS = Vietnam Household Living Standards Survey.

Summary and Conclusion

Vietnam's major challenge in enhancing the technical skills of its current and future workforce is to overcome the disconnects among employers, education providers, and students. These disconnects are driven by information gaps, inadequate incentives, and capacity limitations affecting education and training providers, businesses, and prospective students. The government can be effective in overcoming the disconnects by promoting the flow of information, by setting adequate incentives, and by investing in the enhanced capacity of education and training providers and students to make good choices in response to better information.

Better information, incentives, and capacity are mutually reinforcing. Government can use regulatory or financing incentives to promote partnerships between providers and industry and the generation and dissemination of better information on graduates' employment successes. In turn, better information makes providers more accountable. Ambitious and successful universities and vocational schools want to demonstrate that they have strong links with industry and that their graduates find good jobs and do so quickly. Investments in their managerial and teaching capacity can enable them to do so.

A more connected, responsive skills development system suggests a changed role for government in response to the modern market economy. The government's focus is shifting from controlling inputs (enrollment quotas, curriculum, teaching methods) to incentivizing better outputs (qualifications and competencies of graduates) and facilitating partnerships between businesses and providers, for example, by setting occupational standards. With the transition toward greater autonomy of universities and colleges under way, the government's role in skills development is also in transition, but, as demonstrated in this report, that transition is not yet complete.

Annex 5A: In Depth

Developing Occupational Skills Standards in Vietnam's Tourism Sector

Vietnam is a relatively new tourism destination in Southeast Asia, but is increasing in importance. International tourist arrivals in Vietnam reached more than 6 million in 2011, a 19 percent increase over 2010 according to statistics from the Vietnam National Administration of Tourism. Vietnam's tourism revenue in the first half of 2012 surged by more than 35 percent to VND 62 trillion, or more than US$ 3 billion, compared to VND 45 trillion in the previous 12 months. The government's "Strategy for Tourism Development in Vietnam" for 2011–20 estimates that up to 2.2 million workers will be needed in the tourism sector by 2015 and 3 million by 2020. According to data from the World Travel and Tourism Council, the sector already accounts for 4.3 percent of Vietnam's GDP (gross domestic product) and 3.7 percent of all jobs.

To operate competitively in the international tourism marketplace and to provide internationally recognized standards, the tourism industry needs a workforce with the skills to deliver products and services of appropriate quality. For years, however, the industry has been suffering from a significant shortfall in well-qualified staff. Education and training institutions have been unable to produce graduates with the skills and knowledge required to meet the needs and expectations of the tourism sector.

Responding to the Needs of the Market

In response to this challenge, the government of Vietnam, with assistance from the European Union, launched a project to design and develop occupational skills standards for the tourism industry. The project aimed to train new staff at entry level in the industry, both through the college education system and in-company, especially for hotels and medium to large tour and travel companies. Thirteen occupational standards were developed through analyzing and establishing the tasks that people performed to fulfill the requirements of a specific job. These Vietnam Tourism Occupational Skills Standards (VTOS) include front office, housekeeping, food and beverage service, western food preparation, Vietnamese food preparation, pastry and bakery, small hotel management, hotel security, travel operations, tour operations, and others.

The VTOS Development Process

From the initial job analysis, the required skills and knowledge required for competent job performance was defined and broken down into tasks and subtasks. The tasks were further divided into a sequence of steps and performance levels, along with an explanation of why the process needed to be carried out in a particular way. The resulting standards provided in-company trainers with a clear and systematic set of standards to enable staff to put into practice internationally accepted operating processes and improve the quality of their work.

The program team worked closely and consulted with industry members, trade bodies, colleges, and government agencies to ensure that the needs of the industry were met and that the standards developed were practical and appropriate to entry-level staff. Additionally, technical working groups were set up to review and provide feedback on the standards and the development process. The standards were then pilot tested with the target groups to ensure that they were applicable and subsequently refined and updated.

Impact on the Industry

The final process before implementation of VTOS was accreditation. The Vietnam Tourism Certification Board (VTCB), which is part of the Vietnam National Administration of Tourism, was established to provide the assessment guidelines and quality assurance system for the new occupational standards (figure 5A.1). More than 3,000 trainers were trained and certified by VTCB; more than 140 assessors were trained in work-based assessment techniques with almost 1,100 trainees assessed in their workplaces and the fully equipped assessment centers in the tourism colleges. In addition, 14 tourism colleges signed up to introduce VTOS into their curriculum and became partners in this initiative. This development process is one that could be used effectively by other industries, in particular to ensure that industry practices are in line with international standards and to provide skilled employees with recognition of their existing professional competences.

Future Developments

To address future needs of the tourism industry, including the mobility of labor through the ASEAN Mutual Recognition Arrangement on Tourism Professionals by 2015, the VTOS system will be updated and redesigned for wider use in hotels and tour and travel companies as well as in the curriculum of tourism and hospitality colleges. It will also aim to gain acceptance in all the provinces and to

Figure 5A.1 Functions of the Vietnam Tourism Certification Board

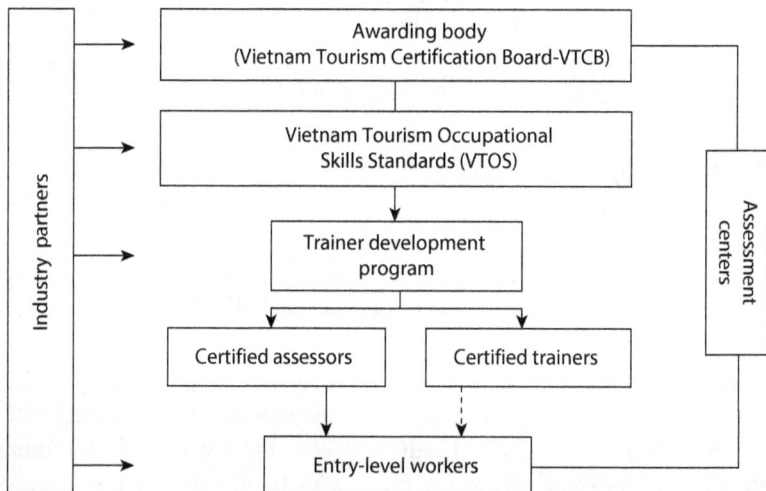

develop new standards for community-based tourism businesses in rural and mountainous areas of Vietnam through developing and improving the quality of their services and thus generating more income and creating employment.

VTOS will also include new standards covering environmental and sustainable practices and expand from frontline staff through to management levels. VTOS will ensure compatibility with the Ministry of Culture, Sports, and Tourism (MCST) occupational standards for tourism and align with the ASEAN Common Competency Standards for Tourism.

Note

1. For a discussion of market failures in skills development, see Almeida, Behrman, and Robalino 2012.

References

Almeida, R., J. Behrman, and D. Robalino, eds. 2012. *The Right Skills for the Job: Rethinking Training Policies for Workers.* Human Development Perspectives. Washington, DC: World Bank.

Bodewig, C., and S. Hirshleifer. 2011. "Advancing Adult Learning in Eastern Europe and Central Asia." Social Protection Discussion Paper 1108, World Bank, Washington, DC.

CECODES (Centre for Community Support and Development Studies), VFF-CRT (Centre for Research and Training of the Vietnam Fatherland Front), and UNDP (United Nations Development Programme). 2013. "The Viet Nam Governance and Public Administration Performance Index (PAPI) 2012: Measuring Citizens' Experiences." Joint Policy Research Paper, Hanoi.

CIEM (Central Institute for Economic Management) and World Bank. 2013. *Workforce Development.* Vietnam SABER (Systems Approach for Better Education Results) Country Report 2012.

Cunningham, W., L. McGinnis, R. G. Verdu, C. Tesliuc, and D. Verner. 2008. *Youth at Risk in Latin America and the Caribbean: Understanding the Causes, Realizing the Potential.* Washington, DC: World Bank.

MOET (Ministry of Education and Training of Vietnam). 2010. *Project on Curriculum and Textbook Renovation from 2015 Onwards.* Drafting committee, Hanoi.

———. 2012. *Early Development Instrument (EDI) in Vietnam.* Hanoi.

OECD (Organisation for Economic Co-operation and Development). 2005. *Promoting Adult Learning.* Paris: OECD Publishing.

Oxfam and Action Aid Vietnam. 2012. *Participatory Monitoring of Urban Poverty in Vietnam: The Fifth Round Synthesis Report (2008–2012).* http://www.Oxfamblogs.org.

Park, D. 2011. *Korean Policies on Secondary Vocational Education: Efforts to Overcome Skills Mismatch and Labor Force Shortage.* Berufsbildung in Wissenschaft und Praxis (BWP). Bonn: Bundesinstitut für Berufsbildung. http://www.bibb.eu/veroeffentlichungen/en/publication/show/id/6663.

Rolleston, C., Z. James, L. Pasquier-Doumer, and Tran Ngo Thi Minh Tam. 2013. "Making Progress: Report of the Young Lives School Survey in Vietnam." Young Lives Working Paper 100, Department of International Development, University of Oxford, Oxford, U.K.

VHLSS (Vietnam [Household] Living Standards Survey). Multiple years. General Statistics Office, Hanoi.

World Bank. 2012a. *Corruption from the Perspective of Citizens, Firms, and Public Officials: Results of Sociological Surveys.* 2nd ed. Hanoi: National Political Publishing House.

———. 2012b. *Putting Higher Education to Work: Skills and Research for Growth in East Asia.* Washington, DC: World Bank.

———. 2013. *Vietnam Higher Education Project 2.* Implementation Completion Report. Washington, DC: World Bank.

Environmental Benefits Statement

The World Bank Group is committed to reducing its environmental footprint. In support of this commitment, the Publishing and Knowledge Division leverages electronic publishing options and print-on-demand technology, which is located in regional hubs worldwide. Together, these initiatives enable print runs to be lowered and shipping distances decreased, resulting in reduced paper consumption, chemical use, greenhouse gas emissions, and waste.

The Publishing and Knowledge Division follows the recommended standards for paper use set by the Green Press Initiative. Whenever possible, books are printed on 50 percent to 100 percent postconsumer recycled paper, and at least 50 percent of the fiber in our book paper is either unbleached or bleached using Totally Chlorine Free (TCF), Processed Chlorine Free (PCF), or Enhanced Elemental Chlorine Free (EECF) processes.

More information about the Bank's environmental philosophy can be found at http://crinfo.worldbank.org/wbcrinfo/node/4.

green press INITIATIVE

www.ingramcontent.com/pod-product-compliance
Lightning Source LLC
Chambersburg PA
CBHW080548220326
41599CB00032B/6403